Economics: The Essentials

WILLIAM M. SCARTH

CONCEPT
PRESS

Harcourt Brace & Company, Canada

Toronto Montreal Fort Worth New York Orlando
Philadelphia San Diego London Sydney Tokyo

This book is produced in association with TVOntario, and is based on the series "Introductory Economics."

Every reasonable effort has been made to acquire permission for copyright material used in this text, and to acknowledge all such indebtedness accurately. Any errors and omissions called to the publisher's attention will be corrected in future printings.

ISBN 0-7747-3502-3

Publisher: *Scott Duncan*
Editor and Marketing Manager: *Ken Nauss*
Projects Manager: *Liz Radojkovic*
Director of Publishing Services: *Jean Davies*
Editorial Manager: *Marcel Chiera*
Production Manager: *Sue-Ann Becker*
Production Supervisor: *Carol Tong*
Copy Editor: *Gail Marsden*
Technical Art: *Aniforms Productions*
Printing and Binding: *Hignell Printing Limited*

This book was printed in Canada on acid-free paper.

1 2 3 4 5   99 98 97 96 95

To Kathy

Preface

Free Trade, Social Policy Reform, Deficit Reduction... One cannot take an active part in public policy debate without running up against economic analysis on a daily basis. Increasingly, individuals feel at the mercy of specialists (interviewed in the news media) in their attempt to form an independent opinion on these issues. But while economic analysis is central to modern life, it is not easy to learn in bits and pieces. It is not surprising, then, that introductory economics is among the three most-taken courses at most universities.

But a principles course at university is often geared to preparing students for specialist training in the discipline. As a result, the typical text is an encyclopedia on the subject. While policy applications are included, the reader must find these discussions within the larger block of material that stresses formal definitions and theorems. Many students become discouraged, since the principles course and text cover more formal material than was really wanted.

Of course, instructors and textbook writers have been aware of this common reaction for many years. Inevitably the response seems to be that this state of affairs is essentially unavoidable - because economics is a difficult and technical subject. There is no point in pretending otherwise by teaching a series of partial truths that will need to be "unlearned" later by students who go on in the subject. More important, students who do not go on will never realize how "dangerous" a little learning may be.

This book is based on my belief that there **is** a way out of this dilemma. This belief is based on the principle that the topics to be covered in an introductory treatment must be carefully selected. Only those that are absolutely required for learning how economists think and how the central policy issues can be understood are included. These topics are then treated rigorously and in a thorough manner. The idea is for readers to learn a limited number of things well. I am convinced that this goal is preferable to having people know just a little bit about a wide set of topics, or having people lose interest when forced to try to master a lot about many less central topics.

Thus, it is through a bold selection of topics, not dropping the level of rigour, that this book imparts an in-depth understanding of economic analysis without ever departing from a focus on policy issues for more than a page or two. Central topics such as: positive versus normative statements, incentives, supply and demand, producer and consumer surplus, competition, monopoly, externalities, marginal productivity, and the determination of GDP, inflation, unemployment, interest rates and exchange rates are covered in detail. But other subjects, such as: detailed elasticity calculations, extended multiplier derivations, indifference curves, oligopoly, monopolistic competition, monopsony, IS-LM and Phillips curves are left out completely. Also, the book is thin on factual (both historical and institutional) material. The rationale is that this material can be picked up elsewhere, and it is the general understanding of the economist's approach to policy questions that is the item which is in short supply.

Obviously, some very valuable insights have had to be dropped. For example, by limiting the formal analysis of market structures to pure competition and pure monopoly, there is no place for considering strategic behaviour. Any one firm in a competitive industry is too small to affect the other firms, and a pure monopolist has no direct competitors. Hence, game theory is not covered at all. Some economists will cringe at this exclusion, but the non-specialist's time constraint must be respected. In any event, the central policy questions to do with imperfect competition (deregulation, the Competition Act, marketing boards, equity and efficiency issues) can all be appreciated without additional formal modelling.

A Summary of What is to Come

The central focus of the book is on what a market system does well and what it does poorly. On each question there is a consistent focus on both efficiency (the concept economists often emphasize) and equity (the issue the general public is often most focused on). Here is a whirlwind tour of the book.

After an introductory chapter, there is a series of eight chapters on each of microeconomics and macroeconomics. Microeconomics, from the Greek "micro" (meaning small) focuses on questions of detail such as the allocation of resources across particular industries and the distribution of income across individuals. Macroeconomics, from the Greek "macro" (meaning large) focuses on the entire economy as a unit, and considers questions such as what determines the overall level of output in the economy, the general level of interest rates faced by all borrowers, the rate of inflation, the exchange rate, etc.

The first two chapters discuss the role of theory, opportunity cost, supply and demand, and the invisible hand. It is shown how the invisible hand fights back when legal restrictions which attempt to overrule the forces of supply and demand are imposed. Also, basic analysis is used to explain how, and in what circumstances, the burden of taxes can be shifted to others.

The next two chapters take a look "behind the scenes" to see why demand and supply curves make sense. The fundamental principle - that any activity should be expanded up to the point that additional benefits are just pushed down to the level of the additional costs - is discussed. It is applied to the household decision concerning which goods to buy, and to the decisions of firms concerning which inputs to hire and how much output to produce. A central insight that is carried into later chapters is that the area under the demand curve indicates the benefit to society of any activity, while the area under the supply curve indicates the value to society of the resources used to produce that item.

Chapters 5 and 9 extol the virtues of free markets, by documenting in detail why a market system dominates central planning (so it is not surprising that so many countries have been giving up on planning in recent years) and by measuring both the benefits and costs of embracing free trade.

The remaining chapters in the microeconomics section of the book (chapters 6, 7 and 8) provide some balance by considering some of the reasons why unfettered markets do not do everything well. Market failure can result from market power and spill-over effects, and many are concerned that income is distributed in an undesirable way by free markets. In chapter 6, we consider monopoly, regulation and competition policy, and in chapter 7 we see why government financing, though not government provision, of public goods is needed. Also in chapter 7, we evaluate the rationale behind subsidizing activities that generate beneficial externalities, and why emission taxes (or tradable emission permits) represent a mechanism whereby market forces can be harnessed to alleviate one of the market's fundamental limitations.

Paying factors of production according to their productivity is efficient, since it ensures that scarce (and therefore expensive) factors are used carefully. But payment according to productivity leads to equity problems since many individuals only own one abundant factor - unskilled labour. Most attempts to redistribute income generate inefficient outcomes, such as the poverty trap that is an integral part of traditional welfare programs. Chapter 8 explains how incomes are determined by marginal productivity, how the international mobility of capital makes it difficult to avoid the fact that some taxes are shifted to those receiving lower incomes, and how a negative income tax may accomplish society's redistribution objectives more effectively.

The study of macroeconomics begins in chapter 10, where the basic measures (GDP, the unemployment rate, and the consumer price index) are discussed. The tools of aggregate supply and demand are introduced, as is the macro-version of the invisible hand. The economy has a self-correction mechanism: wages and prices rise whenever the economy is trying to produce more than it can on a sustainable basis, and wages and prices fall whenever unemployment is high. Debate about the effectiveness of this self-correction mechanism is what lies behind the dispute concerning whether the government should have a stabilization policy (to iron out the fluctuations in economic activity) or whether the attempt to stabilize just adds more unpredictability to the course of the economy.

The government can either adjust its spending and taxes (its fiscal policy) or the nation's quantity of money (its monetary policy) if it wants to try to stabilize economic activity. Chapters 11 and 12 consider fiscal policy by evaluating the multiplier process that follows government initiatives in the short run, and the accumulating debt problem that can develop in the longer run. By focusing on both short and long run aspects, both the costs and benefits of deficit reduction can be appreciated.

Chapters 13 and 14 discuss the development of banking, so that the details of Bank of Canada policy can be understood. It is stressed that, for a country like Canada that represents just a tiny fraction of the world financial markets, there is only a limited ability to affect the level of Canadian interest rates. Thus, monetary policy is treated as the same thing as exchange-rate policy.

An integration of fiscal and monetary policy is provided in chapters 15 and 16. A supply and demand analysis of the economy's markets for both goods and money is used to show that fiscal and monetary policies can sometimes be very ineffective. For example, a "crowding out effect" operates through exchange rates. An increase in government spending (intended to create jobs) can so bid up the value of the Canadian dollar that just as many jobs are destroyed in the export and import-competing sectors. Another important result of the analysis is that Canada must have a flexible exchange rate to have an inflation rate that is different from that prevailing in the United States. Chapter 16 also contains a discussion of the history of the international monetary system, explaining why the system changed when it did.

The final chapter of the book focuses on growth policy instead of stabilization policy. In this context, it is explained that the increase in the material standard of living that Canadians have enjoyed over the last 125 years is due to rising productivity. Productivity growth has dramatically slowed down since the mid 1970s, and policies that might increase this rate of growth are considered. The experience of both the formerly planned and the developing economies is considered, and the debate about trickle-down economics is examined in detail.

The book ends with a reminder of its central theme - that by relying on our knowledge of private incentives when considering social and economic policy, we can minimize the trade-off between our equity and efficiency objectives. Institutional arrangements that allow us to harness the force of private interest in the pursuit of public policy objectives will prove to be durable and effective.

The book contains an appendix which will be useful for readers who are formally enrolled in an economics course. The appendix contains 50 questions and answers that allow you to deepen your understanding of the analysis. Because economics is a technical subject, there is no substitute for simply trying questions, to see whether you have actually mastered the material. Since the practice questions are listed by chapter, it is easy for you to determine which pages you might need to review if the questions identify gaps in your understanding.

The material in this book is related to correspondence courses offered at several Ontario universities. The TVOntario series "Introductory Economics" is an integral part of these courses, and this book is the written version of the series scripts.

Acknowledgements

A number of individuals have helped produce this book. First, Cathy Boak at TVOntario tempted me with the idea of preparing scripts for a television series for students studying economics by correspondence. We planned that series together, and received helpful comments from both Ake Blomqvist at the University of Western Ontario and the late Doug Purvis at Queen's University. The loss of Doug's input beyond the initial planning stage is just one of the countless ways in which I and all other Canadian economists have been set back by Doug's death. Later on, detailed comments on each TVO script were provided by Avi Cohen (York University) and John Palmer (University of Western Ontario) as well as by Ake Blomqvist. These comments very much improved the final programs, as did the many helpful suggestions made by Cathy Boak and the series producer, Susan Murgatroyd. I doubt that any other introductory treatment of economics has benefited as much from detailed input by non-specialists. The resulting increase in general accessibility is very much due to Cathy's and Susan's efforts.

The preparation of this book version of the scripts has benefited from the tireless efforts from several at Harcourt Brace and Company Canada. In particular, Scott Duncan, Marcel Chiera and Liz Radoijkovic have been patient, efficient and encouraging at every turn. I am also indebted to Harcourt Brace and Company for allowing me to adapt the questions and answers from the Study Guide (authored by Craig Swan and I) that accompanies Economics: Principles and Policy (Fourth Canadian Edition) - authored by William Baumol, Alan Blinder and I. Finally, Darrell Spinks and John Milne at Aniforms Productions did an excellent job preparing the graphs for both the television series and this book, and coping with the various time deadlines involved.

In addition to these many debts, I must acknowledge the understanding and flexibility of the people with whom I live. My wife, Kathy, has been a constant support (and advisor), and my sons, Brian and David, have patiently endured my letting the project intrude on our time together. This family support is literally invaluable.

A Note from the Publisher

Thank you for selecting Economics: The Essentials by William Scarth. The author and the publisher have devoted considerable time to the careful development of this book. We appreciate your recognition of this effort and accomplishment.

We want to hear what you think of Economics: The Essentials. Please take a few minutes to fill in the stamped reader reply card at the back of the book. Your comments and suggestions will be valuable to us as we prepare new editions and other books.

Table of Contents

Chapter 1

The Issues and Methods of Economics

This book will introduce you to the tools economists use to understand how the economy functions and it will give insights into the policy decisions governments make. Economics studies the choices that are available to society, choices such as - Which taxes are most conducive to raising income standards? What are the costs and benefits of free trade? What are the most effective ways to reduce unemployment?

The Problem of Choice

Every society faces a problem of choice because its resources - its labour, raw materials, machines, and factories - are limited. Economists emphasize this fact of life with a graph. Most readers will be familiar with the use of graphs to show important **facts** - but using graphs to show **ideas** may be less familiar. Since the study of economics involves an extensive use of graphs in this way, we must master the approach straight away.

We begin our study of society's choices by focusing on just two possible goods that an economy could produce - food and manufactured items. Figure 1 is a graph which indicates at a glance the fact that society faces a trade-off concerning how it can allocate its scarce resources between these two uses. We measure physical units of food out from the origin along the horizontal axis and physical units of manufactured goods out from the origin along the vertical axis. There are no recorded numbers along the axes, since all that is important is that bigger quantities are denoted by points that are further out from the origin, the point denoting zero quantities, along each axis.

Resources are scarce and we cannot have everything. One option for society is to put absolutely every resource into the farming sector and to produce as much food as we can. The large dot on the food axis in Figure 1 marks off a distance that denotes this maximum amount of food that it is possible to produce. But all food and no manufactured goods is a very extreme allocation of resources. The other extreme is to put all our labour, machines, and other resources into the manufacturing sector and to produce as much as we can in that area. The large dot on the vertical axis in Figure 1 indicates that other extreme resource allocation - getting all manufactured goods and no food. Society can choose a number of

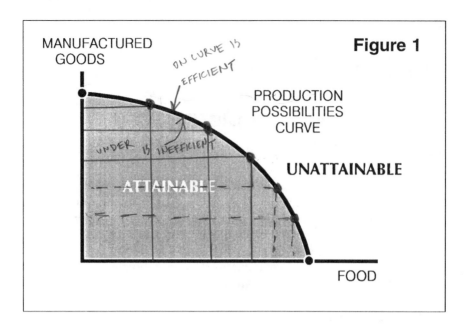

MANUFACTURED
GOODS

ON CURVE IS
EFFICIENT

Figure 1

PRODUCTION
POSSIBILITIES
CURVE

UNDER IS INEFFICIENT

UNATTAINABLE

ATTAINABLE

FOOD

outcomes between these two extremes and the curved line in Figure 1 illustrates the results of all these intermediate possibilities.

Economists draw this line curved in a bowed-out fashion because resources are specialized. Since most resources are more productive when used in particular industries, we lose progressively more of one good (say manufactured goods) as we transfer resources over to the farming sector. We first transfer those workers who are least suitable to manufacturing activities, and only then do we start transferring those who are least suitable for the agricultural sector.

Economists call the line in Figure 1 the nation's **production possibilities curve**, since it marks the boundary of all choices that are **feasible**. All points on or below the production possibilities curve are feasible, or attainable given society's limited resources, but only the outcomes shown by the points right on the curve itself are consistent with society using all its available resources in an efficient manner.

The negative slope of the curve shows at a glance that society faces a choice or trade-off. If we want more of one item we have to move more resources into that industry and that means moving resources out of the other industry so that we have to give up some of the other item. This trade-off is illustrated in Figure 2.

Initially, society is obtaining the combination of food and manufactured goods denoted by point A. Then people decide that they want more food - say the amount given by the distance that point B is to the right of the origin. Figure 2 indicates how many manufactured goods society has to give up (represented by distance AC) to satisfy their bigger appetites (the extra food represented by distance CB).

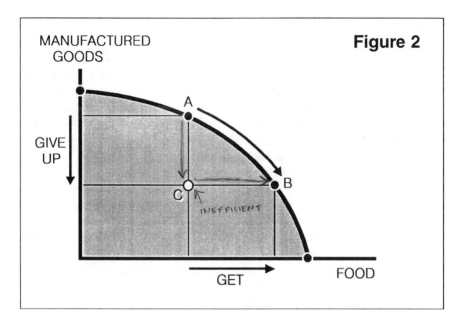

Figure 2

Inefficiency

Society could produce a combination of goods like that denoted by point C in Figure 2, a point that is not even on the boundary of our feasible set. There is clearly something unfortunate in being at some interior point like C, since it is physically possible to move to many points along the production possibilities curve (between points A and B) that involve more of everything. Because these possibilities exist, economists call an allocation of resources that yields outcome C **inefficient**.

How can the economy get stuck at an inefficient point? One reason is a general reduction in economic activity. When we have a prolonged recession, there are unemployed men and women, and unused machines and factories. One job of economic analysis is to help us understand why recessions develop, and this problem is investigated in the second half of the book.

There is another reason for our getting stuck at an inefficient point. Even if we have no unemployed resources, we can have a bad use of those resources. For instance, suppose we had all the people who were particularly good farmers employed in the manufacturing sector and all the people who were good at manufacturing growing crops. Such a misallocation of resources prevents using each resource to its best advantage, and the result is that less of everything is produced. In later chapters, it is explained in detail how misallocations develop and how policy can be used to help avoid them.

Equity and Efficiency

We have seen that point C in Figure 2 is inefficient, while points A and B are not since they are on the very boundary of what is attainable. One implication that might seem to follow from this fact is that being at points A or B is "better than" being at point C. These points are more efficient, but there's another dimension to what makes things good or bad and that is how are those goods distributed. It is true that at all points on the curve between A and B we have more of everything. But at these points, the distribution of goods might be skewed to a particular rich group and others may receive almost nothing. Often government policies that are intended to redistribute income toward the less fortunate force the economy to move from a point like A or B down to one like C.

Throughout this book, we encounter this trade-off between policies that are good on **equity** or fairness grounds but perhaps bad on **efficiency** grounds. One of the main purposes of the book is to indicate what are some of the better policies for minimizing this conflict between equity objectives and efficiency objectives.

Opportunity Costs

We have been using the production possibilities curve to illustrate how economists measure costs. As noted, we say that the choice of increasing our food consumption is that we must incur the cost of giving up some manufactured goods. You will notice that there are no prices mentioned in this discussion - no reference to dollar costs. Economists simply say the cost of food is the **forgone alternative** - manufactured goods.

As an everyday example of this approach, suppose you decide to go to university. In calculating the costs, you add up expenses like tuition and books for a total of something like $5,000 per year. But one of the major costs of your attending university (even though no actual payment is involved) is the earnings you forgo by not taking a job, let's say $25,000 per year - much more than the actual costs paid out to go to university. Economists call this concept of cost - opportunity cost, and it must be understood to avoid confused decision-making in everyday life.

The opportunity cost of any action is the value of the best forgone alternative - that is, it is the value of what you have to give up to take that action.

Specialization, Investment and Growth

Thus far, we have been emphasizing that at each point in time an efficient society faces a trade-off. More of one good requires the sacrifice of another. But many societies have shown that over the years they have more of everything. This simple observation must mean that societies can

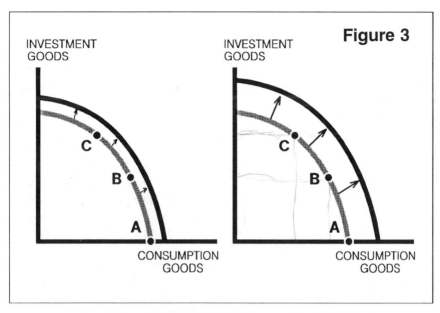

Figure 3

somehow move their production possibilities curve further out from the origin through time. Specifically, how is this expansion possible?

There are two main ways by which we can achieve an expansion in the position of our production possibilities curve. One is to move to production methods involving increased specialization. The more workers do very precise tasks, and get particularly good at them, the more productive they become. As a matter of history, this is one of the very real ways nations get wealthy.

Investment is another way we can move our production possibilities curve out from the origin. By withholding some of our resources from producing either food or manufactured consumer goods today, we can use the leftover resources to invest in more machines and factories and research. By doing this, we pull today's production possibilities curve closer to the origin, but then in the following years, our workers have more machines to work with. This leads to higher productivity which means an expanded position for our production possibilities curve in all those future years. This is why some people are in favour of government policies that stimulate investment in new machines, technical knowledge and education. If labour becomes more productive, workers have higher standards of living.

The increase in future productivity is not free - the opportunity cost is a reduced standard of living today. One way to see this is to divide the goods which society produces into the following two categories - investment goods (like machines), and consumption goods (like CDs and sandwiches). At any point in time, our limited resources force us to choose among the outcomes indicated by a production possibilities curve like that shown in Figure 3. As long as we choose to be at any point other than A (like B), we are consuming less than we could now, but with more machines available next year, the production possibilities curve will be in an expanded position then. If we choose a point like C (and sacrifice a lot of consumption now), we are rewarded with an even bigger increase in our standard of living in the future (as shown in the right-hand panel of Figure 3). Investment is a policy that involves "short-term pain but long-term gain."

The Role of Theory in Economics

The production possibilities curve is a simple model that illustrates the concept of opportunity cost used in economic theory. All theories involve simplifying assumptions, so it is appropriate at this stage to consider whether a theory requires "realistic" simplifying assumptions to be useful. An analogy is instructive. Think of using a map to find your way in a strange city. A map with too much detail is confusing. You just want one that shows the main streets, so you can find your way around more easily. Such a map is like a scientific theory or model - it deliberately leaves out some of the detail, so the essential elements of a problem stand out more clearly. Of course, it is possible to strip away too much detail. A map which just shows the major highways that go around and through a city is of no use for locating even major points of interest within the city.

Just as there is no "right" or "wrong" level of detail for maps (it depends on what the map is to be used for), there is no "right" level of abstraction in science. All theories have somewhat unrealistic assumptions. Indeed, the purpose of theory is to help understanding by deliberately leaving out some detail. The test of whether this abstraction process is helpful or not is whether a theory's predictions are borne out in fact, not whether its assumptions are unrealistic. Throughout this book, you will see that, like all scientists, economists use theory in this way.

Positive and Normative Issues

Another key point that must be appreciated before we go any further in using economic theory is the distinction between positive and normative statements. **Positive** statements are propositions that can be settled by an appeal to the facts. They are either true or false. An example might be "Lower taxes lead people to give more money to charity." Statements like this are the sorts of things that economics can examine and test.

Normative statements involve words like "should" or "ought." "We ought to give money to charity." People cannot settle such a statement on the basis of logic and appeal to fact. The only thing we can say about a normative statement is that it is or is not consistent with a certain set of values. Economists have no right to tell the rest of society what its values ought to be. Thus, economics can clarify positive, not normative issues.

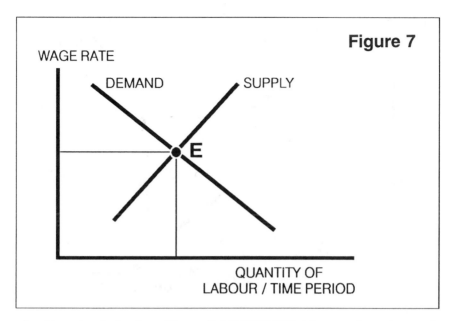

Figure 7

WAGE RATE

DEMAND   SUPPLY

E

QUANTITY OF
LABOUR / TIME PERIOD

alter his or her behaviour. Thus, all adjustments in wage and employment levels come to an end at point E.

We have just described how a competitive bidding process works in a free market, in this case the market for unskilled labour. Economists assume that point E in Figure 7 is the market outcome, if we did not have a minimum wage law.

A Minimum Wage Law

Now suppose the government decrees that the equilibrium wage in Figure 7 is just too low a wage rate for unskilled people to be receiving. Suppose the government passes a law which says it is unlawful for firms to pay any wage rate less than the height of the horizontal that has been added in Figure 8. What would happen?

At such a high price for labour, firms want to hire a smaller number of workers. Firms slide up their demand curve from point E to point B, and some workers are laid off (and this is shown by the leftward arrow along the employment axis). But households want to work more; in terms of work wanted, households slide up their labour supply curve (again, see the arrow along the quantity of labour axis in Figure 8). The result is excess supply of labour, and the more widely known word for this excess supply is unemployment. Thus, the minimum wage law makes the market outcome move from point E to point B, and unemployment results. We get what the government wanted on the vertical axis - the higher wage rate. But we obtain an unintended effect along the horizontal axis - we get unemployment.

So minimum wage laws do not necessarily provide more income for the poor at all. The people who are lucky enough to keep their jobs get

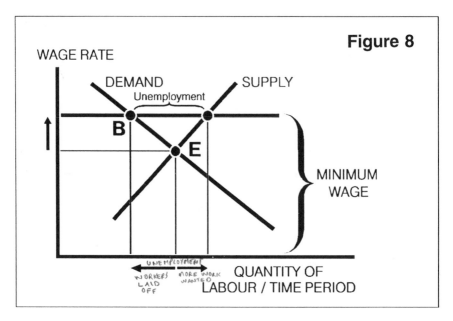

Figure 8

WAGE RATE

DEMAND

Unemployment

SUPPLY

B

E

MINIMUM
WAGE

UNEMPLOYMENT

WORKERS
LAID
OFF

MORE WORK
WANTED

QUANTITY OF
LABOUR / TIME PERIOD

higher income, but quite a few people lose their jobs and so their income goes from a perhaps discouraging low level to no income whatsoever - and that is not a transfer toward the less fortunate. Provincial data clearly shows that the provinces with the highest minimum wage rates are the ones with the highest proportion of their unemployed in the unskilled category. Thus, our simple theory accurately reflects the data. One of the major results of minimum wage rate legislation is to create unemployment among a large number of the people that the policy was designed to help.

Summary

This analysis of minimum wage legislation is an example of what economics can do. It can question the positive elements of a policy, without ever having to get into the thorny issue of whether individuals have the same values. Logically, settling positive issues comes before arguing about values. In the next chapter, the supply and demand model will be developed more extensively, so that we can begin in earnest our study of what a market system can do well, and what it does poorly.

Here is a review of some of the **key concepts** covered in this chapter. We have seen that economics is the **study of choices**. Society must tradeoff one objective for another since our resources are limited. We illustrated this **trade-off** by discussing the concept of **opportunity cost** and by considering the **production possibilities curve**. We saw that there can also be a trade-off between **efficiency and equity** objectives.

We distinguished **positive** and **normative** statements. Economics can make its biggest contribution by focusing on positive issues. Finally, we introduced the tools that will be used throughout the remainder of the book - the tools of **supply and demand**.

Chapter 2

Supply and Demand

In the last chapter, we introduced the tools of supply and demand. But we must dig deeper to fully appreciate how these tools can be used to analyze questions such as what goods are available to you, and what prices, rents, and taxes you have to pay. You may have already been wondering - What determines how steeply we should draw the supply and demand curves? and What determines the position of these curves? This chapter is devoted to exploring these issues. First, we consider the question of slope and this leads us to what economists call elasticity.

The Elasticity of Supply and Demand

It is helpful to review briefly our minimum wage analysis. From Figure 8 on the previous page, you will recall that without the policy, equilibrium exists at point E, where both demand and supply are satisfied. But with the minimum wage, the outcome moves from point E to point B, and the diagram shows the key result of the policy: higher wages for those who keep their jobs, but a decreased quantity of labour demanded leads to layoffs and unemployment. The relative size of the intended and unintended effects of policy is very much affected by the slope of the demand curve for unskilled labour, and this is illustrated by the two alternative graphs in Figure 1 on the next page. Clearly the minimum wage policy is much less appealing in the right-hand panel of Figure 1, since the layoffs problem is dramatically bigger there. What has caused this bigger effect? The fact that the demand curve is flatter.

To understand this effect more clearly, we need some measure of how much the quantity demanded responds to price changes that is independent of the units we choose to measure prices and quantities. We call this measure of responsiveness - **elasticity**. Elasticity is defined as the percentage change in quantity demanded that comes about when there is a given percentage change in price. In calculating this formula, it is customary to ignore the minus sign that is involved, since the demand curve is a negatively sloped relationship.

Consider the two demand curves in Figure 2, that could represent household buying intentions for any commodity. Economists say that the demand curve on the right is "elastic," since there is quite a large percentage change in quantity demanded, and that the demand curve on the left is "inelastic," since there is a much smaller percentage response in quantity demanded, for the same change in price.

Letting P, Q and Δ stand for price, quantity and "the change in" each variable, the price elasticity of demand is calculated as follows:

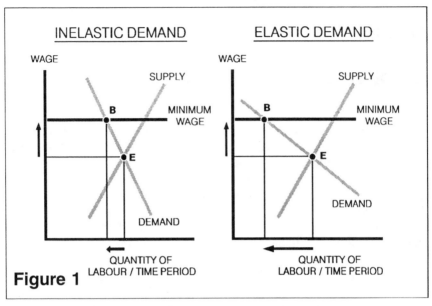

Figure 1

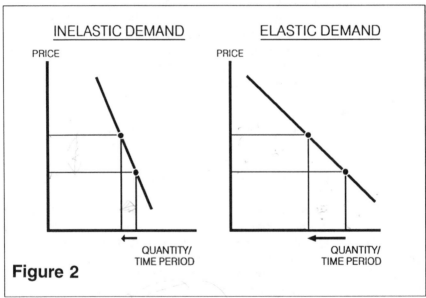

Figure 2

Elasticity = - (% change in Q)/(% change in P)

= - (ΔQ/average Q)/(ΔP/average P)

= - [(Q_2 - Q_1)/(Q_2 + Q_1)]/[(P_2 - P_1)/(P_2 + P_1)]

where the 1 and 2 subscripts stand for the two points on the demand curve (like the two dots on each curve in Figure 2) that define the range over which the responsivity of demand is being measured. Notice that, by inserting a minus sign in the formal definition of elasticity, the price elasticity of demand must always turn out to be a positive number.

Demand is said to be elastic if quantity responds proportionately more than price (that is, if the elasticity coefficient exceeds one) and is inelastic if quantity responds proportionately less than price (that is, if the elasticity coefficient is less than one).

The most important thing that determines the elasticity of demand is whether there are any close substitutes available for the item. For an absolute necessity, demand is completely inelastic. It is drawn as a vertical line to reflect the fact that it must be purchased no matter what the price. An example is the demand for insulin on the part of diabetics. It does not matter how much the price rises; diabetics do not reduce the amount of insulin they demand. The opposite extreme case is an item for which buyers have perfect substitutes available. In this case, demand is infinitely elastic and it is shown as a horizontal line. An example might be a particular brand of soap that is virtually indistinguishable from other brands. If the price of that one particular soap rises much, most buyers switch to another brand.

Elasticity of supply is defined in a similar manner, although no negative sign is added to the definition since supply already represents a positive relationship between price and quantity.

Now that we have clarified how economists measure the responsivity of demands and supplies, we are ready to return to the minimum wage analysis. Unfortunately for unskilled workers, it is easy for firms to find substitutes for them (by simply moving to more automated production methods). Thus, as a matter of fact, the demand curve for unskilled labour is quite **elastic**, so it is the right-hand panel in Figure 1 that is the realistic one. Thus, the unwanted results of minimum wage legislation, the layoffs that result from the policy, are substantial.

We have been focusing on the elasticity of the demand for labour, but as the references to insulin and soap indicate, the same method of analysis is applicable to consumer goods. As an application of supply and demand in this field, we now consider the wheat market. Food is a necessity, so the demand curve for grain is rather inelastic. This fact has forced farm revenues to fall over the years, as we now see.

A Supply and Demand Analysis of Farm Incomes

Figure 3 shows supply and demand curves for grain. One supply curve is labelled as "years ago," because we wish to examine the implications of the vast technological changes that have occurred in farming methods over many decades. These changes have dramatically increased productivity in agriculture, with the result that today's supply curve is much further to the right. We can think of the outcome in the grain markets as moving from an initial equilibrium at point A many years ago, to a new equilibrium at point B. What has happened to the total sales revenue of farms during this period?

Farmers used to receive a high price per unit (indicated by the height of point A) on each of the units they sold (and that total quantity is

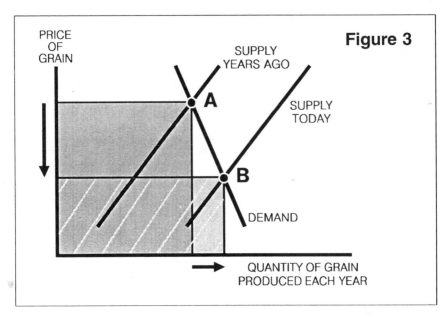

indicated by the amount by which point A is to the right of the origin in Figure 3). Total sales revenue (that is price times quantity sold) was equal to the area of the shaded rectangle with point A at its corner [the base (quantity) times the height (price)].

After the technological improvements lower farm costs, farmers receive a lower price per unit (indicated by the height of point B) on an increased number of units sold (again indicated by point B), so sales revenue is now the shaded rectangle involving diagonal hatch lines with point B at its corner. Because the demand for grain is inelastic, the percentage increase in quantity sold is much smaller than the percentage decrease in price per unit, so farmers' sales revenues have been shrinking rather dramatically. This is the main reason why governments throughout the world have operated major subsidy programs for their agricultural industries. The ultimate cause of this government activity is the combination of three things: a concern for maintaining income standards for farmers, the technological improvements in agriculture, and the price inelasticity of the demand curve for food.

Shifts in the Supply and Demand Curves

The analysis of farm income trends has underlined two general points: knowledge of elasticity is fundamental to understanding many developments in our economy, and we must become familiar with those things that cause the position of supply and demand curves to change. In the last chapter, we supposed that we were the manager of a firm, and we considered only one determinant of the amount of labour demanded - its price, which is the wage rate. The fact that the demand curve is negatively sloped is the geometric way of showing an inverse dependence, that is,

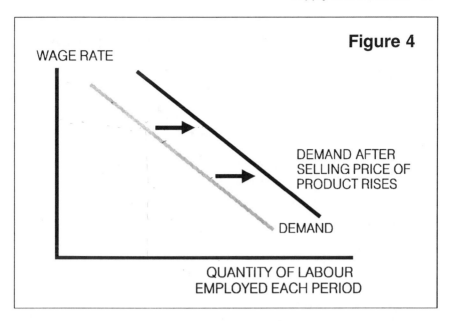

Figure 4

WAGE RATE

DEMAND AFTER
SELLING PRICE OF
PRODUCT RISES

DEMAND

QUANTITY OF LABOUR
EMPLOYED EACH PERIOD

that the quantity of labour demanded is inversely related to the wage rate. (The higher the wage rate - the less labour demanded; the lower the wage rate - the more labour demanded.)

But the wage is only one of the influences on the quantity of labour demanded. There are other important determinants, such as the price of the product that the firm sells. If the price of the product doubled, it would be a great time to sell more commodities and so the firm would try to acquire more labour to produce that extra output. Similarly, if there were a large increase in the price of labour-saving machines, the firm would decide that there was no point in using so many machines, and it would increase its demand for labour to minimize its costs of production. Thus, the higher the price of a substitute input, like labour-saving machines, the greater is the firm's demand for this particular input - labour.

So there are many things that affect the amount of labour demanded (and we have just mentioned three) - the wage rate, the price of the product and the price of other inputs. There is a fourth item in our discussion as well, the quantity of employment itself. The problem is that even with just this partial list, we have four things and we are trying to draw a graph in which there are only two dimensions. The solution is to choose two of the four variables to put on the axes: the wage rate and the quantity of employment. We call this partial relationship "the demand curve." The effect of wage changes on the quantity demanded is shown by the slope of the demand curve. Changes in any of the other determinants have to be shown as a shift in the entire position of the demand curve.

For instance, in Figure 4, we show the effect of a higher selling price for the firm's product price by shifting the demand for labour curve

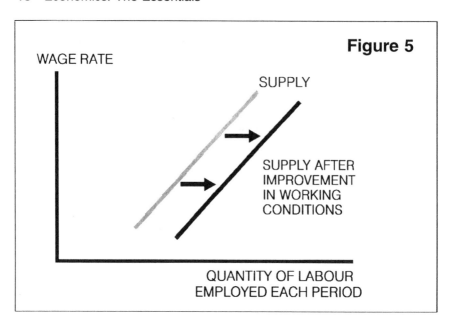

Figure 5

WAGE RATE

SUPPLY

SUPPLY AFTER
IMPROVEMENT
IN WORKING
CONDITIONS

QUANTITY OF LABOUR
EMPLOYED EACH PERIOD

to the right because more labour will be demanded at every wage rate. Similarly, we would show the effect of a lower product price by shifting the demand curve to the left.

The same holds true for the supply curve for labour. The positively sloped line shows that, other things equal, a higher wage rate, leads to an increased willingness to work. A lower wage rate leads to a decreased willingness to work. But there are other influences like job safety and the level of unemployment income benefits. So there are at least four things to talk about on the supply side as well: the wage rate, the level of job safety, the level of unemployment insurance benefits, and the quantity of employment itself. The partial relationship between the wage rate and the quantity of labour supplied is shown by the labour supply curve. A change in any other influence must be shown as a shift in the entire position of that labour supply curve. For example, an increase in the safety of working conditions raises people's willingness to work and so shifts the entire position of the labour supply curve to the right, as shown in Figure 5. At each wage rate, more labour is supplied. Similarly, a decrease in the desirability of the working environment decreases people's willingness to work and we would show this as a shift in the position of the labour supply curve to the left.

Knowledge of these shift factors is useful for evaluating policies that can, over the longer run, increase both the incomes of the unskilled workers and their level of employment. For example, by providing training schemes that make workers more productive, the government can induce firms to increase their willingness to hire workers and so shift their demand curve for labour to the right. Such a development moves the market outcome from point E to point A in Figure 6, so that both income per worker (the wage rate) and the number of workers hired increase. It

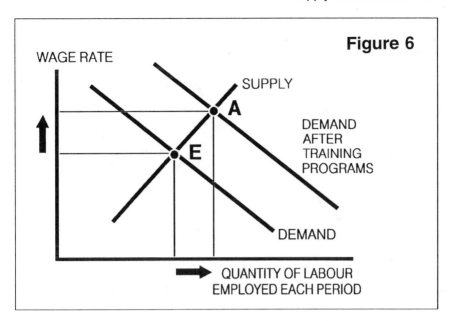

may take a while for polices of this sort to take effect, but at least they do not lead to lower employment the way a minimum wage policy does.

The Invisible Hand

Economists apply supply and demand analysis to all markets - those for things like labour that we call input or factor markets, and those for things produced, like cars, we call output or product markets. Supply and demand is the basis for understanding free market economies. The alternative to free markets is central planning, and many people think an economy will be totally disorganized if we do not have central planning. On the other hand, most economists feel that a decentralized system of individual consumers and firms - each just looking after their own self-interest - actually does a pretty good job of allocating society's scarce resources.

To see why economists have this confidence, consider a major change in consumer preferences. Suppose many of us decide we now want to drive small cars. We used to like big gas guzzlers but we do not have those tastes any more. The question is: without a central planner, will the economy transfer a lot of its resources over to the small-car industry and out of the big-car industry? Economists say "yes" because the market will adjust as if guided by an invisible hand.

We can understand how this transfer of resources works by considering supply and demand diagrams for both the small-car and the large-car markets (see Figures 7 and 8). These supply and demand curves are drawn for particular values of all those "other" influences that (if changed) would shift the position of one of the curves. For example, the drawing of the supply curves assumes a given level for the cost of the

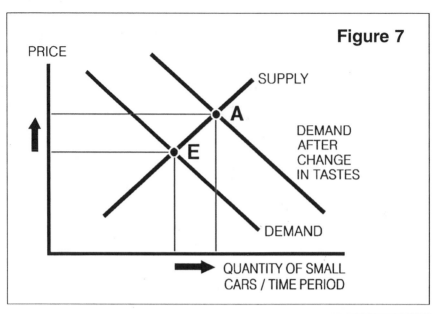

Figure 7

PRICE

SUPPLY

A

E

DEMAND
AFTER
CHANGE
IN TASTES

DEMAND

QUANTITY OF SMALL
CARS / TIME PERIOD

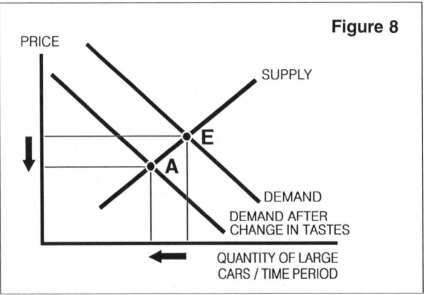

Figure 8

PRICE

SUPPLY

E

A

DEMAND

DEMAND AFTER
CHANGE IN TASTES

QUANTITY OF LARGE
CARS / TIME PERIOD

factors of production used to make cars (like the price of steel and the wage rate paid to auto workers). If tastes change in favour of small cars, then the demand curve for small cars shifts out to the right. At every price, people now want to buy these small cars. Similarly, in the large-car market, the change in tastes means that demand has shifted back to the left, indicating a decreased willingness to buy. Figures 7 and 8 clearly show the "before" and "after" outcomes in each industry. For example, in the small-car market, the intersection of the original demand and supply curves (point E) indicates what things were like before the change in tastes. After the change in tastes, A has become the equilibrium point. The lines drawn from A to the axes show the results. The shortage at the original price has driven the price up and that is what makes it privately profitable for firms to slide up their supply curve, producing more of exactly what the people now want. The firms are making this adjustment in their own profit interest, without any social directive.

Similarly, in Figure 8, with the reduced demand for large cars, the equilibrium point in that sector moves from point E to point A. The fall in the price of large cars means that losses are going to be incurred by the producers of large cars, and so there will be shutdowns and layoffs in this segment of the auto industry. So the resources move from the declining sector to the expanding sector, not because a planner has somehow noticed the change in people's taste and then tells the resources to move, but simply because people are looking after their own self-interest. The owners of the firms want to earn as much profit as they can, so they enter the industries where the products are selling better and at higher prices. Thus, firms migrate from the large-car industry to the small-car industry. These firms get the resources like labour to go with them by offering them higher wage rates. All we need to assume is that firms want to maximize their profits and that income earners (households) want to maximize their income. These assumptions ensure that resources will be transferred in the very direction that the change in tastes wants them to go. So a decentralized system can do a pretty good job of responding to people's tastes.

Adam Smith, an economist writing some 200 years ago, was the one who coined the term "invisible hand." According to Smith, self-interest is the invisible hand which guides the allocation of society's scarce resources, so that they are placed in precisely those areas where a planner would want them.

Government policy makers often seem rather unimpressed with the invisible hand, since they are concerned with what they regard to be "unfair" outcomes of the market system. Policy makers frequently try to overrule the forces of the market. Often they impose controls to keep prices from rising. If we did that in our car example (that is, if we kept prices from rising in the small-car industry), then the profit incentive would not be there, so the resources would not get transferred. So high prices for certain items are exactly what we want in the longer run, because they provide the necessary profit signals to get the desired resource transfers to occur. But often, governments are worried about the short run, and about income distribution or equity problems, not long-run resource allocation issues. Thus, they impose price controls.

Price Controls

A classic example of government intervention to limit price increases is rent control, and to evaluate this policy, we turn once again to supply and demand. Figure 9 shows both a demand curve and a supply

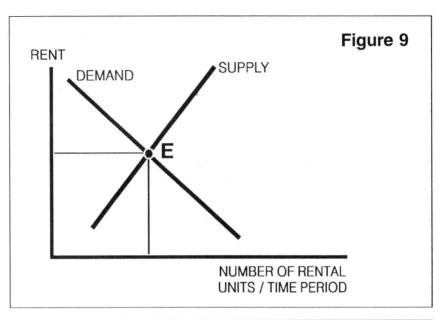

Figure 9

RENT

DEMAND

SUPPLY

E

NUMBER OF RENTAL
UNITS / TIME PERIOD

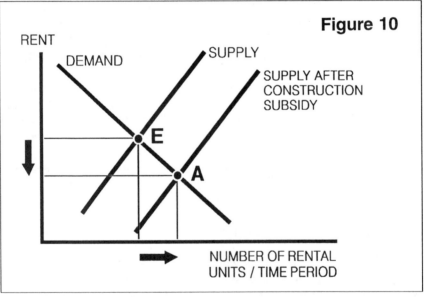

Figure 10

RENT

DEMAND

SUPPLY

SUPPLY AFTER
CONSTRUCTION
SUBSIDY

E

A

NUMBER OF RENTAL
UNITS / TIME PERIOD

curve for housing units. You might wonder why the supply curve is not a vertical line, indicating that there is a fixed number of apartments available at any point in time. The reason that there is some slope to the supply curve is that apartment units can be converted fairly quickly to other uses, such as offices or basement recrooms. If the rent is not high enough, many owners can and do opt for these alternative uses.

In a free market without rent controls, the equilibrium is at point E in Figure 9, because that point shows the only price for which the quantity of housing units demanded just equals the quantity supplied. But

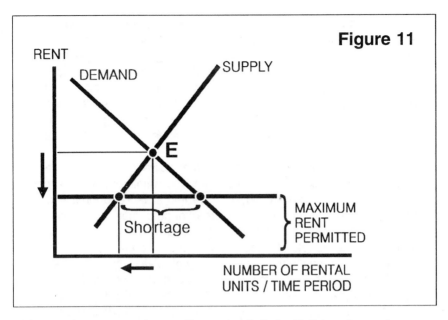

Figure 11

RENT

DEMAND

SUPPLY

E

Shortage

MAXIMUM
RENT
PERMITTED

NUMBER OF RENTAL
UNITS / TIME PERIOD

voters and governments are often not satisfied with this outcome because they regard this rent as too high for some people to pay.

One policy that could address this concern might be to subsidize the production of new housing units. This policy would shift the supply curve out to the right, as shown in Figure 10, so that the equilibrium would become point A. Figure 10 shows that this policy would both lower rents and increase the quantity of housing. Of course, to implement this policy, the government would have to levy taxes, borrow more, or cut back on other programs to come up with the money for the production subsidies.

Policy makers frequently think it is less costly not to attempt a shift in the supply curve, but simply to pass a law stipulating that no one may charge a rent above the amount indicated by the height of the horizontal line in Figure 11. What are the effects? At this low rent, many people want apartments so there is an increase in the quantity of apartments demanded. But the owners are not interested in making so many units available. It is not profitable for them to do so at the lower rent, so we see a shrinkage in the quantity supplied (as shown by the arrow along the quantity axis in Figure 11). We end up with an excess quantity demanded or a shortage - many people wanting apartments who cannot find them. There was not any shortage before the rent control was enacted, but there is afterward.

Whenever we observe a shortage like the one illustrated in Figure 11, we have it because of policies that refuse to allow a higher price to ration the scarce item. Economists like to summarize things this way: when we try to overrule the invisible hand, the invisible hand fights back, giving us outcomes we do not really want. What happens so often in these cases is that a very arbitrary means of allocating the shortage emerges instead. For example, apartment owners discriminate against certain types of potential renters. Or they end up charging "key money" - thousands of dollars just to obtain the key to the apartment. Thus it happens that either the overall cost of renting an apartment is not lower (especially if discrimination or an underground market develops and arrangements like key money become common) or the law is effective and overall payments to landlords are lower. But in this case, landlords will use the space in other ways so that the quantity supplied of rental housing falls and there is an increase in the housing shortage. Neither outcome is what the government intended.

We have now seen that both maximum price laws (like rent control) and minimum price laws (like the minimum wage) cause scarcities. This is not what policy makers intend, so economists do not recommend such attempts to overrule market outcomes. Economists feel that in many of these areas, the market mechanism should be allowed to operate. If some people cannot afford the prices involved, we should transfer income directly to them through a general tax and income-support system. This way, those with lower incomes can be protected from market outcomes. Chapter 8 explains in detail how this can be done.

It is important to remember that not all of our analyses have shown that government policy works out badly. We have seen that a policy of educating and training the unskilled can raise both their wages and their level of employment. And a policy of zoning and increased supply of land for low-income housing can both lower rents and increase the supply of rental units. As these examples indicate, it is possible for governments to design policies that work through the forces of supply and demand, rather than try to overrule those forces.

Excise Taxes

Governments seem to appreciate the forces of supply and demand when they decide how to raise money through taxation. For example, an excise tax is a charge levied on certain goods - like a charge for each litre of gasoline you buy. We now explain how supply and demand analysis can clarify which excise taxes yield the greatest revenue for the government.

Figure 12 shows the demand curve for a commodity on which the government is thinking of imposing an excise tax. To keep our analysis simple, we assume that this good can be produced at a constant price (given by the height of the horizontal, or infinitely elastic, supply curve shown in Figure 12). If an excise tax is levied on the sellers of this good, they are going to have to charge precisely that much more per unit to cover the tax (and still pay all their other costs as before). So with the tax included, the supply curve shifts up by the amount of the tax per unit. This means that the equilibrium moves from point E to point A. The higher price resulting from the tax induces consumers to reduce their consumption, and this is shown by the arrow along the quantity axis in

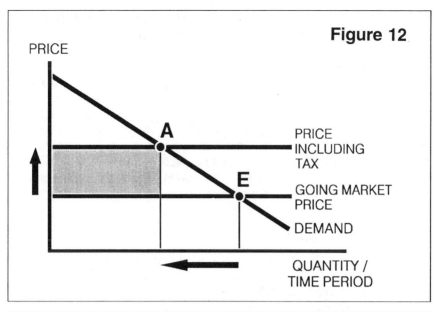

Figure 12

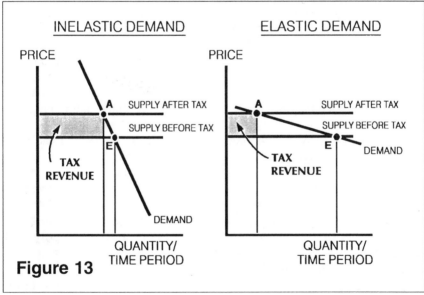

Figure 13

Figure 12. The shaded rectangle shows the amount of tax paid by consumers. The height of the rectangle is the tax per unit, the width of the rectangle is the quantity purchased after the price increase, and the product of the tax per unit times the number of units (height times width of the rectangle) gives the total taxes paid.

There has been some "tax avoidance" in the sense that buyers have avoided making some of the purchases that they had previously made. Clearly, the tax would not generate much revenue for the government if the reduction in the quantity demanded were dramatic. An example of that problem is shown in the right-hand panel of Figure 13. For that highly elastic demand curve, the tax causes purchases to drop fairly dramatically so the tax raises very little revenue (see how small the shaded rectangle is). By comparing the two shaded rectangles in Figure 13, we can see that, to maximize its tax receipts, the government should concentrate its taxes on commodities for which the demand is inelastic.

Does the government actually use this analysis? Not completely, since there is no tax on insulin, which has an extremely inelastic demand. However, the highest excise taxes in Canada have been levied on gasoline, alcohol, and tobacco, all goods which tend to have very inelastic demands. So in the excise tax area, at least, most policy makers seem to appreciate the principles of supply and demand.

Summary

The analysis in this chapter has shown that the market system can work pretty well, and that government attempts to override the forces of supply and demand often lead to unintended and undesirable effects. But there are some areas within our economy where we simply cannot rely totally on market forces. Some government involvement is definitely required to solve such things as pollution problems, and Chapter 7 is devoted to these issues. We emphasize this point now so you do not think that this book is dedicated to claiming the market system can do everything. Pollution is just one issue that proves that it cannot. The central question that we keep returning to is what the market does well and what it does poorly. In any one chapter, space constraints may force us to stress one side of the issue or the other. But taking the book as a whole, we hope there is adequate balance to give you the tools to form your own overall opinion.

Here is a review of some of the **key concepts** covered in this chapter. We have furthered our understanding of the basic economic tools of **supply and demand**, and we have learned how economists use **elasticity** to measure how much demand and supply respond to price. We have discussed some of the factors that cause **shifts in supply and demand curves**. Many individuals think that central planning is needed to avoid economic chaos. But we have seen how the **invisible hand** of self-interest (working in free markets) can duplicate the outcome of an effective planning process, and that this automatic guiding of society's scarce resources toward the outcomes that accord with people's tastes can break down when **price controls** are imposed. Finally, we have learned that **taxes** levied on **commodities with inelastic demands** yield the **greatest revenue** for the government.

Chapter 3

Demand Theory: Household Behaviour

So far in this book, we have justified the slopes of the supply and demand curves quite simply on the basis of the notion that suppliers like price increases while demanders do not. But more insight can be gained from these tools if we think more carefully about what lies behind the demand and supply curves. So the job for this chapter (and the next one) is to embark on two major excursions. First, we take a closer behind-the-scenes look at the demand curve, and this involves our studying what economists call the theory of household, or consumer, behaviour. Then, in the next chapter, we look at the supply curve and study what economists call the theory of the firm. Once we have completed these two background studies, we will be able to use the demand and supply tools to ask and answer many more particular questions. So we now begin these excursions, with the trip behind the demand curve.

The Law of Diminishing Marginal Utility

As consumers, we make many decisions every day, like how many pieces of pizza to buy for lunch. We now use this example to explain the basic assumption economists make about human behaviour to explain the negatively sloped demand curve. Economists assume that consumers buy goods because we get satisfaction from them and that a consumer's goal is to maximize the satisfaction that can be had from a limited budget. To proceed, we need to know how satisfaction varies as a person buys more or less of any good or service. Our basic psychological assumption is called the law of diminishing marginal utility.

Let us focus on each of these words in turn. **Law** is just a scientific word for **assumption**. It makes an assumption sound plausible, since the professionals within that discipline call it a law. Economists do this since there is a lot of accumulated evidence consistent with this assumption about human behaviour. **Diminishing** means **getting smaller** or less. The word **marginal** is just a word meaning **additional** or incremental. **Utility** is the word used by John Stuart Mill, a nineteenth century philosopher, to talk about **satisfaction**. It is just another word for satisfaction. Economists assume that the more people buy of any one particular commodity, the more total satisfaction or utility they get from consuming that commodity, but that each subsequent unit of the good adds less to this accumulated total amount of utility. For instance, when you buy pizza, you get a lot of satisfaction or utility from the first slice or

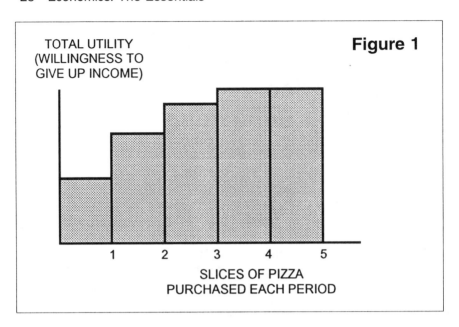

TOTAL UTILITY
(WILLINGNESS TO
GIVE UP INCOME)

Figure 1

SLICES OF PIZZA
PURCHASED EACH PERIOD

two. But once you get full, you do not get as much extra utility from your third and fourth slices. Economists say that this is an example of the diminishing additional or marginal satisfaction provided by the additional units of a good that you purchase.

The assumption of diminishing marginal utility is shown in Figure 1. We measure the number of slices of pizza along the horizontal axis, and the total or cumulative amount of utility on the vertical axis. We need some unit of measurement for utility, so we measure it in terms of the amount of a person's income that she is willing to give up to have each possible amount of a good. So in this case, we are measuring the satisfaction derived from slices of pizza in willingness to part with income.

In the example shown in Figure 1, when this person eats one slice, she gets an amount of satisfaction equal to the first shaded rectangle on the left. That is the amount she is willing to pay for the slice of pizza. When she eats the second slice, she gets some more satisfaction. That higher total satisfaction is shown by the second (somewhat larger) rectangle in Figure 1. The second rectangle is larger than the first, but since the second rectangle is not double the size of the first, the amount of additional satisfaction our consumer gets from eating the second slice is not quite as much as from the first one (because she is not so hungry). Then the third slice raises her total utility even higher, but the incremental utility - that is what we mean by marginal utility - is even smaller still. The fourth slice is hardly worth eating, since it does not add much to the size of the total utility rectangle. Finally, the last (fifth) slice is worth nothing to the individual pictured here, since the total utility rectangle for 5 slices is no bigger than the total utility rectangle for 4 slices. So the additional or marginal utility of the fifth slice is zero.

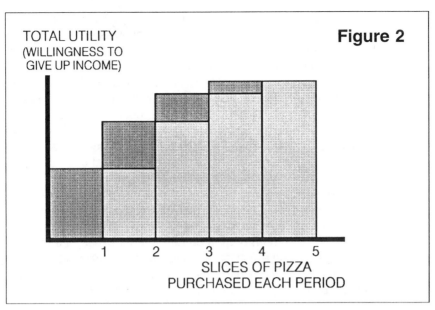

TOTAL UTILITY
(WILLINGNESS TO
GIVE UP INCOME)

Figure 2

1   2   3   4   5

SLICES OF PIZZA
PURCHASED EACH PERIOD

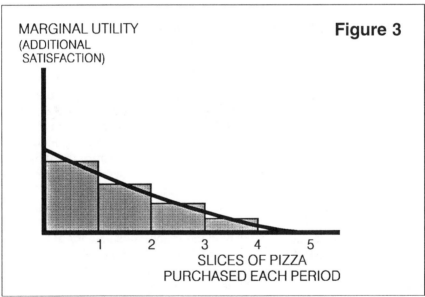

MARGINAL UTILITY
(ADDITIONAL
SATISFACTION)

Figure 3

1   2   3   4   5

SLICES OF PIZZA
PURCHASED EACH PERIOD

We can show the marginal utility of each slice of pizza by shading (in a darker fashion) the amount by which each slice makes the accumulated total bigger, and this is shown in Figure 2. There is no dark bit for the fifth slice since its marginal utility is zero in this example. There are two ways we can tally up how much total satisfaction our consumer gets from five slices of pizza. One is simply to measure the area of the fifth lightly shaded rectangle. The other way is to add up all the additional bits of utility, the marginal utility. When we add up these four dark-shaded areas, we get the same total.

Another thing we can do is to show marginal utility on the vertical axis in a separate graph, as in Figure 3. This just involves transferring the dark-shaded rectangles down so that they are the only things appearing in the graph. Notice how the heights of the rectangles get smaller as more slices of pizza are consumed, illustrating diminishing marginal utility. Since the satisfaction derived from five slices of pizza is given by the sum of the four dark-shaded rectangles (wherever we have located them in Figures 2 and 3), we see that the area under the jagged marginal utility "curve" in Figure 3 measures the total benefits derived from that much pizza.

To explain the assumption of diminishing marginal utility in terms of a common example like purchasing pizza, the graphs have been drawn so that each slice is represented by a very noticeable distance along the horizontal axis. This has resulted in marginal utility appearing like a set of stairs. But when examining economic issues more generally from now on, we will find it easier to smooth out the corners of this series of steps, by considering that each single unit of our good can be represented by a very tiny distance along the quantity axis. Thus, from now on, we will deal with smooth marginal utility curves, like the one that also appears in Figure 3.

The Household's Optimal Purchase Rule

We have been focusing on pizza to have a specific example, but economists believe that people's tastes follow this pattern for essentially all commodities. Except for cases where addiction, for example to a drug, is involved, marginal utility falls as the quantity consumed rises. But how does this fact help a consumer decide how many slices of pizza to buy? The answer to this question can be understood by considering Figure 4.

In Figure 4, we see the smoothly drawn version of the marginal utility curve for any commodity, such as pizza. For simplicity, it is shown as a straight line. Each commodity has a going market price, and in this case, that going price of pizza is given by the height of the horizontal line in Figure 4. The price line shows the cost to the consumer of buying more pizza (that is of moving to the right in the graph), because for every slice of pizza that she buys, she must pay that price. She must give up that many dollars worth of the other things she could otherwise buy. So the extra cost to her of consuming more pizza is equal to the going market price. And the addition to her benefits - her satisfaction - is the height up to her additional utility or marginal utility curve.

Should the consumer pictured in Figure 4 move from zero pizza consumed to a little bit of pizza purchased? Yes she should, because the height up to her additional benefits line is much higher than the height up to the line showing the cost of purchasing it. For this consumer, buying a bit of pizza is obviously a good deal - so she will move to the right. This reasoning suggests that she will keep buying until she reaches the point at which the additional satisfaction of another slice of pizza is just balanced by the price of buying that slice. Thus, she should increase

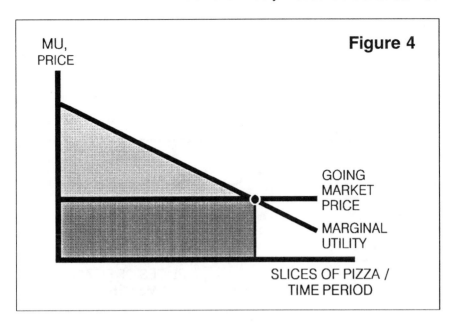

MU,
PRICE

Figure 4

GOING
MARKET
PRICE

MARGINAL
UTILITY

SLICES OF PIZZA /
TIME PERIOD

purchases just to the point indicated by the large dot in Figure 4. By focusing on this point, we can deduce what economists call the optimal purchase rule for households. They should govern their spending so that the **marginal utility** they are getting from each item consumed is just **equal to the price** they have to pay for that item.

Consumer Surplus

In Figure 4, we see that this person's total willingness to pay for her optimal amount of pizza is the entire area under the marginal utility curve, up to the amount consumed. We must remember from the previous graph with the stairs, if we add up all the additional bits of satisfaction for having moved all the way over to the optimum point, we get the total utility that is received. Thus, the total willingness to pay for the chosen amount of pizza in Figure 4 is the entire shaded trapezoid (which is partly shaded light grey and partly shaded dark grey). But all that the market is making our consumer pay for each unit of pizza is the going market price. So the total payment is just that price times the number of units consumed, that is, the dark-shaded rectangle in Figure 4. So the consumer is getting a bargain. Her total willingness to pay (the whole trapezoid) exceeds what she is having to pay (the dark-shaded rectangle), so she is getting the lightly shaded triangle for nothing.

Economists call this free bit **consumer surplus**. It is the excess of total benefit over total expenditure. We use this concept extensively in later chapters.

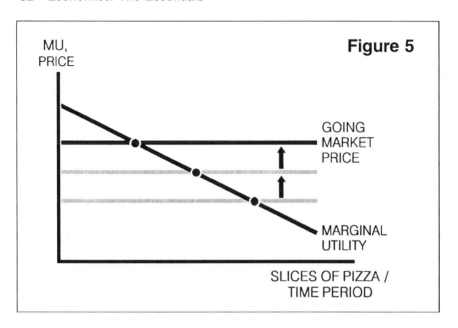

Figure 5

The Demand Curve

The final point that follows from marginal utility theory is that an individual's demand curve and her marginal utility curve can be thought of as one and the same thing. Remember back in Chapter 1 when the demand curve was first introduced, we noted that you can think of it as the summary of what an interviewer would get if everyone were asked how much they would consume at a whole series of prices. If consumers are successful in arranging their buying so that they maximize their satisfaction, then they must be behaving as if they were following the optimal purchase rule (even if they do not use the economist's language).

So as the interviewer suggests all possible positions of the going market price line, a consumer who follows the optimal purchase rule answers by indicating all the points on his or her marginal utility curve, as shown in Figure 5. Thus, given that we are measuring utility in terms of willingness to part with income, the demand curve and the marginal utility curve are identical. The overall market demand curve is simply the adding together (horizontally) of all these individual demand curves. Thus, when economists statistically measure both the position and the elasticity of that overall demand curve, and they calculate the area under it, they have a measure of society's total willingness to pay for any quantity of that item. Indeed, this is exactly how economists measure the total satisfaction provided by any commodity.

For the rest of this chapter, we illustrate how this theory of consumer behaviour can help us understand some specific problems. We

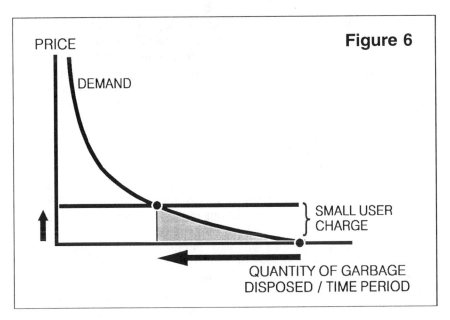

Figure 6

PRICE

DEMAND

SMALL USER CHARGE

QUANTITY OF GARBAGE DISPOSED / TIME PERIOD

focus on two questions: "What are the effects of user fees charged for public services?" and "Who actually pays excise taxes - the producers of goods or the buyers of those goods?"

User Fees for Public Services

As an example of public services, we consider garbage disposal. All of us generate a lot of garbage. For some of this litter, the benefit we get from being able to move it away from our homes and our children is extremely high; for other items we throw away, the additional benefits we receive from its disposal through the municipal garbage collection system are trivial. The cost of options such as composting and reusing containers is very low. Despite this fact, we often still opt for garbage disposal since the cost we are charged per item is even lower - it is zero. But our landfill sites are reaching capacity and our government budgets are overdrawn. For these reasons, it seems reasonable to many economists that households should be charged a user fee for garbage disposal - that is, the price paid for this public service should depend directly on the number of items set out for collection.

To understand this suggestion, consider Figure 6, which shows a demand curve for garbage disposal services. Since we measure utility in terms of people's willingness to part with income, and since the demand curve coincides with the associated marginal utility curve, we can view this demand curve as showing the marginal benefit to society of various levels of garbage disposal services. The optimum purchase rule says that households will consume every item (including garbage disposal services), up to the point at which the marginal benefit is reduced to an extent that it hits the going market price line. If we are not charged for a good on a per-use basis, then the going market price for an additional unit of it is zero, and the market price line coincides with the horizontal axis.

No wonder we demand a tremendous amount of these services and have a scarcity of landfill sites when, at the margin, disposing of garbage is free to each individual. We are pricing garbage collection so that reasonable consumers - maximizing their utility - go right out to their optimal consumption point, and demand a lot of disposal services.

The marginal benefit curve for garbage disposal is very high for the first few items but it flattens right out to approach zero at high quantities. This is because some amount of garbage disposal is extremely valuable. It might be difficult to avoid serious disease without this minimal quantity of garbage removed. But of course the last few items which we throw out do not involve anything that is life-threatening at all, so the marginal benefit for these units falls to near zero.

What would happen if we raised the user charge (for example, so much per bag) from zero to something rather small? The marginal benefit curve shown in Figure 6 suggests that this pricing policy might result in a dramatic reduction in the quantity of garbage we put out each week. As before, people go to the marginal-utility-equals-price point, but that point is no longer far over at the right hand edge of the graph. Such an incentive for the increased re-using of containers and for composting would likely make a noticeable difference to our landfill problems (as shown by the large move along the quantity axis in Figure 6). Yet the loss in total satisfaction for society would just be the shaded triangle of consumer surplus, that is no longer being enjoyed. At a zero price, the entire area under the demand curve was surplus. This whole area may be very large. But the loss that follows the introduction of a user fee is very small by comparison to this.

Economists have advocated that user charges be seriously considered for other items such as medical services. But some of the suggested applications call into question the concept of "universality" in public services. Some people could not afford even a small user charge, and that is one consideration that keeps quite a few policy makers from implementing user charges in areas such as medical care. We really have two problems: an **efficiency** issue - how to avoid squandering scarce resources - a problem that comes from removing the price incentive mechanism when services are offered free on a per-use basis, and an **equity** or income redistribution issue - can all citizens enjoy those services that our society considers necessary? Thus, a user charge generates a "win/lose" outcome: it helps solve an efficiency problem, but it can worsen an equity problem.

Since we have two policy problems, we really need two policy instruments. First, on the equity side, we need to have a tax structure and an income-support system that can effectively redistribute income in the desired way. Chapter 8 is devoted to this topic. Second, if we can achieve effective income redistribution using this other policy instrument, then we can advocate a wider reliance on user charges. The incentive provided by

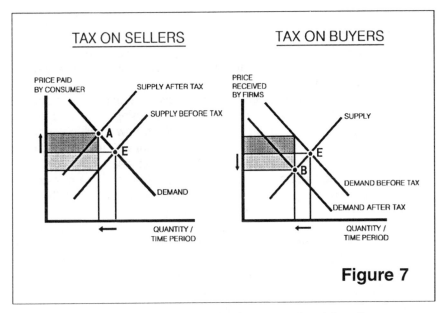

Figure 7

these taxes makes a major contribution toward solving the resource wastage and government deficit problems, while an income redistribution policy copes directly with the equity issue. By using the two policies together, we can achieve a "win/win" outcome concerning both our efficiency and our equity objectives.

Tax Incidence:
Who Really Pays an Excise Tax -
Consumers or Producers?

Perhaps this is a good time for a bit of review. We have discussed taxes a couple of times now - excise taxes in Chapter 2 and now user charges in the present chapter. But the analysis so far has been oversimplified, since it has been presumed that firms can fully "pass on" the burden of any tax to consumers. Let us now use supply and demand analysis to see whether this assumption is a good one. This analysis allows us to deepen both our understanding of a fundamental tax-policy question, and our ability to manipulate supply and demand curves.

In Chapter 2 we saw that when the supply curve is completely elastic, and a tax is levied, the product price goes up by just the amount of an excise tax, so the firms "pass on" the tax to consumers. But can firms do this in the more standard case of a positively sloped supply curve? To find out, we focus on the left-hand panel of Figure 7.

Before any tax is levied, the market equilibrium is point E. Now suppose the government taxes firms a certain number of dollars per unit sold. If an interviewer asked the firms after that policy was put in place: "What price do you now need to justify each level of production?", the interviewer would receive the obvious answer: "A price that is higher than was needed before the tax." And the margin of increase would be just the per-unit amount of the tax, no matter which level of output is chosen. In other words, just as with the horizontal supply curve case, the supply curve shifts up vertically by the amount of the per-unit tax at every point along the supply curve.

This after-tax supply curve is also shown in the left-hand panel of Figure 7. The intersection of the now-relevant supply curve and the people's demand curve is point A, and this is the new equilibrium point. We see that an excise tax means higher prices. But with the higher price, consumers buy less of the product, and so we get less output produced and consumed. Notice that the vertical distance between the no-tax and with-tax supply curves is the amount of the per unit tax, but that the amount of the price increase is only a fraction of that distance. This difference means that the firms have passed on the tax to some extent, but not completely. The total tax collected by the government is the tax per unit times the number of units that are still being bought and sold - that is the sum of the dark- and lightly shaded rectangles.

Since the price paid by consumers increases by only a fraction of the tax, the net-of-tax price received by firms falls. Thus firms are able to pass on only the top lightly shaded part of the total tax payment, and they have to bear the lower dark-shaded part themselves. The analysis shows that, in general, taxes will only be partly passed on (not completely passed on) by firms. How much gets passed on turns out to depend on the elasticity of the demand and supply curves. If demand is very inelastic or (as we saw before) if supply is very elastic, the upper lightly shaded part becomes the whole thing. You can verify this result by experimenting with graphs on your own.

In any event, to have a judgement about whether a tax is really paid by consumers or producers, we have to talk about particular industries one at a time and go out and statistically estimate the demand and supply elasticities, as economists have done for all major commodities. It is no good people just saying, "I think firms are profit maximizers so that they will always pass it on." Consumers are maximizers, too, and because they maximize their utility, firms cannot make them buy as much as they did before the price went up. It is not a matter of instinctive belief: the amount of the tax passed on depends on the elasticities.

There is another way of considering the imposition of an excise tax on this commodity. Suppose that instead of taxing the firms every time they sell a good, the government taxes consumers every time they buy the good. In this case, we do not move the supply curve at all, because the firm has nothing to do with the collection of the tax. When the tax is collected from consumers, it is the demand curve that shifts. The tax decreases consumers' willingness to make payments to firms by the amount of the tax, (since that is what must be sent to the government).

In this alternative presentation, which is shown in the right-hand panel of Figure 7, we simply shift down the household willingness to pay line (the demand curve) by the amount of the per-unit tax, making the new equilibrium point B. The consumers pass on to the firms some of the tax that was levied on them. As before, the total tax paid is the sum of the two shaded areas, and just as before firms pay only the lower dark-shaded part, since the price that they receive net of tax has fallen.

Figure 7 allows us to compare the tax on sellers and the tax on buyers at the same time. We see that whomever is formally taxed, all rectangles are the same size in both panels. The conclusion is that it just does not matter whether the tax is nominally on firms, or on households. The distribution of the tax revenue burden is the same. The only thing that matters (concerning who really pays the tax and how much tax revenue is actually raised) are the elasticities of demand and supply, as the diagrams make abundantly clear.

If you are like most people, you will find this conclusion quite surprising. When they rely on intuition, people often think that taxes should be collected from firms (since firms can afford to pay) rather than from households (since many households cannot afford to pay). But our supply and demand analysis has just demonstrated that the actual distribution of tax burdens between households and firms is exactly the same, no matter whether the tax is applied to sellers or buyers. This is true whatever anyone thinks about who ought to be taxed. With this insight (that some of your intuitive presumptions about economic issues may have reflected limited understanding) you are in a position to realize that your investment in learning economics is really starting to pay dividends.

Summary

Here is a review of some of the **key concepts** covered in this chapter. We have studied the theory of consumer behaviour, which is the thinking underlying the demand curve. We have examined the **law of diminishing marginal utility** which helps us understand households' **optimal purchase rule**. This rule clarifies the logic underlying decisions to buy. We have seen that one implication of diminishing marginal utility is the existence of **consumer surplus**, and we applied that concept to evaluate **user fees** for public services. Finally, we answered the question of **tax incidence** - Who really pays an excise tax, consumers or producers?

In the next chapter, we take an excursion that is similar to that just accomplished. We go behind the supply curve instead of the demand curve, and examine the theory of the firm.

Chapter 4

Supply Theory: The Behaviour of Profit-Maximizing Firms

This chapter represents the second of our excursions behind demand and supply curves, this time it's the supply curve's turn. We start off by considering a situation which is analogous to our theory of household behaviour. In that theory, each individual household was assumed to be a very small part of the whole market, so that the going market price of each commodity was independent of how much that individual consumer purchased. The analogous situation for firms is called a competitive industry. Each firm is such a small part of the overall industry that it cannot affect either the price of the output good that it sells, or the price of the inputs that it uses to produce that good. Strictly speaking, this theory is literally descriptive of only a few Canadian industries, such as the large number of farmers who produce a homogeneous brand or quality of a particular food item. Nevertheless an analysis of competition is a useful starting point, and rest assured, we consider other forms of industrial structure later. For example, in Chapter 6, we consider monopoly, a situation in which one firm has no competitors at all.

The Theory of the Firm

To follow the reasoning in this chapter, it is helpful to think as if you are the manager of a simple firm who must decide how many units of an input should be hired to maximize the firm's profit. Profit is simply what is left over after you subtract your input costs from the sales revenue that you obtain by selling your output. We talk about output being produced by inputs or factors of production and there are all kinds of inputs. For example, there is labour, fertilizer, machines, and factories.

Some factors can be adjusted very quickly, that is in a short space of time. Other factors, like the size of a plant, can only be changed if considerable time is available. So economists find it useful to talk about the theory of the firm in terms of two different time horizons. The first we call the **short run** and that is a period that is short enough that only some, but not all, of the factors can be varied. The **long run** is a period that is long enough that firms can vary the amount (that is, the number of units used) of all the inputs to the production process.

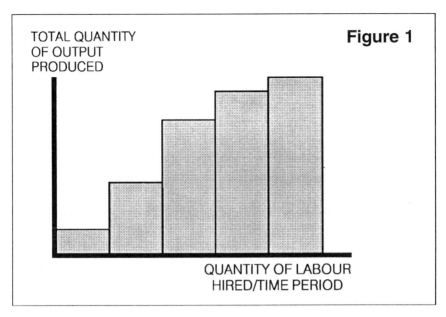

TOTAL QUANTITY
OF OUTPUT
PRODUCED

Figure 1

QUANTITY OF LABOUR
HIRED/TIME PERIOD

To keep our discussion simple, let us have just one variable-in-the-short-run factor and one constant or fixed factor; and let us have the easily varied factor be called labour and the fixed factor in the short run be capital equipment or just capital for short. Figure 1 illustrates what we call the input-output function for any representative firm in the short run. With a fixed size of plant and equipment, the only degree of freedom the firm has is to hire more or less labour. And the implications for how much output that will be generated by the firm's operations is given by this graph. As we increase our hiring of labour, that is, as we move out from the origin along the labour input axis, the total output obtained from hiring all workers is shown by the height of each rectangle. Clearly the height gets bigger and bigger; we get more and more output as we hire more and more of the variable input, labour.

But notice something more particular. Output not only increases as we hire more input but, for a while, it increases at an increasing rate. This is shown by the fact that the second rectangle which shows the output for two workers is more than twice the size of that for one worker. Then, as more workers are hired, the increases in output get proportionally smaller.

This pattern is more apparent in the left-hand panel of Figure 2, where the dark-shaded rectangles highlight the additional output of each new worker hired, as we first move out along the employment axis. In the early range of hiring, the dark rectangles become larger as we hire more workers. If we only have one worker, we cannot divide up tasks and specialize. But if we have two or three workers, we can specialize and have more output than just three times that of the first worker. So output is increasing at an increasing rate over this initial rate of expansion. But if we keep increasing the number of workers hired, diminishing returns set

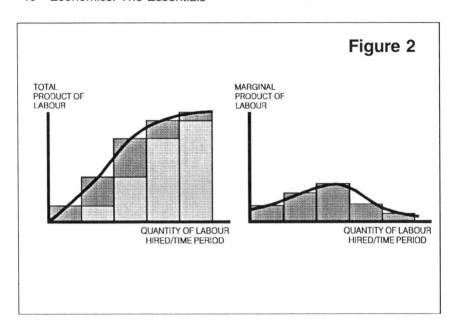

Figure 2

TOTAL
PRODUCT OF
LABOUR

MARGINAL
PRODUCT OF
LABOUR

QUANTITY OF LABOUR
HIRED/TIME PERIOD

QUANTITY OF LABOUR
HIRED/TIME PERIOD

in. Each dark rectangle becomes smaller. We have more and more workers and they are all trying to share the one machine. Since each worker has less of a machine to work with, eventually workers get less and less productive. Economists call this effect the **law of diminishing marginal returns** - the proposition that beyond some point the hiring of more labour brings ever smaller additions to total output.

When developing our theory of consumer behaviour, we found it helpful to focus on marginal utility. The same strategy is very useful in talking about the theory of the firm. The additional or marginal product of each worker is shown by the dark rectangles in the left-hand panel in Figure 2, and these marginal product amounts have been transferred down to the axis in a new graph (in the right-hand panel of Figure 2) which shows just the marginal product of labour. Once labour has been hired out to the point that its marginal product is falling (that is, beyond the third worker in this example), we are in the range where diminishing marginal returns have set in. For the remainder of our discussion, we will squeeze the space we reserve for each unit of labour on the horizontal axis, so that our total product and marginal product curves can be represented as smooth functions.

You will find this material easier by keeping in mind the strong analogy to our theory of consumer behaviour. For consumers, we assume that households maximize their satisfaction and that there is diminishing marginal utility. Similarly, we assume that firms maximize their profits, and that there is diminishing marginal productivity of the inputs that go into the production process. That is the basic set-up and, just as we had an optimal purchase rule for households, this same format leads to an optimal hiring rule for the firm.

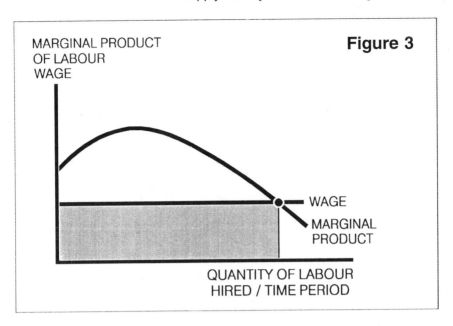

The following labels appear in the figure: MARGINAL PRODUCT OF LABOUR WAGE (vertical axis), **Figure 3**, WAGE, MARGINAL PRODUCT, QUANTITY OF LABOUR HIRED / TIME PERIOD (horizontal axis).

The Optimal Hiring Rule

As with any activity, hiring should be expanded up to the point that the marginal benefits are just balanced by the marginal costs of the activity. The benefit of hiring one more worker is the value of the marginal product of that new worker, while the cost is the going wage rate (expressed in the firm's output units, for proper comparison). These curves are shown in Figure 3. We must compare the height of the marginal product curve to the height of the going wage rate line. Should the firm hire the first worker? Yes, because the height up the marginal product curve is higher than the height up the cost-of-labour line. We can keep adding to our profits if we keep expanding employment until we get to the point that the extra benefit (the marginal product) and the additional cost (the going wage we have to pay for labour) are just the same. So the profit-maximizing level of employment is given by the dot in Figure 3.

Just like the analogous graph for households, the firm is getting a bonus. All the firm has to pay for each unit of labour is the going wage rate, so the total wage bill is equal to the shaded rectangle in Figure 3. But the total amount of output the firm gets to sell is the sum of all the workers' marginal products, that is, the whole area under the marginal productivity curve up to the optimum point. So the firm has some **producer surplus**, and like consumer surplus, it is equal to the area above the going wage line. This surplus represents profits. Since firms try to **maximize profits**, they would be giving up some of this triangular-shaped area which represents profits, if they did not expand employment all the way out to the amount given by the intersection.

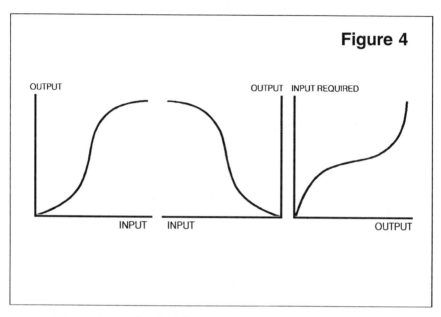

Figure 4

Thus, the **optimal hiring rule** is: Hire any factor up to the point that the value of its marginal product is just equal to the price that must be paid for that factor.

The Optimal Output Decision for a Competitive Firm

So far, our theory of the firm has been limited to determining the optimal level of an input (such as labour) to hire in the short run. But given the input-output relationship, once that hiring decision has been made, there is nothing more to choose. The amount of output that can be produced is dictated by the technology that is summarized by the input-output function. So the optimal hiring rule and the optimal output decision represent the same decision. But we can gain many more insights for policy by recasting our theory of the firm to focus on the output decision.

To determine how its profits vary with output, a firm must know how its sales revenue and its costs of production vary with its production level. Let us continue with the cost side, we derive what economists call the **total cost curve**. All firms have some capital, the factor of production that is fixed in the short run, and since there are costs associated with owning that capital, economists call these expenditures **fixed costs**. Firms also have **variable costs** which in our case simply equal the wage rate times however many workers have been hired.

The best way to appreciate how we should draw the total cost curve is to focus on the input-output function that we discussed earlier. We had the input of labour measured along the horizontal axis and the output of goods measured along the vertical axis as is shown in the left-hand panel of Figure 4. Now consider flipping and rotating this graph. First, flipping it over, so that the labour input axis runs out to the left

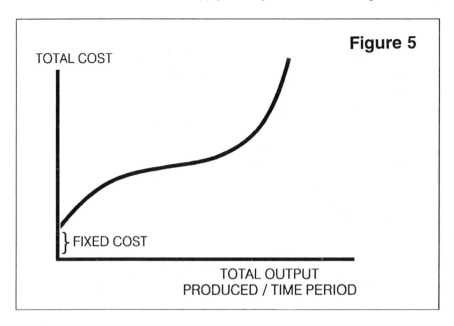

Figure 5

TOTAL COST

} FIXED COST

TOTAL OUTPUT
PRODUCED / TIME PERIOD

instead of to the right, we have the middle panel in Figure 4. Then, by rotating 90 degrees we end with the right-hand panel. The graph on the left shows how much output we get for each level of employment; the graph on the right shows exactly the same thing but from the reverse - it shows how much labour input we need to produce any level of output.

Since labour costs (the variable costs for this firm) simply equal the labour requirement for each level of output times the going wage rate, the variable cost curve is just like the curve in the right-hand panel of Figure 4. The height of that curve at each point has to be multiplied by the wage rate that must be paid to each worker. Thus, the variable cost curve has to have this shape. Variable costs increase, first at a decreasing rate, but then at an increasing rate once diminishing marginal returns set in.

The **total cost** curve looks much the same, as we see in Figure 5. It is arrived at by moving the variable cost curve up from the origin by the amount of the fixed cost associated with owning the fixed factor (in this case, capital).

Remember, we started drawing all these graphs so we could determine the rate of output that will generate the highest possible level of profits for this firm. Since profit is the excess of total revenue over total cost, we need to add a total revenue function to Figure 5, so let us take a look at the revenue side of the picture now.

When firms take the going market price as given, the total revenue line is an easy thing to draw. We multiply the total number of units that the firm is selling by the price, and the result is the total amount of sales revenue. So total revenue, when drawn as a function of quantity sold as in Figure 6, is simply a straight line with the slope equal to the price of the product.

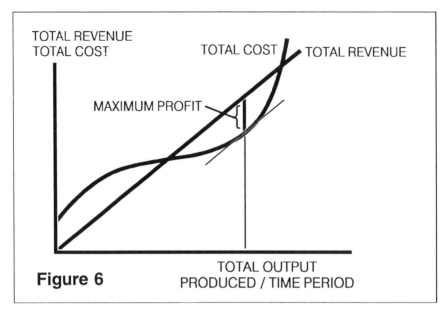

Figure 6

TOTAL OUTPUT
PRODUCED / TIME PERIOD

Putting the total cost curve and the total revenue curve together, as in Figure 6, we can determine the profit-maximizing level of output. What we are looking for is that point along the output axis at which the vertical gap between the total revenue line and the total cost function is the greatest. Clearly producing next to nothing is not such a good level of output to pick because the firm is losing money. Its costs are greater than its revenues. And at the intersection of the two curves, it is making precisely zero profits, since total revenue and total cost exactly equal each other. The biggest positive gap, between revenues and costs is shown in Figure 6.

Economists often think of this profit-maximization decision in terms of the slopes of the total revenue and total cost curves. The intersection of the total revenue and total cost curves on the left in Figure 6 cannot be the profit-maximizing rate of output because the slope of the total revenue function is very different from the slope of the total cost function. With different slopes, it must be the case that as we move more to the right, the profit gap is widening. Similarly the intersection on the right cannot be a profit-maximizing rate of output either because there the total cost line has a much steeper slope than the total revenue line. If we move back and reduce production, it must be the case that the profit gap widens, again because the slopes are different. In between these two extremes, then, we have the biggest profits when the slope of the total cost function (as shown by the tangent in Figure 6) is precisely equal to the slope of the total revenue line.

Economists define the slope of the total revenue line to be **marginal revenue,** and the slope of the total cost curve to be **marginal cost**. Given these definitions, we can say that profit-maximizing output occurs where **marginal revenue equals marginal cost**.

A **competitive** firm that takes prices as given can sell all it wants at the going market price. By increasing output by one unit, the additional or marginal revenue for the firm is simply the going market price. The slope of its total revenue curve is just the going market price and so marginal revenue is just another name for price. For this special case of a small competitive firm, then, the profit-maximizing rule can be restated as: Produce that rate of output for which **marginal cost equals price**.

There are many uses of this analysis. For example, governments raise money through a variety of taxes and some of these taxes are levied on firms. The theory of the firm allows us to compare how firms react to these different kinds of taxes. We often hear firms claiming that if the government imposes a tax, the firm will have to lower output and lay off some workers. Is this kind of lobbying just a bluff? To have an informed opinion about tax policy, we must appreciate which taxes are appropriate in different circumstances.

Which Taxes Cause Firms To Cut Production in the Short Run

One of the taxes that governments impose on firms is a license fee. For example, this tax is used when a restaurant is allowed a franchise along a limited access highway. The firm often has to pay an annual fee for being allowed to be the only restaurant that is available to motorists in that region. This type of fee is something the firm pays just for being there. It is not a fee that varies with the level of sales. It is a one-time payment that is part of the firm's fixed costs. It is just like the fee for a license plate for your car - the amount charged does not vary with the amount you drive.

We show the imposition of a license fee in Figure 7. Since it increases fixed costs, the license fee simply moves the total cost curve up by exactly the same distance at every point. This means the point at which we have the biggest profit gap remains at exactly the same rate of output as before. It will be a smaller gap so the firm will not like it, but the firm is not going to cut its output since that would just lower profits even more. The analysis shows that so long as our assumption of diminishing returns and profit maximization are reasonable, any threat by a firm to lay off workers in response to this type of license fee is likely to be a bluff. Firms may use such a threat to try to discourage the government from imposing the fee, but if the government does impose it, a profit-maximizing firm will not want to worsen it's profit picture in the short run, by moving away from the profit-maximizing rate of output.

But other taxes do cause short-run adjustments. For instance, if an excise tax is imposed, under which the firm pays a certain amount per unit of output, then the total cost curve rotates upward and counter-clockwise as shown in Figure 8. The excise tax does not change fixed cost at all because it is a tax per unit of output, and if the firm does not produce anything, then of course it does not incur any taxes. So the

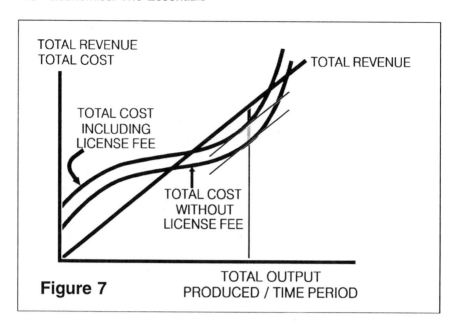

Figure 7

TOTAL REVENUE
TOTAL COST

TOTAL REVENUE

TOTAL COST
INCLUDING
LICENSE FEE

TOTAL COST
WITHOUT
LICENSE FEE

TOTAL OUTPUT
PRODUCED / TIME PERIOD

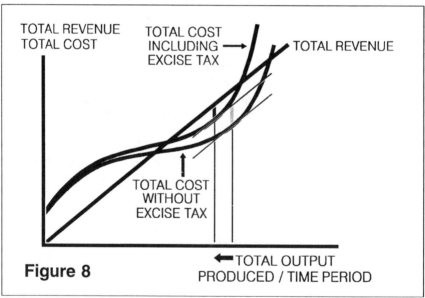

Figure 8

TOTAL REVENUE
TOTAL COST

TOTAL COST
INCLUDING →
EXCISE TAX

TOTAL REVENUE

TOTAL COST
WITHOUT
EXCISE TAX

←TOTAL OUTPUT
PRODUCED / TIME PERIOD

intercept of the total cost curve does not move up at all. But the more output is produced and sold, the more taxes the firm has to pay, and the distance between the old cost curve and the new one increases as output increases. Clearly this policy raises the slope of the total cost curve at every quantity. The result is that the maximum-profit-gap outcome must then occur at some point further to the left. So with an excise tax, we find that firms do cut their output because it is in their profit interest to do so. As a result, this tax does result in immediate layoffs.

One value of economic analysis is to make clear that not all taxes are the same. Some are good for one purpose and bad for another. Which tax should be used depends on what the goals of the government are. If the government is concerned about income redistribution, and the tax is designed to take some profits away from the owners of firms (and to use the funds to make transfers to the less well off), then the license fee is a good idea. We get the income transferred without any layoffs. But if the reason we are taxing is to have less of this activity (because for example, it is an industry that causes a lot of pollution) then we do want a reduction in output, so the excise tax is desirable.

Average Cost and Marginal Cost Curves

Just as we found it useful in our analysis of household behaviour to move away from the total utility function to look at the marginal utility function, it is useful to move away from the total cost curve to look at the **marginal** cost curve (and while we are at it, the average cost curve).

To do this, we start with the standard total cost curve shown in the left-hand panel of Figure 9. Next, we draw the line that goes through the origin of this graph and is just tangent to the total cost curve. Average cost is simply the ratio of total cost to the quantity of goods produced. For the output level that is highlighted in the left-hand panel of Figure 9, it is the ratio of the height of the large dot to the distance that the dot is to the right of the origin. We graph this ratio as the height of the large dot in the right-hand panel of Figure 9. That dot is one point on the average cost curve. At output levels below and above this one, the ratio of total cost to output is higher since the ray to the origin in the left hand panel is steeper. Thus, the average cost curve must be U-shaped, as shown in Figure 10.

As noted earlier, marginal cost is the slope of the total cost curve. As is indicated by the tangents in the left-hand panel of Figure 11 this slope is high at low output levels. As output increases, this slope falls and then rises again. And so, when we record the value of this slope as a height in the right-hand panel in Figure 11, the marginal cost curve must also be U-shaped. Also since the tangent and the ray through the origin in the left-hand panel must coincide when the ray is at its smallest slope, average cost and marginal cost must be the same amount at this output. Thus, the marginal cost curve must cut the average cost curve at its minimum point.

The Long Run

The long run is a time horizon during which firms can change not only the amount of labour they hire but also the amount of capital equipment they use. When the amount of capital is varied, the entire position of all the short-run cost curves (that we have just derived) is shifted. If larger amounts of capital equipment permit more automation, then the firm's cost curves are lower.

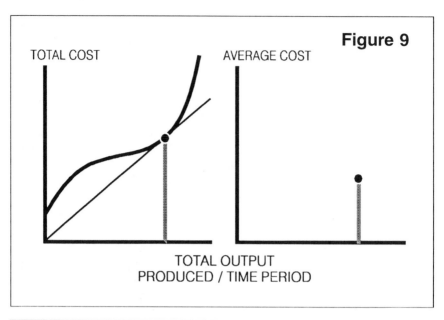

Figure 9

TOTAL COST AVERAGE COST

TOTAL OUTPUT
PRODUCED / TIME PERIOD

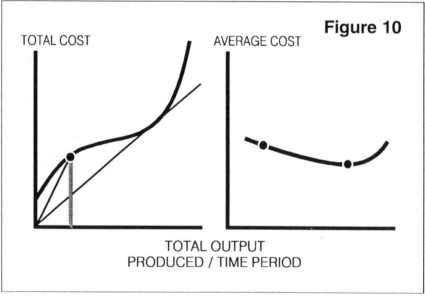

Figure 10

TOTAL COST AVERAGE COST

TOTAL OUTPUT
PRODUCED / TIME PERIOD

We see two such positions of the firm's short-run average cost curve in Figure 12. Also, a curve which summarizes these, and a host of other possibilities appears as well. Economists call this summary the firm's **long-run average cost curve**. There are three general possibilities for the shape of this long-run average cost curve.

For many industries, it turns out that firms can achieve the economies of large scale operation fairly quickly, without reaching a very high rate of output. Then they can continue to expand simply by replicating their existing plants. The result is that doubling both the labour

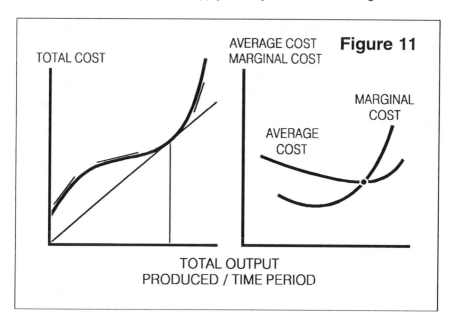

TOTAL COST

AVERAGE COST
MARGINAL COST

Figure 11

MARGINAL
COST

AVERAGE
COST

TOTAL OUTPUT
PRODUCED / TIME PERIOD

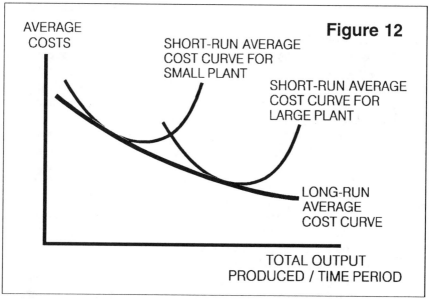

AVERAGE
COSTS

Figure 12

SHORT-RUN AVERAGE
COST CURVE FOR
SMALL PLANT

SHORT-RUN AVERAGE
COST CURVE FOR
LARGE PLANT

LONG-RUN
AVERAGE
COST CURVE

TOTAL OUTPUT
PRODUCED / TIME PERIOD

and capital inputs just doubles the rate of output. Economists call this **constant returns to scale** and it is characterized by a horizontal long-run average cost curve. For some industries, however, a firm's attempt to expand involves a severe co-ordination problem within the firm (as the enterprise becomes very bureaucratic), and costs rise as output expands. Economists call this a **decreasing returns to scale** industry, and it is characterized by a rising (or positively sloped) long-run average cost curve.

Finally, for other industries, the long-run average cost curve declines over the entire relevant range of output (and this is the case that is shown in Figure 12). Any industry that has large set-up costs like a telephone network or a public utility with a grid of pipes or power lines is in this position. We call this type of industry an **increasing returns to scale** industry and they often tend to lead to what we call **natural monopoly**. Such an industry cannot remain competitive because once one firm gets bigger than the others, it achieves lower unit costs. It underprices the other firms and eventually drives them out of business. So we simply cannot talk about this kind of long-run average cost curve in a competitive environment.

Whatever is the shape of the long-run average cost curve, this relationship represents the supply curve for that commodity in a long-run time horizon.

Summary

Here is a review of some of the **key concepts** covered in this chapter. We have outlined the theory of the firm which is based on the assumption of **profit maximization**. This theory allowed us to understand two alternative ways of stating what firms must do to maximize profits. First, the **optimum hiring rule** is what firm managers use when adjusting input levels. Each input is hired up to the point that its **marginal product** is pushed down to the level of its price. Second, we recast this hiring rule so that we could indicate how a firm manager can determine the optimum output level for a competitive firm. Output is expanded up to the point that **marginal revenue** is equal to **marginal cost**.

We considered several ways to illustrate a firm's revenue and cost data by deriving the marginal revenue curve and the average and marginal cost curve. To illustrate why policy makers need to be aware of this analysis, we used the theory to explain which **taxes** cause firms to cut production in the short run, and which do not cause layoffs.

Finally, we discussed why some industries are characterized by constant **returns to scale** in the **long run** and why others involve decreasing and increasing returns to scale.

In the next chapter we focus on constant returns-to-scale industries and we compare a competitive market economy to a centrally planned one. Then, in Chapter 6, we consider increasing returns-to-scale industries (that is, monopolies), and we discuss competition and regulation policy.

Chapter 5

Competition vs. Central Planning

In this chapter, we discuss the operation of a perfectly competitive industry in some detail. This is not because economists think there are a lot of industries that are perfectly competitive; indeed they do not. It turns out that the model of a perfectly competitive industry forms an ideal against which we can evaluate all other outcomes. Our first job in pursuing this is to establish how the theory of the firm that we examined in the last chapter is used to derive the supply curve of a commodity in the short run.

The Short-Run Supply Curve in a Competitive Industry

We begin with a reminder from the last chapter. Perhaps you should glance back at Figure 11 on page 49. The short-run total cost curve for a firm involves first an increasing returns region, and then a decreasing returns region at higher levels of output. As a result, costs increase at a decreasing rate over the low-output range of production, but then increase at an increasing rate at higher output levels. This same pattern is represented by the average and marginal cost curves. Both these curves are U-shaped because there are increasing returns in the early phase of operations, with diminishing returns setting in at higher outputs. This fact makes per unit costs first fall, then rise. In the current chapter, we focus on the average and marginal cost way of picturing the behaviour of a firm's costs.

Economists argue that every activity should be carried on to the point that the marginal benefits of the activity are brought down to just equal its marginal costs. In the case of a firm, the marginal benefits of selling more output are the additions to total revenue. Recall that we have named these additions, marginal revenue. And for a competitive firm, marginal revenue is just the going market price for which the firm can sell the product.

So the market price line shown in Figure 1 represents the additional benefits line or marginal revenue line associated with increasing output. The marginal cost curve shows the additions to total cost. The firm will maximize its profits if it keeps choosing a higher level of output, that is if it keeps moving to the right in Figure 1, so long as the additions to revenue more than make up for the additional cost of that expansion. As long as the height up to the additional revenue line is greater than the height up to the additional cost line, the firm should expand. Similarly, if

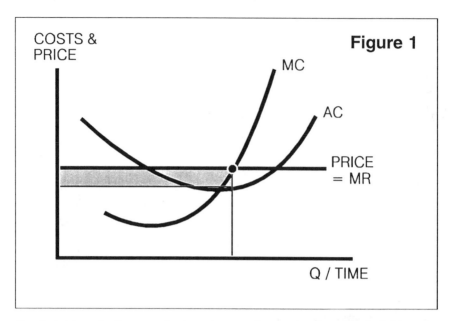

the height up to the marginal cost curve is greater than the height up to the going price line, the firm must have expanded too much, because the last unit produced has added more to its costs than to its revenue (thus decreasing its profits). So to maximize profits a competitive firm must operate where marginal benefit - that is, the going market price - is just balanced by the marginal cost of production, and that is right at the large dot in Figure 1.

Now glance back at Figure 6 of the last chapter (on page 44). When discussing that graph, we said that profit maximization occurs at the point where the slope of the total revenue curve and the slope of the total cost curve are exactly the same, since that point gives the firm the biggest profit gap. But in Figure 1 here, we are showing marginal cost and marginal revenue not as slopes but as heights in a diagram on their own. That is why it is the intersection of marginal revenue and marginal cost that illustrates that same profit-maximizing level of output for the firm.

Why is the average cost curve shown in Figure 1? Because with it we can measure exactly how much profit is being made by the firm. Since revenue per unit is the height up to the price line, and cost per unit is the height up to the average cost curve, then profit per unit is the difference between those two heights. The height of the shaded rectangle indicates the profit per unit, and the width of that rectangle is the number of units involved. Thus, the area of the shaded rectangle is total profits.

When the supply curve was first introduced in Chapter 1, we said that it can be thought of as the tabulation that an interviewer would record after talking to all firms and asking them a series of if-then questions. If the price is high, how much would you want to produce? If the price is lower, how much would you produce and so on. Now we know that a profit-maximizing, perfectly competitive firm would arrive at its answer by

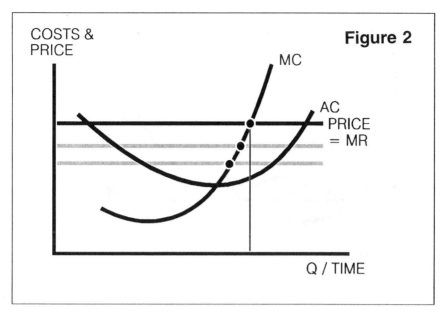

Figure 2

drawing in a price line for every different output price that the interviewer asks it to consider, as shown in Figure 2. The firm answers the interview by stating the quantity of output that corresponds to the point where the price line cuts its marginal cost curve. So when the firm answers the interviewer, all the firm is really doing is tracing out points on its marginal cost curve. The firm's short-run supply curve is therefore nothing more than the relevant range of its marginal cost curve.

The overall market supply curve in the short run is constructed by adding the quantities supplied by each individual firm (at each price), so it is simply the horizontal summation of all the individual firms' marginal cost curves.

How Firms React to Losses

So far, we have focused on prices that are high enough to ensure that firms make a profit. But what happens at lower prices? Figure 3 shows the price = marginal revenue line below the minimum point of the average cost curve. If the firm were to produce at all, the level of output given by the large dot would be its best rate of output. By extending a vertical line through this point, we can assess whether the firm will produce at all.

Its cost per unit is given by the height up to the average cost curve, and this is greater than its revenue per unit (the height up to the price line). So the firm is making a loss on each unit of the good produced equal to the height of the shaded rectangle. That per-unit loss means a total loss on all units equal to the area of the shaded rectangle.

Why should the firm operate if the best it can do is incur this loss? The simple answer is that the firm will not stay in this business very long

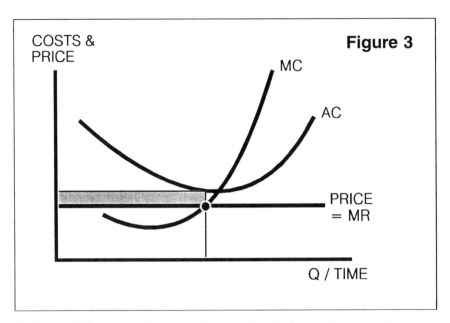

COSTS & PRICE

Figure 3

MC

AC

PRICE = MR

Q / TIME

if it is possible to move its capital into another industry. But remember, our graph shows the short run. We cannot vary or move capital until the long-run when capital becomes a variable factor of production, along with all the other inputs.

In the short run, the firm is stuck with having to pay its fixed costs, that is - the costs associated with owning or leasing its capital equipment. If it chooses not to operate in the short run, it still has to pay these fixed costs. Thus, in the short run, the firm shown in Figure 3 should pick the outcome that involves the smallest losses. If it shuts down, its losses equal its fixed costs. If it operates at the quantity given by its price equals marginal cost intersection, its losses equal the shaded rectangle. So, for prices just a little below the minimum point of the average cost curve, the firm will still operate in the short run. But, for prices that are below the minimum point of the average cost curve by a wide margin, the firm will shut down because then its losses would exceed its fixed costs. It would do better just to shut down and lose only its fixed costs.

You must remember, though, all of this is for the short run. In the long run, if a loss is incurred, firms will not stay in the industry. They would rather employ their capital in some other industry in which profits can be earned.

How can we define full long-run equilibrium in a competitive economy? We say that firms will not have reached the end of their migration from one industry to another until all firms are making the same rate of profit in every industry, since only then will firms no longer have any incentive to move. So it is having the same profits earned everywhere that defines long-run equilibrium.

Economists use profits in a little different way than do accountants and everyday people and we must clarify this now. The way of defining profits according to standard accounting methods is simply to take total sales revenue minus all the costs that firms actually pay out for the factors of production that they are using, and that they do not already own themselves. But economic profits involve the notion of opportunity cost. Economic profits are accounting profits minus what the firm could be viewed as forgoing by not renting out the factors of production it owns (to some other firm and getting paid for them). If the owner of the firm uses her own labour time and uses some machines that she owns, then it is true that she does not have to pay herself to use them. But by using them, she is forgoing the opportunity of being paid by someone else. To make the correct profit-maximizing decision, she must realize that she has incurred these costs by forgoing those opportunities.

So what is the opportunity cost incurred by having the firm's own capital being tied up in this industry? The firm's owner is giving up the opportunity of earning those profits that her capital could have earned in some other industry. In the full equilibrium of a competitive economy, the same profit rate is being earned everywhere. This means that the forgone earnings in potential profits elsewhere are exactly what the firm's capital is earning here. So **economic profits** will be profits that she's earning here, minus the profits that she could earn elsewhere, in other words, zero. So another way of stating what we mean by equilibrium in a fully competitive economy is that all firms earn economic profits of zero, or just a normal rate of return on their invested capital. We have included all these opportunity costs when drawing all cost curves, and so we are using the economists' way of defining profits.

The Invisible Hand in a Competitive Industry

We discussed the invisible hand in Chapter 2. This expression summarized the notion that self-interest can provide the necessary incentive for individuals and firms to behave so that outcomes in the economy are the same as what an all-knowing central planner would try to accomplish. We can now describe this process in more detail.

Figure 4 depicts a competitive industry - the whole industry in the right-hand panel, and the situation for any one representative firm in the left-hand panel. Initially, the industry is in long-run equilibrium. Demand and supply intersect at point A in the right-hand panel, and the height of point A determines the going market price. The market price line is extended over to the left-hand panel, where it is interpreted as the marginal revenue line. Each firm is at its marginal cost equals price outcome at point A in the left-hand panel, earning zero economic profits. So we begin with a long-run, competitive equilibrium - with the market clearing, no economic profits are being made, and the optimal output-setting rule (price = marginal cost) being obeyed.

Now let us assume there is a change in tastes. If the change in taste is in favour of this commodity, the demand curve in the industry part of the graph moves to the right. In the short run, we move from point A to

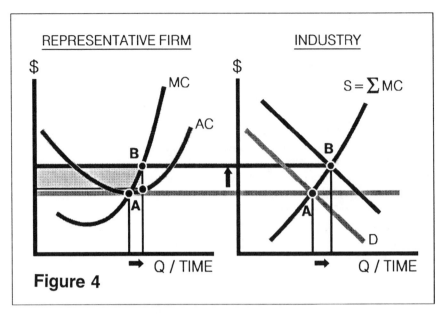

Figure 4

point B - the intersection of the now-relevant demand and supply curves, in the right-hand panel of Figure 4. For every firm in the industry, the price line is now the higher horizontal line in Figure 4. So the profit-maximizing point for each firm is the intersection of marginal revenue and marginal cost at point B in the left-hand panel of Figure 4.

Each individual firm increases output and this adjustment is shown by the arrows along the quantity axes in Figure 4. In the short run, all of this new output has to come from existing firms. In the short run, there is not enough time for capital to be adjusted within these firms or for new firms to enter this industry.

But the shift to point B is not the end of the story. At point B, revenue per unit is greater than cost per unit, so firms are receiving positive economic profits (shown by the area of the shaded rectangle in Figure 4). Positive economic profits means more profit than anybody else is earning in any other competitive industry. Lots of people will want to get into this industry. Thus, in the long run, more firms enter the industry. Thus, there are more marginal cost curves to add up to get the industry supply curve, so the industry supply curve shifts out to the right.

How far does the supply curve shift? For simplicity, we assume that this industry is characterized by constant returns to scale in the long-run sense. This means that the supply curve will have to move out to the point that the market price gets competed down to precisely where it was before (as shown by point C in the right-hand panel of Figure 5). If the price does not fall all the way to where it was before, then the intersection of the price line and the marginal cost curve is still going to be above the average cost curve and there will still be a positive profit rectangle (like the one pictured in Figure 4 only smaller). And if above normal profits still exist, there will still be an incentive for more firms to enter.

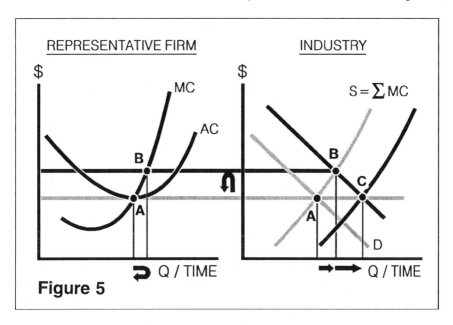

Figure 5

So the full long-run competitive equilibrium occurs when enough firms enter the industry to force the price all the way back down to where it was in the first place. We get more industry output, but each individual firm will have returned back to its lower level of output and be at zero economic profits again. There will simply be more firms.

The Advantages of Competition

The foregoing analysis makes one thing quite clear. The way a decentralized system of free markets works is that **temporary profit opportunities** open up in the areas that people want expanded. Then, the selfish pursuit of those profits causes the resource re-allocation that the people wanted to occur.

While the resource allocation process requires profit incentives to get it to happen, it does not involve permanent income redistributions. This is because the profit rectangles appear only in the short run, and they are competed away in the long run. Nobody is in a position of permanently receiving above normal profits, and that is an outcome that many people seem to like.

The second desirable feature of a competitive industry is that the outcome is **efficient**. When we get to full equilibrium, society is getting the commodity for the minimum possible unit price. Point A in Figure 5 is the lowest point on the unit cost curve, and that is efficient. We are tying up the least amount of society's scarce resources to produce each unit of each good.

The third appealing feature of this outcome is that even without a central planner, the outcome is coincident with what a perfect, all-knowing planner would do if one really could perform such a job. If the planner actually had all the data and the computer ability to do a perfect job of planning, it would end up replicating this competitive outcome.

Here is why a planner can do no better. In a competitive economy, consumers are going about their selfish way obeying the optimal purchase rule - making their purchases so that:

marginal utility equals price (MU = P).

Firms know nothing about these people's tastes directly, just as the households know nothing about the production processes of the firms. The firms just selfishly go about setting their output decisions so that:

price equals marginal cost (P = MC),

because that is what is in their best private interest. But since the price the firms are receiving and the price the households are paying is the very same thing, we have:

marginal utility equals marginal cost (MU = MC),

even though no firm or household has made any attempt to ensure that this happens.

The marginal utility equals marginal cost outcome is exactly what a perfect planner would want to achieve, because a planner must keep expanding any industry for which the extra benefit somebody in society receives from the last unit being produced is greater than the value of the resources that the economy is using up to produce that last unit. But further expansion drives up marginal cost which is the value of the forgone resources, and further expansion drives down marginal utility which is the extra benefit that someone receives from consuming the last unit. Thus, the planner's rule is marginal utility equals marginal cost, and that is automatically satisfied in a competitive economy.

Economists use the optimal planner's rule as a benchmark against which to judge all departures from the competitive ideal. We say that any industry for which marginal cost is greater than marginal utility is over-expanded. Similarly, if marginal utility is greater than marginal cost, we say that we do not have enough of that activity going on. This theme is pursued in the next two chapters on monopoly and pollution. By viewing such varied issues as examples of the same generic problem (a gap between marginal utility and marginal cost), economists have developed a unified approach to economic policy problems.

But you may well ask, why do economists want a system that can replicate a perfect planning outcome? Why not just adopt a centrally planned system in the first place?

Central Planning

To appreciate how impossible efficient central planning is, consider an economy with just three goods: steel, coal, and electricity. To set the output levels of just these three industries efficiently, the planner needs at least twelve pieces of data. First, the planner must know people's tastes to determine the desirable amounts of the three goods to be made available to the consumers. Second, the planner must know how much coal is needed to produce each unit of coal itself, each unit of electricity, and each unit of steel; then, how much electricity is needed to produce each unit of coal, electricity, and steel, (and so on), and there are (3x3), or nine data requirements here.

Now consider an economy with a million items, and this is still a gross under estimate of the number of different products there are in the real world (think of all the different sizes of nuts and bolts there are and how useless these items are unless they are properly matched). For this economy, there are one million times one million or one trillion pieces of data for the planner to collect! The fact that a competitive **de**centralized system can replicate the job of an all-knowing planner without anybody having to collect all this information, and know how to use this data, is a **very** powerful result. There seems to be little option but to try making our actual economy approach this competitive ideal.

Given that so many countries have tried and rejected central planning, there seems to be fairly strong support for the strategy of trying to fix what a market system does poorly, rather than giving up on the market completely as a planned system does. For the remainder of this chapter, we return to our familiar supply and demand curves to analyze the shift from a state-controlled system to market-determined prices.

Moving to a Market System

In centrally planned economies, state-controlled prices are usually set below what would clear the market, as in Figure 6. Who gains and who loses when there is a policy change to do away with state-controlled prices and let a market economy emerge? Figure 6 shows that the observation point moves from the initial outcome, point A (with its low price, low level of output and shortages), to point E. As a result, more goods are produced and sold to consumers.

We now realize that, since the demand curve is the horizontal summation of all the marginal utility curves, the area under the demand curve (between points A and E) represents the total benefits that people derive from this extra quantity of the good that comes from moving to a market system. And since the supply curve is the horizontal summation of all the individual firm's marginal cost curves, the area under the supply curve (between points A and E) is the extra cost to society of having this additional amount of output.

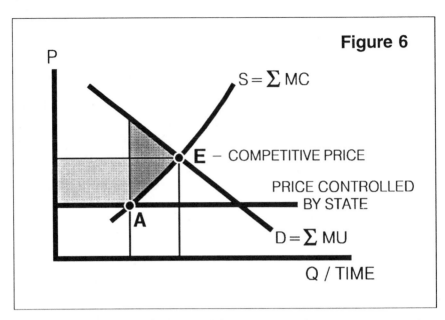

The extra benefits exceed the extra costs by an amount equal to the dark grey triangle in Figure 6. That area is the net efficiency gain. Economists can measure areas such as these in all markets. The total is a large amount of material welfare that a planned system essentially throws away **every** year. The magnitudes involved help explain why so many countries have rejected planning, and are trying to rely increasingly on market forces to achieve these efficiency gains. These gains come with a cost however, in terms of people's concerns about income distribution.

To appreciate these concerns, focus on the range of output to the left of point A in Figure 6. The height of the shaded rectangle indicates the amount by which the product price has risen, so the area of this rectangle is the extra amount consumers have to pay for what they were previously buying, once the market is freed up. It is no wonder that some of the people in the formerly Communist countries have resisted the move toward free markets. They are likely the ones who are hit hardest by higher prices, and who have suffered the loss of the shaded rectangle in Figure 6. Overall, society is better off to the tune of the dark shaded triangle every year, but this gain is not shared equally. Thus, it is not surprising that there are sizeable pockets of disagreement about the advisability of moving toward freer markets.

What is the attitude of economists to this dilemma? When there is a trade-off between efficiency gains and redistribution effects that definitely involve some losers, economists push for a package approach that involves two policies. We should pursue the efficiency gain, while at the same time putting in place an income redistribution program which ensures that winners can and do compensate the losers. In this way, we do not have to give up an efficiency gain in the name of defending equity.

Summary

Here is a review of some of the **key concepts** covered in this chapter. We have derived the **short-run supply curve** for a **competitive industry**, and we have seen what determines **long-run equilibrium**. We used these concepts to provide a more detailed account of the **invisible hand**. We identified some of the desirable features of this competitive outcome, one of which was that it duplicates what an efficient **central planning** system tries to achieve - have **marginal utility equal to marginal cost** for each commodity. We saw why efficient central planning is impossible. Finally, we studied the shift from state-controlled prices to market-determined prices, and the resulting tension between efficiency gains and redistribution effects.

In the next chapter, we consider industries where competitive forces do not exist - a situation we call **monopoly**. We will evaluate government attempts to regulate monopolies, and to control their behaviour through the Competition Act.

Chapter 6

Market Failure: Monopoly

In the last two chapters we have seen what the market system does well. The basic message was that if there are many buyers and sellers for each commodity, then competition forces firms to arrange society's scarce resources in just the way that a perfect planner would, without any need for the impossible calculations that central planning involves. But it will be obvious to all readers that in some industries in our economy there are not many firms, so there is limited competition. This lack of competition is the problem we explore in the present chapter. We focus on the extreme case economists call a monopoly - a situation in which there is only one seller of a commodity.

There are two ways a monopoly can develop: through deliberate government policy, and (without government intervention) through one private firm taking over all competitors through a series of mergers. We start by considering a very common form of government-created monopoly - a marketing board.

Marketing Boards

Some of the most competitive industries that we could have in Canada are in the farming sector. For example, consider the egg industry where there is a large number of farms, each producing a very homogeneous product. For years we have had provincial marketing boards for eggs and other products. All producers within a province must sell their eggs to the marketing board. The marketing board then acts as a monopolist and sells the eggs to the rest of the community, after making sure it withholds enough supply to keep the price up. The rationale is to raise the income of farmers.

Figure 1 clarifies how a marketing board works. Initially, we assume perfect competition. In the industry part of the graph (the right-hand panel), demand and supply intersect to determine the going market price. This price is taken as given by each individual farmer, who is pictured in long-run equilibrium in the left-hand panel of Figure 1.

Now suppose a marketing board is created, and it assigns a quota to each producer which limits output. In the overall industry, with the total amount of eggs being reduced by the quota, market price rises by a large amount. Each individual firm (farm) is allowed to sell at this price per unit, but each farm is limited by its share of the overall quota.

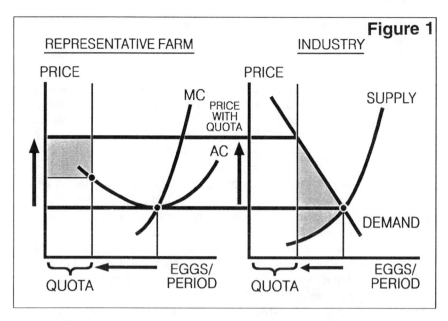

Figure 1

Total revenue is the new high price shown in Figure 1 times the number of units allowed by the quota. This revenue is represented by the area that is below the high price line and to the left of the quota line in the left-hand panel of Figure 1. Total cost is the cost per unit (given by the intersection of the average cost curve with the quota line) times the same number of units allowed by the quota. Total revenue exceeds total cost by an amount given by the shaded rectangle in Figure 1. Thus, with the marketing board, the farmer makes positive economic profit equal to the shaded rectangle each period.

This outcome is bad for consumers because they are getting less output at higher prices. In the competitive outcome without the marketing board, society obtained this good at the lowest conceivable price, since each farm was operating at the minimum possible point on its average cost curve. That was an efficient outcome. Now we see that by producing fewer units through the monopoly selling arrangement, average cost is higher than its minimum point. So from society's point of view, a monopoly of this kind is less efficient than a perfectly competitive industry. Also, it causes equity concerns as poor people pay more for food to increase the profits of farmers.

Another way of appreciating this inefficiency is by focusing on consumer and producer surplus. Society loses the amount of eggs indicated by the arrow along the quantity axis in the right-hand panel of Figure 1 each period, as a result of the quota policy. The area under the consumers' demand curve for the product is their willingness to pay for that output that they are no longer getting to consume. So the total loss to consumers due to this restriction on the rate of output is the whole area under the demand curve over that range of output. But society has saved some resources by curtailing the output in this industry and the area under the marginal cost curve (over this range of output) is the value of the alternative uses of these resources. So society gains the area under the marginal cost curve. But society's loss (the area under the demand curve) exceeds society's gain (the area under the marginal cost curve) by the shaded triangular-shaped area in the right-hand panel in Figure 1. This area is the annual net loss to society of having the marketing board.

The existence of this loss each year is what convinces many policy analysts that marketing boards should be eliminated. While acknowledging this inefficiency, others defend the policy since they feel that income redistribution toward farmers is a good thing. That is, they support the policy on the grounds that this equity gain is worth the loss in efficiency. But is there really a redistribution to farmers? The answer is "yes," but only for those individual farmers who were in operation way back when the marketing board was originally established.

The reason for this is that the quota - the right to sell a specified number of eggs - was originally given to each farmer who was involved in the industry back then. This quota has a value and it can be bought and sold. It adds to the value of what the farmers own in just the same way a house or barn does. For new producers to enter the industry at a later date, they must buy both a farm and a quota. The additional payment for the quota raises the fixed costs (but not the marginal costs) for the new entrant. Competition among new entrants to acquire the above-normal profits forces the price of the quota (and therefore fixed costs and so the position of the average cost curve) to increase to the point that the average cost curve cuts through the intersection of the quota line and the going market price line. Once this has occurred, the excess profits are completely eliminated. In full long-run equilibrium, then, farmers (as producers) gain nothing from the marketing board. All the marketing board creates is a once-and-for-all capital gain for the original set of quota owners.

Monopoly Without Government Intervention

A marketing board is a monopoly that could not have existed without government intervention. Now we consider a monopoly that exists without legislation, to see whether government intervention can improve the outcome from the consumers' point of view. We focus first on the demand curve of a monopolist.

With a complete monopoly, there is only one seller of a commodity. This means there is no distinction between the demand curve for the entire industry and the demand curve for the product for that one firm. The downward-sloping demand curve means that to get people to voluntarily purchase a bigger quantity of the good each period, the monopolist must reduce the price on all units of the product that are sold, since in most cases, the monopolist cannot separate one buyer from another. This means that when the firm increases its output, the extra revenue that comes in is less than the market price.

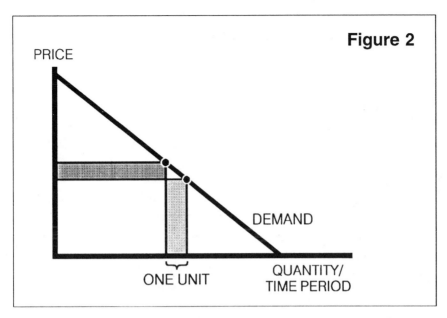

Figure 2

PRICE

DEMAND

ONE UNIT

QUANTITY/
TIME PERIOD

To see this, we focus on the demand curve in Figure 2. Suppose the firm considers increasing output and sales by the one unit shown in Figure 2. The extra revenue that is obtained is not just the lightly shaded rectangle on the right, whose height is the going market price. To get the extra sale, the firm has to reduce its price a bit, so it loses a bit of revenue on all the other units that were already being sold at the higher price. This loss in revenue is shown in Figure 2 by the flat but wide dark grey rectangle. The net additional revenue, what economists call marginal revenue from increasing sales by this one unit, is the going market price (the lighter grey rectangle) minus the little bit of lost revenue on all the other sales (the darker grey rectangle). So marginal revenue is less than price, and it can even be negative.

The gap by which marginal revenue is less than price is larger at higher levels of output. If the firm were increasing output just above zero, the dark grey rectangle hardly exists at all, but as the firm moves to the right in the graph, the dark grey rectangle becomes large and the light grey rectangle becomes ever smaller. This means that the marginal revenue line is almost as high as the demand curve near the zero sales level, but it falls farther and farther below the demand curve at larger and larger levels of sales, as shown in Figure 3.

How a Monopolist Operates

Now we combine these marginal revenue and demand curves with the marginal and average cost curves we derived in Chapter 4. All four curves are shown in Figure 4. We have learned in previous chapters that any activity should be expanded up to the point at which the marginal benefits are just balanced by the marginal cost of expanding the activity.

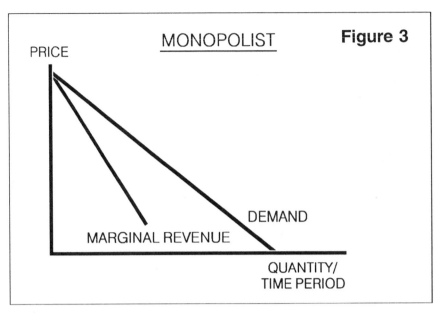

MONOPOLIST   **Figure 3**

PRICE

DEMAND

MARGINAL REVENUE

QUANTITY/
TIME PERIOD

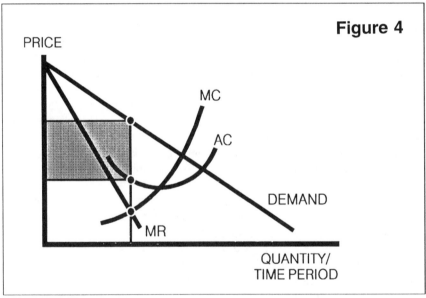

Figure 4

PRICE

MC

AC

DEMAND

MR

QUANTITY/
TIME PERIOD

In the monopolist's case, the marginal benefits are the additional revenue as shown by the marginal revenue line, and the additional costs are given by the marginal cost curve. So the profit-maximizing rate of output is given by the intersection of marginal revenue and marginal cost, and this level of output is highlighted in Figure 4. A vertical line drawn in at this level of output is extended up to the demand curve to see the households' maximum willingness to pay for this quantity. The monopolist charges this price. Even though a monopolist has no competitors and could charge an even higher price, it will not do so. If it did, people would buy less and the firm would be operating at a level that generated lower profits.

The height up to the demand curve is the revenue per unit that the firm receives and the height up to the average cost curve is the cost per unit. The gap between these two heights is the profit per unit, and since the firm is earning this profit per unit on each unit, the shaded rectangle is the total profits earned. The economic reasoning which we have just used, that profit-maximizing output is given by the intersection of the marginal cost and marginal revenue curves, is the same as we used to analyze perfect competition. The only difference is that things are a little more complicated in this application since, for the monopolist, the marginal revenue and demand are two distinct curves.

The Invisible Hand Breaks Down With Monopoly

In the last chapter, we saw that the invisible hand works well in a competitive environment. In that case, consumer tastes were the ultimate authority in deciding the allocation of society's scarce resources. But without competition, a monopolist does not have to serve consumer interests so directly.

Recall that the invisible hand relies on three things:

1. that self-interest leads households to arrange their purchases so that marginal utility equals price:

$$MU = P;$$

2. that self-interest leads firms to set output so that marginal revenue equals marginal cost:

$$MR = MC;$$

3. that for competitive firms, marginal revenue and price are one and the same:

$$MR = P.$$

These relationships imply that marginal utility equals marginal cost:

$$MU = MC.$$

Thus, for the last unit produced of any good, the additional benefit for someone in society is just equal to the value of the resources that society has to use up to produce it.

When a good is produced and sold by a monopolist, households still set marginal utility equal to price:

$$MU = P;$$

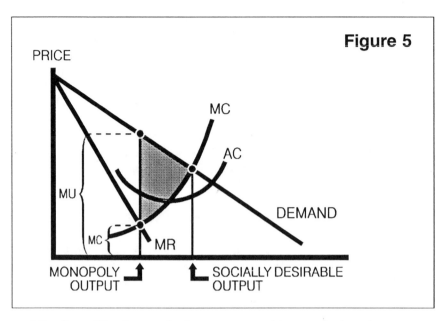

Figure 5

and the firm still sets marginal revenue equal to marginal cost:

$$MR = MC.$$

But since price exceeds marginal revenue:

$$P > MR,$$

the three relationships imply that marginal utility is greater than marginal cost:

$$MU > MC.$$

Society gets too little of any good produced by a monopoly, since at the margin, society values that commodity at an amount greater than the value of the resources that are needed to produce it.

We can see this result by comparing the output for which MR = MC with the output for which MC = P in Figure 5. Marginal utility exceeds marginal cost at the monopoly output, and the net loss to society of keeping output below the social optimum is (as before) the shaded area. Consumers lose the trapezoid under the demand curve, but some resources are saved by the monopolist operating at a lower rate of output, and the saving is the area under the marginal cost curve. The net loss to society is the shaded triangular-shaped area. This loss to society is incurred every period.

We refer to this loss as the efficiency aspect of the monopoly problem. The other element of monopoly, which we call the equity aspect of the monopoly problem, is the fact that above normal profits (the

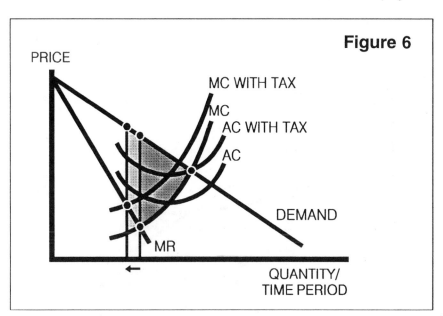

Figure 6

PRICE

MC WITH TAX

MC

AC WITH TAX

AC

DEMAND

MR

QUANTITY/
TIME PERIOD

economic profits shown in Figure 4) are being earned. Some individuals are uncomfortable with the knowledge that others are earning above normal profits, especially in the case of a monopoly, where no new entrants may appear to compete away these profits. Also, the existence of the above normal profits can lead to a further waste of resources. Individuals become tempted to engage in takeover battles and lobbying efforts as they compete to become the ones who receive this extra income. This so-called **rent seeking** activity involves labour being diverted away from productive activities (which could create more goods) toward activities which are unproductive from society's point of view (since they just involve fighting over the goods that already exist).

What can a policy maker do about these problems? Some people think it is obvious - just tax the monopolist. If all we are concerned about is the equity problem, then a tax might be fine. For instance, if we impose an excise tax on the sales of this good, it will shift both the marginal cost and the average cost curves up by the amount of the tax, successfully taking away some of the monopolist's profits. But, as can be seen in Figure 6, this makes the profit-maximizing rate of output occur even farther to the left. The efficiency loss increases, from just the dark grey area to the sum of both the dark and lightly shaded areas in Figure 6. Thus, the trouble with using an excise tax to reduce a monopolist's profits is that while making progress on the equity dimension of the monopoly problem, we worsen the efficiency aspect of the monopoly problem.

The result is quite different if we impose a license fee on a monopolist. In this case, the tax adds to fixed cost, so the average cost curve shifts up, while the marginal cost curve does not. The size of the profit rectangle is reduced, while the size of the efficiency loss triangle is not increased. Thus, if it were not for the fact that higher fixed costs create

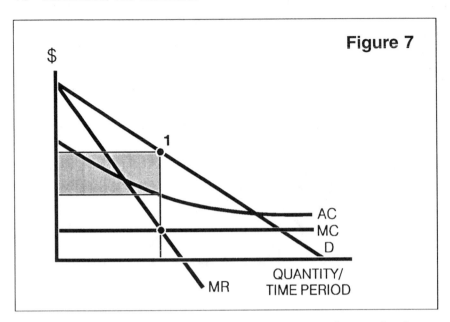

Figure 7

a bigger barrier to entry for would-be competitors, a license fee is an effective tool for reducing monopoly profits.

Because excise taxes worsen the efficiency dimension of the monopoly problem, and because license fees make it harder for new firms to enter an industry to compete with a monopolist, public policy makers have considered other approaches - such as direct government regulation of monopolies and the passing of the Canadian Competition Act. But before we evaluate these policy measures, it must be emphasized that all we have considered about monopoly so far is how that firm's demand curve differs from that of a perfect competitor. As we now see, it is possible that the structure of production costs may differ for monopolists as well.

The Cost Curves of a Monopolist

Often an industry becomes monopolized because there are very large fixed costs involved. Think of the major monopolies in our economy such as a public utility like the telephone system. Such operations involve major set-up costs to get the whole grid of wires into place, and rather low (basically constant) marginal costs to add new users to the network. The large fixed cost makes it very difficult for a new entrant to come into the industry in a small, step-by-step fashion.

This typical cost structure is shown in Figure 7. There is a low and constant marginal cost curve, and an average cost curve which starts off very high because there is a large fixed-cost component. The average cost curve becomes lower and lower as output is increased, because the fixed cost is spread over more and more units to calculate average cost. And it never turns up because the marginal cost is constant.

This pattern of costs creates what is called a **natural monopoly** - a situation where average cost is failing over the entire range of output. Once a firm like this becomes big, it can underprice all smaller would-be competitors and become, or remain, a monopolist.

Broadly speaking, there are three approaches to coping with monopoly power. One is to have direct government **regulation** of monopoly, as we used to have in the airline industry, for example. A second is to rely on prosecutions through our **Competition Act**. And the third is to rely on the discipline imposed by **foreign competition** when free trade is allowed. We consider each alternative in turn.

Regulation of Monopoly: the Theory

What are the pros and cons of regulating natural monopolies? Up until the 1980s, many people thought regulation was best, but since then, many analysts are less convinced. We now consider this debate.

Before we use our graphs to evaluate a policy of government regulation of natural monopoly, we remind ourselves where a monopolist would operate without any regulation. As before, the intersection of marginal revenue and marginal cost determines the profit-maximizing rate of output, if the firm is not subject to any regulation. We extend this line up to the demand curve, to point 1 in Figure 7, to get the profit-maximizing price. Revenue per unit is that price and cost per unit is the height up to the average cost curve. So profit per unit is the height of the shaded rectangle, and total profits earned by the unregulated monopolist are represented by the shaded area.

Compare this outcome to the most efficient outcome from society's point of view, that given by MU = MC. Since the demand curve shows marginal utility, it would be efficient for production to be expanded all the way to the point that the demand curve crosses marginal cost at point 2 in Figure 8. With this much more output, society would achieve extra satisfaction equal to the area under the demand curve between points 1 and 2, and society would incur extra cost equal to the area under the marginal cost curve over this same range of output. Thus, the shaded triangle in Figure 8 is the extra net benefits that society is throwing away by letting the monopolist maximize its profits in an unregulated fashion.

It certainly seems appealing to set up a regulatory board, which can collect data and then require that this firm not charge a price any higher than its marginal costs. The trouble is, this policy cannot force a firm to operate at the socially optimal point. To see why, consider how much profit the firm would earn if it actually did operate at point 2. This is shown in Figure 9. The price per unit would be the height up to the demand curve, while the cost per unit would be the height up to the average cost curve, which is higher. So there would be a loss per unit equal to the difference between these two heights. Multiplied over the total number of units, total losses equal the shaded rectangle, if we regulate the monopolist this way. Clearly, this monopolist will not stay in business

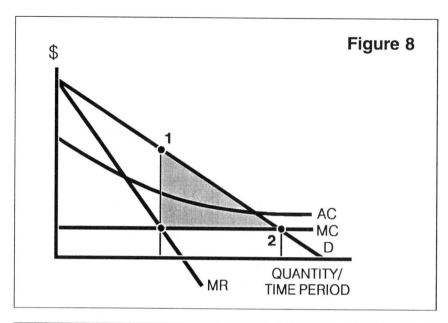

Figure 8

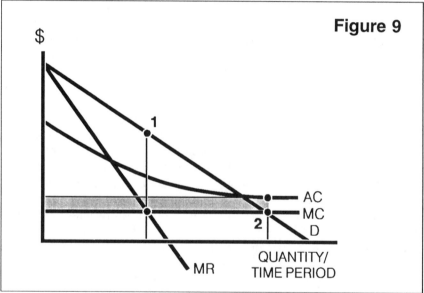

Figure 9

only to suffer these regulation-induced losses. With this regulation policy, this firm will quit the industry and society will get none of this commodity.

The general approach in the history of regulation is to try to push the firm as much from point 1 toward point 2 as we possibly can, without forcing the firm out of business. With this goal in mind, we can go no further than the point where the average cost curve intersects the demand curve because at this point, point 3 in Figure 10, the height up to the demand curve and the height up to the average cost curve are equal, making economic profits zero. So essentially what regulators have done

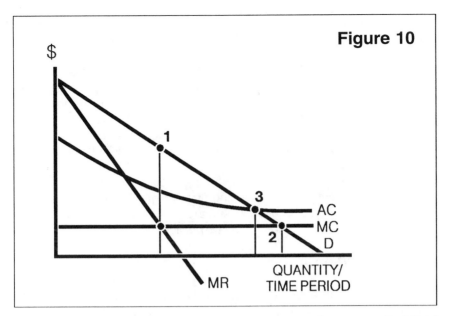

Figure 10

is to try to calculate what price would just yield the firm a so-called "fair" rate of return - a profit rate equal to what can be earned in competitive industries - and to impose the corresponding regulation on price. Thus, trying for point 3 through regulation is a compromise, getting as close to point 2 as we can without driving the firm out of business.

Regulation of Monopoly: the Experience

There are two issues which the basic theory of regulation overlooks - that the process of regulation may affect the monopolist's productivity, and that the monopolist may be able to limit the technical information that the regulator acquires, with the result that regulation may actually further the monopolist's own interests. We consider each issue in turn.

What does regulation do for the firm's incentive to invest in cost-saving technology? Normally, firms invest in new techniques to lower costs and so create extra profits. But if the regulation process pushes down the allowable price every time costs are reduced, then the firm will get no payoff from investing in cost-saving techniques. One way our policy makers have tried to limit this low-productivity problem is to have a lag in the regulatory process. The lag is intended to be long enough to make it worthwhile for the firm to invest in new technology, but not so long as to generate vast profits for the small group of individuals in society that are the majority shareholders of these firms.

Have regulators become captives of the regulated firms? The best way to answer this question is to see what happened during the process of deregulation that took place during the 1980s. In many deregulated industries, the number of firms increased and prices fell. According to

Figure 10, the removal of regulation was supposed to cause a move from point 3 back up to point 1. The fact that prices fell with the removal of regulation can mean only one of two things. First, it could mean that the cost savings that come from new investment, and that are ignored in basic theory of regulation, are substantial, and that the regulatory process was limiting this investment to a very large extent. Second, it could mean that many of the industries that were regulated were, in fact, not natural monopolies at all. This second explanation is supported by the fact that many new firms entered a number of the deregulated industries. What really may have happened with regulation then, is that it provided a government agency which served the monopoly, not consumers, by keeping out new entrants and keeping prices high. The result of all this experience is that many economists are now quite skeptical about regulation as an approach to competition policy.

The Competition Act

The second approach to monopoly problems, which also has a long history, is to pass laws like our Competition Act. This legislation defines many business practices, such as rigging prices and misleading advertising, as unlawful. Ever since 1889, Canada has had some form of Competition Act, but these laws have had quite limited accomplishments. For one thing, the fines were trivial compared to the benefits firms could derive from breaking the law. A second problem was that early interpretations of the Act set the precedent that a guilty verdict was warranted only if competition was completely eliminated, not just lessened. A third problem was that the Act was part of the criminal code, not the civil code. Since a conviction under the criminal code requires no reasonable doubt, and the courts have limited knowledge concerning particular industries, there frequently was some reasonable doubt, and convictions were very rare.

We had a major revision of the Competition Act in 1986. Fines and prison terms for company executives were made much stiffer, and many offenses were transferred to the more flexible civil code of law, involving a new competition tribunal replacing the standard courts. The authority of the competition tribunal was challenged in a series of Supreme Court cases, but since the government won all these cases in the early 1990s, many economists have just recently acquired a renewed but cautious optimism concerning this legal approach to competition policy.

Summary

Here is a review of the **key concepts** covered in this chapter. We have studied how the invisible hand breaks down when competition is limited. We discussed **monopoly** and we have seen that it results in **inefficiency**. When monopoly is government-created, as with **marketing**

boards, the inefficiency can be eliminated by dismantling the marketing board. With a **natural monopoly**, however, it is very difficult to eliminate the inefficiency. There are three ways of trying to do so. First, we can have government **regulation** of the monopoly; second, we can apply the **Competition Act** through the courts and the Competition Tribunal; and third, competition can be enforced by dropping tariffs to permit new market entrants from other countries.

Given the limited success of regulation and the legal approach to monopoly problems, many economists favour relying on the discipline of the market - which can be made more effective through free trade. We devote an entire chapter to free trade later in this book (Chapter 9). But before examining this alternative, we look at another reason why free markets can fail to operate efficiently. That problem is the phenomenon of spill over effects that arise from the production process, effects like pollution. It is to these issues that we turn in the next chapter.

Chapter 7

Market Failure: Externalities

Thus far, we have spent most of the book discussing how a decentralized market system performs. In the last chapter, we saw that the market mechanism can fail to deliver an efficient outcome for society if some individuals or firms are big enough to have market power. But market power is not the only problem that can develop. Another is the existence of spillover effects. An example of this problem is second-hand smoke. Neither smokers, nor the tobacco companies that create cigarettes, have to pay anything for spillover costs of this sort, so a market system does not take them into account.

Some spillover problems are so pervasive that economists have defined a term called **public goods** to distinguish them from what we have been studying up to now - the provision of private goods and services.

Public Goods

An apple is an example of a private good. It has a feature economists call excludability, which means it is very easy for an individual to keep the apple for herself. Everyone else can be excluded from having it. This all seems obvious but some goods, which we call public goods, do not have this property.

Consider a lighthouse, for example. The fact that one ship has sailed by, seen the lighthouse, and avoided crashing into the rocks does not curtail another ship from deriving the same safety services from the lighthouse. Once the lighthouse is built and operating, there is no way that anyone can exclude passing ships from seeing it and benefitting from the service it provides. Thus, the services are not excludable and so a lighthouse is an example of a public good.

The important thing to realize about a public good is that because users cannot be excluded from enjoying it, it is unlikely that individuals, operating in their own self-interest, will offer to pay enough to cover its costs. Everyone hopes the costs will be paid by others. Because most people try to "free ride" on others, private profit-oriented firms do not find it in their interest to produce a public good. After all, it would cost them something to produce a lighthouse, to return to our example, and once it was built, they would get no sales revenue from its operation, since there is no mechanism by which they can force consumers of the lighthouse services to pay. The only way we will have such public goods produced in our society is to have the government coerce people to pay a share of the costs through the levying of taxes. But this does not mean that the government must actually build and operate the lighthouse. These tasks can be tendered out to competing private firms, to see which can do these tasks most efficiently.

There are many examples of public goods - national defence, city streets, and our legal system, to name just a few. It is important to recognize that the **actual provision** of public goods is very much a separate issue from the government **financing** of them. As far as the underlying logic is concerned, the notion of publicness only justifies the government financing of these services, but not the government providing them. The institutional arrangement of using tendered bids from private firms is quite common for the construction of highways and public buildings and many analysts think that this practice should be expanded into other public-sponsored activities such as education.

Beneficial Externalities

We now consider goods which are a mixture of public and private goods. Education does not represent a pure public good, since each student certainly uses up a spot in the classroom, and each student benefits more from her own education than others do. But there are certainly some positive spillover effects involved. We all benefit from the fact that the level of education at our workplace, and in society in general, is reasonably high.

Education is not unique in this regard. There is a whole range of goods and services which generate favourable spillover or external effects - for example, garbage collection, good health, and street lighting. A public good is really just a beneficial externality in an extreme form - one in which the external beneficiary enjoys the service just as much as the primary "consumer." To analyze the mixed case - a private good with beneficial externalities - we focus on Figure 1, and consider an individual's decision to attend university.

There are two benefits from a person's going to university. One, which we call the private benefit, is the higher income and the general intellectual satisfaction received by that individual. As with the consumption of any item, diminishing marginal utility applies, so the private marginal benefit curve is downward sloping in Figure 1. The second benefit from a person going to university is that society at large gains from having that more informed and productive person to work and interact with. These extra benefits to society are incorporated within the social marginal benefit curve in Figure 1. It includes both the private benefits to the individual being educated plus the spillover benefits to others. (For a purely private good, there is no difference between the private and social marginal benefit curves. Since we focused exclusively on private goods in earlier chapters, we did not distinguish private and social benefits.)

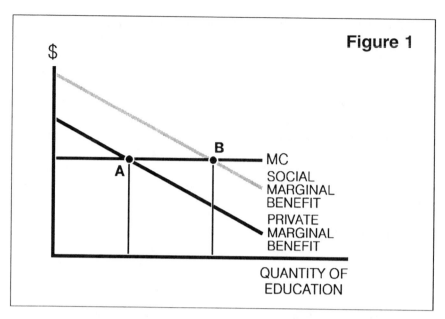

The third curve shown in Figure 1 indicates the marginal cost of educating a person, which must be paid by that individual if there is no public subsidy for education. For simplicity, we assume that this marginal cost is constant. If left to her own devices, this individual's private optimum is to go to the intersection of the private marginal benefit curve and the marginal cost curve, that is to point A. But this is not the best outcome from society's point of view, since at this level of education, marginal benefit exceeds marginal cost. From society's point of view, the best point is B, and this involves providing this individual with more education. The reason she stops short of seeking as much education as is in the public interest, is that she does not receive the benefits that go to society in general and so, acting as a rational maximizer, she attaches little or no weight to them in making her own decision.

How can the individual be induced to get more education, that is, to move from the quantity given by point A to that given by point B in Figure 1? One solution is to subsidize education. With a subsidy, the cost to the individual would shift down. If the subsidy is the amount shown in Figure 2, there will be a coincidence between what is in this individual's private interest, and what is in the public interest. With the subsidy, the individual will choose point C - the intersection of her private marginal benefit curve with the subsidized cost curve. But points C and B involve the same amount of education, so the original problem has been solved. Economists refer to the subsidy as a way of "internalizing the externality" because it causes the private decision maker to attach weight to what was previously only an external benefit received by others. This then is the ultimate justification for subsidizing education, health care, and many other activities. There remains much debate, however, since there are many different views concerning the size of these beneficial externalities.

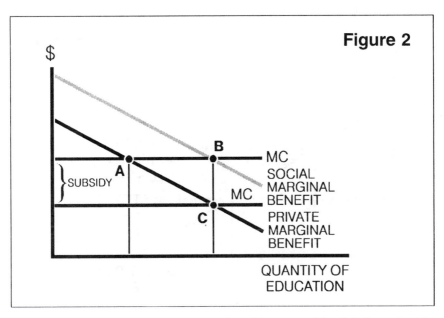

Just as with pure public goods, with externalities it is important to stress the difference between the government financing of services and government provision of these services. The positive externality argument only justifies government financial support of education; it does not mean government employees should actually do the educating. Many policy analysts think a system of "education vouchers" could handle this and related cases very effectively. We could subsidize the pursuit of education by giving out vouchers, and then letting individuals spend the vouchers at whichever institution provides them with the kind of education they think is the best. If the government takes over the process of actually providing the education, we lose the efficiencies that come with competition. In that case, we are solving a beneficial externality problem, but at the same time introducing a monopoly problem. A voucher system solves the externality problem without introducing the monopoly problem.

Detrimental Externalities

Spillover effects can be negative as well as positive, and the classic example of these negative externalities is pollution. In Figure 3, there is both the demand curve for some manufactured good and the constant marginal cost curve involved in producing that good. This supply curve is labelled the private marginal cost curve because it includes only those costs which the producers actually have to pay - such items as the costs of labour and raw materials. The private cost curve does not include the spillover costs that are imposed on third parties. For example, suppose the production process in this industry involves the generation of an effluent that is poured into streams and rivers, and that this effluent makes the water unsuitable for drinking or recreational purposes. When

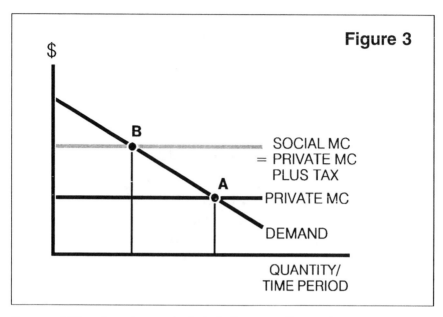

these additional costs are included, the overall marginal cost curve is located at a higher position. This all-inclusive cost curve is labelled the social marginal cost curve in Figure 3. The vertical distance between the private and the social marginal cost curves represents the magnitude of the negative spillover effects - the negative externality that is imposed on the downstream users of the water in the streams and rivers.

The basic problem in situations of this sort is that there is often no mechanism to force private decision makers to take account of the spillover costs. The free market outcome is at point A, since that is the intersection of the relevant demand and supply curves. But at this rate of output, marginal cost from society's point of view is greater than marginal utility, so the industry has expanded beyond what is socially optimal. If, instead, the negative spillover effects were included in this decision, the firms would choose to operate at point B - the intersection of the demand curve and the cost curve that is relevant for all of society.

How can this divergence between the desirable outcome (point B) and what occurs in a decentralized market (point A) be closed? One option is to levy an excise tax on the production or sale of the good whose production is causing the pollution. In this example, a tax per unit imposed on the sellers just equal to the gap between private and social marginal costs would do the trick. It would make the private marginal cost curve including the tax be coincident with the social marginal cost curve. Thus, just as beneficial externality effects can be "internalized" through a subsidy, detrimental externality effects can be "internalized" with a tax.

An emissions tax forces firms to care about pollution, but not because it makes firms care less about private profits and more about the public interest. Instead, the emissions tax forces firms' private interests to coincide with what is in the public interest, since the tax converts what was an external cost that firms could ignore, to an internal one. As with subsidies for beneficial externalities, though, the appropriate size of this tax has been the subject of intense debate.

Environmental Policy

As we have just seen, the economist's solution to externality problems, whether they are beneficial or detrimental externalities, is to close the gap between private incentives and the overall effects on society, through the use of subsidies and taxes. Let us pursue this approach in more detail, in the case of pollution. Until recently, the common approach to pollution has been either to exhort citizens and companies to be more socially responsible, or to pass broad legislation imposing specific limits on the quantity of pollution that will be permitted in the future. For example, all firms in a province might be forced to cut pollution emissions by 50 percent within a five year period.

There is a problem with exhortations to care more about the public interest. This strategy ignores the fact that shareholders generally replace firm managers if they are not trying to make the highest profit possible. The problem with direct quantity reductions, like a 50 percent emission cut for everyone, is that these rules take no account of the fact that some firms find it fairly easy to lower pollution, while others find it very costly. An efficient solution to our pollution problems should exploit these differences, rather than pretend they do not exist.

Technological options vary across different industries. Some firms, like those operating a chemical factory, may quite legitimately claim that if they have to reduce their pollution emissions dramatically, they will literally have to go out of business. They simply do not know how to produce the product any other way, and so there will be many job losses as part of the anti-pollution program. Other firms, like those operating an electricity power generator, can install scrubbers as part of their smokestack system, with the result that significant pollution abatement is possible without any threat to jobs.

Every company has an incentive to tell the government that it is one of the firms that cannot adjust easily. As a result, whenever the government proposes the kind of pollution abatement policy that requires all firms to cut their emissions by the same percentage, they are deluged with requests from firms seeking exemptions. The poor bureaucrats find it costly and difficult to determine the extent of exaggeration, if any, in each specific appeal. So inevitably we get stalled on our time deadlines with this kind of approach. It is more efficient to have a system whereby we achieve our aggregate pollution reduction target by encouraging a massive adjustment on the part of the firms who find it easy to adjust, and little or no adjustment at all for the few firms that cannot adjust and still produce profitably.

An emissions tax accomplishes this weeding out automatically. If it really is costly for some firms, like the chemical factory, to cut pollution, then many of those firms will pay the emissions tax and go on polluting. But if other firms find it quite easy to change their production methods and to cut down, perhaps almost totally eliminating pollution, that strategy will be less costly for them than paying the relatively high tax. They will change their production methods and reduce or eliminate the pollution they cause. In the end, the only firms who actually pay the tax will be the ones who find that the cheapest thing to do. In other words, they are the ones that would truly generate a lot of job dislocations if we forced all firms to cut pollution by an equal percentage.

Thus, without any bureaucrat ever having to know anything about any of the industries, we obtain the response to our pollution troubles that respects the technological differences across industries and which imposes the smallest possible cost in terms of forgone manufactured goods and employee dislocations. So the emissions tax approach is far preferable to the equal-percentage-reduction approach which has, until recently, been the favoured policy of many governments.

Some commentators are so concerned about emission control that they think that it cannot be important to argue about more or less efficient approaches to pollution abatement. They think any policy that makes a positive contribution is good. Most economists disagree. Many share the deep concern for our environment expressed by activists. But they are also concerned that an inefficient approach to pollution will make the trade-off in terms of job losses, and standard of living generally, so expensive, that there will be no real action toward pollution control.

Individuals have always demonstrated their reluctance to make sacrifices unless they are convinced those sacrifices will be effective. Thus, it is important that our pollution abatement schemes be efficient. This realization leads economists back to the idea of vouchers, in this case, for pollution. The basic mechanism for this use of vouchers is to have the government print up a set of tickets, which are known as **tradeable pollution permits**. Anyone who owns a permit is allowed to pollute a certain amount each year. Since pollution without a ticket carries a very stiff penalty, the aggregate quantity of pollution is controlled quite simply by limiting the number of permits that are printed.

One way to distribute the tickets is through an auction. As we noted earlier, some firms find it very costly to stop polluting, while others can clean up at rather low cost, and these various possibilities are shown in the left-hand panel of Figure 4. Since the cost of not polluting is exactly the same as each firm's maximum willingness to pay for a pollution permit, the demand for vouchers in the right-hand panel of Figure 4 will be the mirror image of the cost of not polluting curve. The price of a ticket is determined by supply and demand. The firms that really need to keep polluting, if they are to produce at all, will be prepared to pay a very high price for the vouchers. And the firms who find it relatively easy to cut emissions will just ignore the auction and change their production methods. (The benefit to them of continuing to pollute is less than the price of a ticket.) So an emissions permit program involves all the

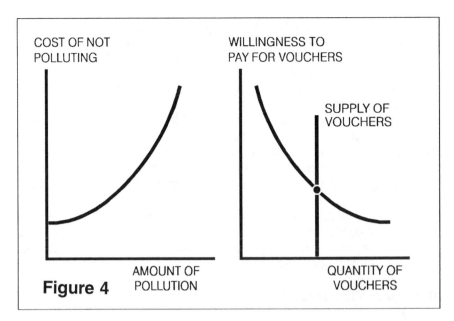

Figure 4

COST OF NOT POLLUTING

WILLINGNESS TO PAY FOR VOUCHERS

SUPPLY OF VOUCHERS

AMOUNT OF POLLUTION

QUANTITY OF VOUCHERS

efficiency gains of the emissions tax approach. But with a system of tradeable permits, the government does not even have to figure out what level of tax it should set. It just sets an overall quantity limit and lets the auction determine the amount of the emissions tax in the form of the auction price for permits.

Now consider what happens when firms react to this price incentive to find cost-effective methods for reducing pollution. If some firms invest in cleaner technology, their cost of not polluting curve will shift down. This means that, overall, the demand curve for pollution vouchers shifts down too. As a result, the price of a ticket falls. The falling price is a signal to the government that firms are finding it easier to make pollution abatement adjustments. So each year the government can reduce the number of tickets it sells. Over time, by cutting the supply of vouchers (thereby keeping the price of vouchers high) the government can force more and more firms to use production methods that generate less pollution.

In short, by issuing vouchers to create a market in pollution rights, we harness all the efficiency aspects of the market mechanism. In this way, market incentives can go a long way toward curing one of the fundamental problems with the market system itself. Unfortunately, pollution vouchers cannot solve all our problems. On an international scale, deciding which government should have the right to print the tickets is still an unresolved issue. To complicate matters, many of our environmental concerns stem from activities in less developed countries. The residents of these countries obtain farmland by cutting the rainforest, and often, the only refrigeration techniques that they can afford are bad for the ozone layer. A voucher system must be coupled with other programs to tackle these issues.

The pollution permits idea is not just ivory tower rhetoric. This scheme has been used effectively in a number of U.S. states for several years. Indeed a second-hand market in tickets has developed. Some firms had to buy a ticket for two or three years because initially they had no cost-effective way to stop polluting. But the cost of the ticket was an ongoing incentive to force the firms to invest in new machinery that operated more cleanly. The moment firms got such a process installed, they had no further need to hold the pollution permit, so they put an ad in the paper and sold it to somebody else. The more firms that do this, the more they flood the market with tickets and the price falls. This is an ongoing signal that society can afford more ambitious pollution abatement targets.

The pollution vouchers proposal has been endorsed at every international conference on the environment in recent years and various governments are now using such schemes. Economists find this development very encouraging.

Resource Conservation

A decentralized market system works on the basis of mutually agreeable trades between individuals and firms. Such trades cannot be arranged unless private property is well-defined and enforced. After all, no one will pay you very much for an item if they are not sure it is really yours to sell. Badly defined property rights lie behind our resource conservation problems, and to see this, we consider deforestation as an example.

Suppose we lease a large tract of forest land to a forestry company for a rather short interval, say 15 or 20 years, and stipulate that the land will remain public property after the lease expires. It is then in the private interest of that firm just to cut down everything and walk away. There is no point in putting resources into reforestation because the new trees will only be of benefit 50 to 70 years after the lease has expired and perhaps some other firm might then get the new lease. So by keeping the land publicly owned, we have precluded the chance of the firm acting responsibly from society's long-run point of view. But if we lease the land to the firm for a long length of time, then it is clearly in the firm's interest to do the reforestation. Otherwise, by just cutting down the trees and not doing any reforestration, it would very quickly drive the value of what is then its own asset to near zero.

History provides many examples that this is the way people react. For instance, in the frontier west, herds of cows were private property. Nobody killed all their cows; they always kept some alive to keep the herd going year after year. To do otherwise would have deprived them of their own livelihood. So it was in their own private interest to not let the resource get squandered. But the buffalo were publicly owned; nobody owned particular parts of the herd. And so there was no private incentive not to kill off nearly all of them, which was precisely what happened. The same thing has been happening with whales, despite numerous international treaties. It seems that, whether we like to admit it or not, people look after their own, private resources, and they tend not to look after something that they do not privately own.

Summary

Many concerned citizens worry about whether economic activity can be sustained in a world of finite resources. They have called for a rejection of both the profit motive and the institution of private property. Economists look to history and see that scarce resources have been used wisely only when the force of self-interest has been harnessed effectively. Most economists think it is better to base social policy on human nature as we know it. This calls for designing our tax system so that private interest and the public interest coincide. In this way, the force of self-interest can be used to secure the public interest, and this seems more constructive to economists than simply wishing the force of self-interest would go away.

Here is a review of the **key concepts** covered in this chapter. We learned that when **spillover effects** are dramatic, we encounter the **public good** problem that these items must be **financed, though not necessarily provided by government**. We saw that when spillovers are less extensive, we have **beneficial** and **detrimental externalities**. Pollution - the classic example of a detrimental externality - is most efficiently limited through the use of **effluent charges** and **tradeable emission permits**. For similar reasons, we found that an increase in **private ownership** is one of the most effective ways to foster **resource conservation**.

The main problem with the private ownership of resources is that it can lead to unequal incomes. Thus, we devote the next chapter to investigating the distribution of income that emerges from market economies and how best the government can affect that income distribution.

Chapter 8

Income Distribution and the Tax System

One thing many people find unappealing about a decentralized market-oriented economy is that it seems to produce a very wide distribution of incomes. Some individuals become extremely wealthy, while others remain very poor. The analysis in this chapter helps to explain why this distribution of incomes occurs. It also explores several features of our tax and welfare systems, with a view to identifying an efficient way of redistributing income from rich to poor.

But before we explore these questions of tax policy, we must understand how the pattern of high and low incomes occurs in the first place. This pattern depends on the productivity of the factors of production owned by each individual, so we start with a review of marginal productivity theory.

Marginal Productivity

When developing the law of diminishing marginal returns in Chapter 4, we simplified the analysis by concentrating on just two inputs to the production process: labour and capital. We continue that simplification here. In Chapter 4, we considered the firm hiring increasing amounts of labour, while holding its amount of capital fixed. The left-hand panel of Figure 1 shows the diminishing marginal productivity of labour. When we first derived this curve, it had an increasing portion for very low quantities of labour, but we deal only with the downward-sloping portion from now on. Recall the rationale for the negative slope: as the labour force gets bigger and the stock of machines does not, each individual worker has a smaller quantity of machines to work with, and so is less productive.

There is a second way of viewing this same phenomenon of diminishing marginal returns, and that is to consider the firm hiring more and more capital, while holding the size of its labour force fixed. The right-hand panel of Figure 1 follows this approach, and it shows the diminishing marginal productivity of capital. As the quantity of capital gets bigger, with the size of the labour force fixed, each additional machine has a smaller quantity of labour to work with, so it adds less to the firm's total output.

It is important to remember that the sum of all the additional outputs yields total output. Thus, the area under a firm's marginal productivity curve measures the total amount that the firm has produced. We can apply this idea to both graphs in Figure 1. To have a concrete

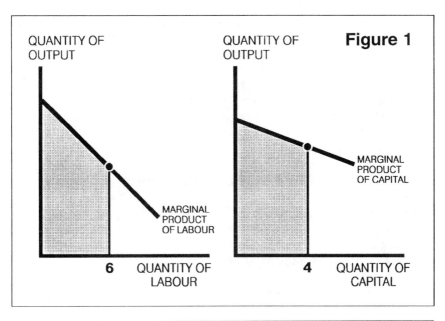

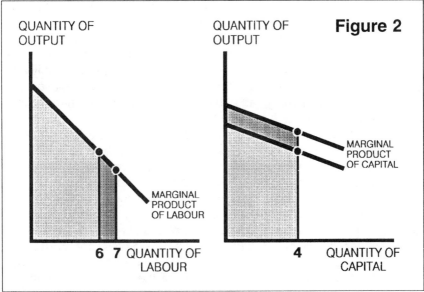

discussion, we assume that the firm whose operations are shown in the graphs has hired 6 units of labour and 4 units of capital. The total output of the firm is shown by the grey area in either of the panels. (The shaded regions are intended to represent exactly the same area.)

If the firm keeps its machine stock constant, but hires one more worker, its total output would increase. The amount of additional output is shown by the darkly shaded area in the left-hand panel of Figure 2. The firm has moved out along the labour input axis by one more unit (from 6 workers to 7 workers), and the extra output is the additional area under the marginal product curve. This extra output is shown in a different way in the right-hand panel of Figure 2. Since we are discussing a case in which the firm has not hired any more machines, there is no movement out to the right along the capital input axis. Instead, the 4 units of capital now have 7 instead of 6 units of labour to work with, and so each unit of capital becomes more productive. The entire marginal product of capital curve shifts up, as shown in Figure 2. The extra output that results is shown by the additional darkly shaded area under the new higher marginal product of capital curve.

It is worth emphasizing once more that the two panels in Figure 2 are just alternative ways to show exactly the same thing. Thus, the total output of the firm before hiring the seventh worker is the light grey area, and the additional output that follows from the hiring of that seventh worker is the dark grey area - whether we view these areas in the left or the right panels of Figure 2. The two light grey regions are the same area, and the two dark grey regions are the same area.

How Incomes are Determined

We are now in a position to see how these marginal productivity relationships determine people's incomes. We know from the optimal hiring rule that was discussed in Chapter 4 that the marginal product curve is the firm's demand curve for that factor. Thus, to find out whether a certain factor, say labour, receives a high or low payment, we simply add together the marginal product curves for all firms (to get the overall demand curve for labour), and then see where that demand curve intersects the supply curve for labour.

Equilibrium in the labour market is shown in Figure 3. The overall supply curve for labour is shown as completely inelastic. You might find this surprising, since you probably know some people who move in and out of the labour force depending on the wage rate. For example, so-called second earners in families, especially low-income families, tend to respond positively to wage rate changes. Higher wages provide an incentive for second earners to leave the home and enter the work force. However, there are other individuals, for example, professionals like some lawyers, who tend to cut hours of work when their wages go up. Higher wages allow these individuals to achieve all the income they want by working less, so higher wages induce these individuals to opt for more leisure (and therefore a smaller labour supply). When we add up everyone's reactions, the positive and negative responses to higher wages appear to just about cancel each other out, so that overall the supply of labour is inelastic.

The labour supply and demand curves shown in Figure 3 are for the whole economy. As a result, the total income available to all the citizens is equal to the value of total goods produced, and graphically, this is the area under the marginal product curve (up to the quantity of labour available). The intersection of supply and demand determines the wage

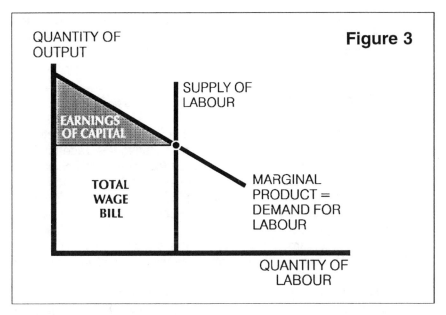

Figure 3

QUANTITY OF OUTPUT

SUPPLY OF LABOUR

EARNINGS OF CAPITAL

TOTAL WAGE BILL

MARGINAL PRODUCT = DEMAND FOR LABOUR

QUANTITY OF LABOUR

rate received by each worker. This wage rate per worker, multiplied by the number of workers, gives the total wage bill received by all workers. Geometrically, this total wage earnings is given by the area of the white rectangle in Figure 3. (The height of this rectangle is the wage rate and the width is the number of workers. Total labour income (the area of the rectangle) is the product of these two items.) By subtracting this wage bill from the total value of output (the entire trapezoid under the marginal product curve), we see that the owners of capital receive the shaded triangle. So the graph shows how national income is divided between labourers and the owners of capital.

The second thing that follows from this marginal productivity explanation of income distribution is that the owners of scarce factors of production receive very high incomes, while the owners of abundant factors of production get very low incomes. Let us consider each of these cases in turn. If labour was very scarce, the supply curve would be far over to the left in Figure 3, indicating that only a very few units are available. An example might be star singers or hockey players. The equilibrium wage (which clears the market for such a scarce factor) is very high. Similarly, if labour was abundant, the supply curve would be far over to the right, indicating that there are a great many units of this factor of production available. An example might be unskilled labourers. The market-clearing wage of such an abundant factor is very low.

These outcomes lead to an efficient use of factors by society. From an efficiency point of view, we want scarce factors to carry very high prices. If it costs firms a lot to use them, firms will use such scarce items only where they are especially valuable. As a result, society will get the most material welfare that is possible, given our scarce resources. Thus the way factors get paid in a market economy is efficient, but the outcome can be pretty discouraging on income distribution grounds. For many individuals, especially those that own only a little bit of just one very abundant factor of production (unskilled labour), this system of factor pricing leads to poverty.

Income Redistribution

Once again, we confront the trade-off between efficiency and equity. To many economists, the sensible response to this trade-off is as follows. Let factors be paid their marginal products, so that we achieve the efficiency gains that accompany the using of scarce factors very carefully; and then redistribute some of the resulting incomes from rich to poor.

There are three possible ways to redistribute income among individuals. The first is a political solution - we can simply redefine who owns the factors of production. This is the socialist approach and a common example from poor agrarian economies is to give a piece of farmland to every family.

The second approach to redistributing income is to leave the ownership of factors as it is, but to impose regulations on markets, such as a minimum wage law or a rent control act. These kinds of maximum and minimum price laws are intended to redistribute income, but as we have already seen in earlier chapters, almost every time we consider such a policy, large and undesired side effects occur. As a result, economists have concluded that this second strategy is usually not a good one to follow.

The third strategy is to leave the ownership of factors alone, leave markets working, let factor prices be what they may (so that resources get used efficiently), but then use a very general income tax system to redistribute some income from the rich to those with lower incomes.

General vs. Specific Forms of Taxation

In a general tax system, the same tax rate applies to all forms of income, whatever is the source of that income. When there are different taxes for different kinds of income, the government creates incentives for people to change their market behaviour, in an attempt to get their income into the lower-taxed form. These incentives lead to inefficiency and a frustration of the initial income-redistribution objective. To see the inefficiency of using particular taxes as opposed to general taxes, let us consider two examples of specific taxes.

The first is a payroll tax, imposed on firms for their use of labour, but not their use of capital. We have several payroll taxes in Canada; the prime examples are the contributions we and our employers make to the Canada Pension Plan and to the Unemployment Insurance fund. Let us examine a version of this type of tax, one in which firms must pay to the government a specified amount of money for each employee. Before the tax is levied, the labour market is as shown in Figure 3.

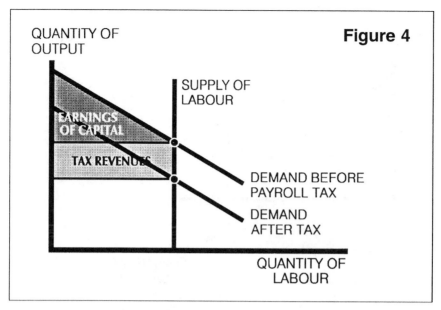

QUANTITY OF
OUTPUT

Figure 4

SUPPLY OF
LABOUR

EARNINGS
OF CAPITAL

TAX REVENUE

DEMAND BEFORE
PAYROLL TAX

DEMAND
AFTER TAX

QUANTITY OF
LABOUR

The tax decreases the amount that firms are willing to pay their employees. After all, firms have to reserve some of what they were previously paying workers to cover the tax. This decreased willingness to pay employees is shown in Figure 4 by the downward shift in the labour demand curve. The vertical distance between the original and the after-tax positions for the labour demand curve is equal to the amount of the payroll tax (measured on a per-worker basis). The intersection of the after-tax demand curve with the labour supply curve gives the new equilibrium. It is clear from Figure 4 that the equilibrium wage drops by exactly the amount of the tax. Thus, even though the tax was levied on firms, the employees are the ones who actually bear the burden of the tax.

The total revenue collected by the government is equal to the payroll tax per worker times the number of workers, and this amount is shown as the lightly shaded area in Figure 4. By comparing Figures 3 and 4, we can see that this entire revenue rectangle comes out of what used to be labour's earnings. The return to capital is still the same dark grey triangle. Thus, firms have shifted the burden of the tax to employees (through lower wages). At the intuitive level, the reason that firms are able to fully shift the payroll tax burden, is because (in the aggregate) labour is a "captive" factor of production, and this is indicated by the supply curve being inelastic.

Of course, it is possible that the wage rate is not pushed down by the payroll tax. For example, some workers are paid at the legal minimum wage. But in this case, the payroll tax only exacerbates the unemployment problem caused by the minimum wage, as firms reduce the amount of labour they want to hire. In this case, then, labour bears the burden of the tax through job losses, instead of through a reduction in wages. In either case, firms avoid paying the tax.

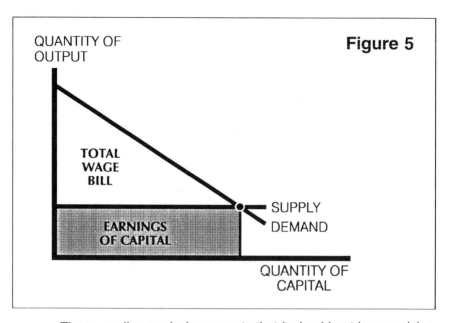

The preceding analysis suggests that it should not be surprising that the labour movement is opposed to payroll taxes (whether they are nominally levied on the employer or the employee). We have just seen that labour bears the full burden of the tax in either case. Given this result, you might also expect that labour would favour a corporate profits tax. But the Canadian corporate profit tax is another very specific levy. It taxes only income that is derived from owning capital that is employed in our country. This is quite different from taxing a Canadian's income, whether that income is labour earnings or a return on capital that is employed anywhere in the world. Because the corporate profit tax is so different from this general scheme, it does not have the effect that most people expect. Indeed, we will now see that labour is even worse off with the corporate profit tax, than it is with a payroll tax!

To examine the effect of a tax on the earnings of domestically owned capital, we focus on a graph depicting the market for capital, as in Figure 5. There we see the downward-sloping demand curve for capital, and a perfectly elastic supply curve for capital. As usual, the demand curve follows from the hypothesis of diminishing marginal returns, and the optimal hiring rule. The supply curve follows from the willingness of foreign owners of capital to let their capital be employed in Canada, as long as we cover its opportunity cost. Thus, as long as capital can earn in Canada as much as it can in any other country, owners are willing to supply Canada whatever quantity it wants. We show this availability by drawing the supply curve of capital as a horizontal line whose height is equal to the yield that is available to capital in the rest of the world.

Before any tax is levied, capital market equilibrium occurs at the intersection of supply and demand in Figure 5. Capital owners receive the internationally competitive yield times the number of units of capital that

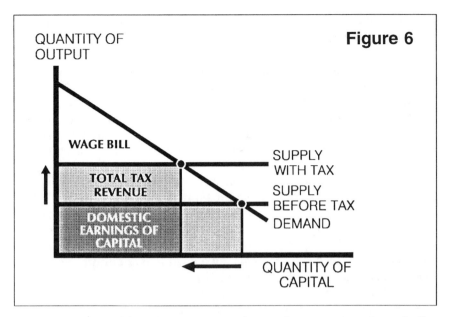

Figure 6

QUANTITY OF
OUTPUT

WAGE BILL

TOTAL TAX
REVENUE

DOMESTIC
EARNINGS OF
CAPITAL

SUPPLY
WITH TAX

SUPPLY
BEFORE TAX

DEMAND

QUANTITY OF
CAPITAL

are employed within our country, so the total payment to them is the shaded area in Figure 5. Labour's income is the residual white triangle.

Suppose a 50 percent tax on the earnings of capital employed in Canada is introduced. Not surprisingly, owners of capital are going to demand double the rate of return on a pre-tax basis - so that on an after-tax basis they will receive what they can still get elsewhere in the world. If capital owners cannot continue to cover opportunity cost, they simply move their capital to another country. As usual, then, we move the position of the supply curve up by the amount of the tax (on a per-unit basis). The intersection of the new, higher supply curve with the demand curve is shown in Figure 6. The arrow along the quantity axis shows how much capital is no longer demanded in Canada. This capital leaves the country. The government receives total revenue equal to the specified tax per unit of capital times the amount of capital that is still employed in Canada. That total tax revenue is indicated by the lighly shaded rectangle in Figure 6. Notice that it comes entirely from what used to be labour's triangle of income.

The capital that is still employed in Canada continues to get the same return per unit as before (on an after-tax basis). The net income involved is shown as the dark grey rectangle in Figure 6. Capital owners appear to lose the light grey rectangle on the right-hand portion of the graph, but they have not. That rectangle represents the income earned by the capital that has left the country. This income used to be earned in Canada, but after the tax the same amount is earned elsewhere.

The tax does generate a loss to the nation as a whole. The total output that is produced within our country has shrunk by the area of the trapezoid under the labour demand curve formed by the vertical lines drawn down from both the initial and the after-tax equilibrium points.

Because labour previously earned the small white triangle part of this trapezoid, it is labour, not the owners of capital, who suffer an income loss. Indeed, as noted already, the entire tax revenue rectangle comes from what used to be labour's larger triangle. As a result, this tax is worse for labour than the payroll tax, because labour not only pays 100 percent of the tax (as labour does with payroll taxes), but labour also bears the additional loss represented by the small white triangle to the right of the tax revenue rectangle in Figure 6. So labour pays more than 100 percent of this tax. If labour had to choose between a payroll tax and this one, they ought to choose the payroll tax.

Labour supporters may find this analysis very discouraging. Is there any tax that is at least partially paid by the owners of capital? The answer is "yes" - a tax on Canadians who earn income from capital that is employed anywhere in the world. The main moral of this analysis is that unintended things happen when we tax particular forms of income differently. We can avoid problems if we have a very **general personal income tax system** in which individuals pay the same tax on all income whether it happens to be labour income, earnings on capital employed here in Canada, or earnings on capital that is employed elsewhere.

Unfortunately, even our personal income tax system is not fully general. This fact is most easily appreciated when we consider our welfare arrangements. When combined with welfare programs, our personal income tax system creates incentives that discourage many individuals from working at all.

Disincentives to Work and the Poverty Trap

Figure 7 summarizes the tax table that you consult each year when filing your tax return. The table tells you how much tax you have to pay for each level of before-tax income that you could have earned. For example, if you have zero income, you don't have to pay any taxes. You can earn up to your basic personal exemption (several thousand dollars) before you have to pay any taxes at all. When summarized as a graph, as in Figure 7, the tax schedule is coincident with the horizontal axis until you use up your basic exemption. Then, at higher income levels, you move into the lowest tax bracket and you start paying taxes. In the graph, the tax rate is given by the slope of the tax schedule. As your income continues to increase, your tax payments increase proportionately - with the factor of proportionality being that lowest tax rate. Then, as income increases further, you move into the higher tax brackets, and the tax schedule becomes progressively steeper, as shown in Figure 7.

In addition to the income-tax system, we have another program which is fundamental to redistribution - the welfare system. It involves giving subsidies to people at the low end of the income scale. Since our objective is to examine the welfare and personal income tax system simultaneously, we use the rather unfamiliar language of referring to an individual's receipt of welfare as the payment of negative taxes.

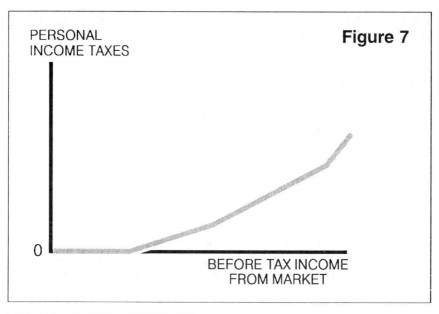

PERSONAL
INCOME TAXES

Figure 7

0

BEFORE TAX INCOME
FROM MARKET

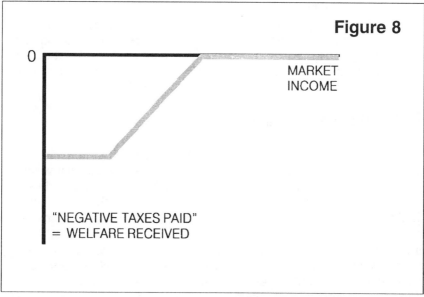

Figure 8

0

MARKET
INCOME

"NEGATIVE TAXES PAID"
= WELFARE RECEIVED

    The basic feature of our welfare system is that if you receive no income from market activities, you qualify for a certain amount of welfare. This amount of subsidy (that is, this amount of negative taxes paid) is represented by the vertical intercept of the welfare schedule graphed in Figure 8. As individuals start earning market income, and move out to the right along the income axis, there is no reduction in welfare payments, at least at the beginning. But after a limit specified by the welfare legislation, welfare dollars start getting withdrawn from individuals as they earn more market income. It varies by municipality, but on average individuals lose about 75 cents of welfare every time they earn one more dollar in the market place. As a result, people at very low income levels are effectively in a 75 percent tax bracket!

Things are even worse for individuals at these low income levels, and this fact can be appreciated by graphing the personal income tax and welfare systems together, as is done in Figure 9. The net implication of the two programs is shown by the dashed line in Figure 9. As can be seen, some individuals (those just emerging from being on welfare) face an effective tax schedule that has an even steeper slope than 0.75. These individuals lose welfare at an implicit tax rate of 75 percent, and they pay positive income taxes at a combined federal and provincial rate that is just over 25 percent. All things considered, the overall tax rate is just over 100 percent! Would you go out to work if your discretionary income actually fell as a result?

When combined, then, the income tax system and our welfare programs involve a tremendous disincentive to get a job. This is important since, short of returning to school, the only way low-income individuals can escape the poverty trap is by acquiring skills while on the job. Only with higher skills will their marginal productivity be higher, and only then will they command a higher wage in the marketplace.

Why do we levy the highest marginal tax rates on such low-income individuals? It was never intended; it is simply a byproduct of the different programs devised by different levels of government at different times. Economists' suggestion for solving this problem is called the **Negative Income Tax**.

A Guaranteed Annual Income

Another name for the negative income tax proposal is a Guaranteed Annual Income. It is based on the proposition that we must remove the steep section and the abrupt kinks in the net tax schedule (the dashed line that incorporates both taxes and welfare) shown in Figure 9. The proposal is simply that the kinked line be replaced by a smoother one, such as the solid line in Figure 10. The new-policy line must have a flatter slope at lower income levels to make sure that we are not taxing punitively that segment of the population that can least afford to pay. A flatter net tax schedule involves a smaller disincentive to work, and the effective tax rate must be less than 100 percent before there is any chance for individuals to escape remaining in poverty.

From the administrative point of view, there would be significant savings in having one integrated system. No separate welfare department would be needed, because all citizens would simply fill out tax forms on a regular basis. Those with higher incomes would pay positive taxes, and those with lower incomes would automatically qualify for negative taxes. With the income tax system extending smoothly into the negative range, there would be no unintended situations in which low income individuals would face tax rates that make economic activity completely unappealing.

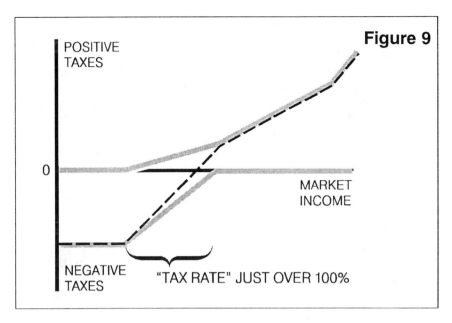

Figure 9

POSITIVE
TAXES

0

MARKET
INCOME

NEGATIVE
TAXES   "TAX RATE" JUST OVER 100%

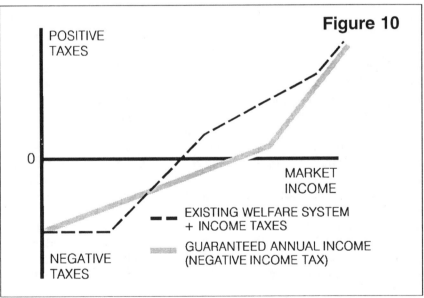

Figure 10

POSITIVE
TAXES

0

MARKET
INCOME

EXISTING WELFARE SYSTEM
+ INCOME TAXES

GUARANTEED ANNUAL INCOME
(NEGATIVE INCOME TAX)

NEGATIVE
TAXES

The maximum amount of negative taxes would go to an individual who could earn no income. That guaranteed annual income is equal to the vertical intercept in Figure 10.

The basic problem with this proposal is that there may be a problem of affordability. The moment we flatten the net tax line somewhat (to remove work disincentives) we transfer a set of people from the tax-paying group to the welfare-receiving group. One way of appreciating this concern is by noting the break-even level of income that separates subsidy receivers from positive taxpayers. That break-even level under the existing programs is given by the point where the dashed line crosses the horizontal axis in Figure 10. The break-even level for the negative income tax proposal occurs where the solid line crosses the market income axis in the same figure. Between these two income levels, it appears that individuals might change from being taxpayers to subsidy receivers, if the negative income tax proposal was implemented. The fear is that the government might have higher welfare costs.

One solution that is sometimes suggested for dealing with this affordability problem is to shift both the slope and the intercept of the tax-subsidy schedule. That is, as the schedule is flattened to lower the net tax rate for those with low (but positive) incomes, the entire position of that flatter line could be moved up. The flattening lowers the work disincentive problem, and the parallel shift up decreases the break-even level of income, and so lessens the affordability problem. But the remaining trouble with this suggestion is that it puts a real squeeze on the most destitute - those with no income at all. By shortening the vertical intercept of the net tax schedule we are shrinking the amount of the guaranteed annual income, perhaps to an unacceptable level.

Defenders of the negative income tax proposal argue that concerns about affordability are based on a misunderstanding. The whole point of this institutional change is to remove the disincentive to work, and so encourage people to move out to the right along the market income axis. Thus, despite the pivoting down of the tax-subsidy schedule, many individuals may increase their market earnings enough to pay more, not less, taxes, and others may qualify for less, not more, welfare.

During the late 1970s, several communities in Manitoba were chosen by the Federal government to try out the negative income tax proposal. Various combinations of slope and intercept were involved in the experiments. The result of these and related experiments in the United States suggested two things. First, the cost of supporting those already receiving payments under a traditional welfare program did not increase. Individuals either worked more, or found a job that was better paying enough, that the cost to the government was no higher - even though welfare was "taxed back" at much lower rates. But the second finding has confirmed the affordability worry. A significant number of individuals who were not previously receiving welfare were pulled into the subsidy receiving group.

Overall then, the negative income tax proposal involves more redistribution, and so it is a more expensive program. This fact has made governments hesitant to adopt this reform. But many analysts have concluded that the removal of the fundamental reason for the poverty trap (the 100 percent effective marginal tax rates for the poor) is worth an increase in cost. The negative income tax plan has been endorsed by every Royal Commission that has investigated poverty issues in recent years.

Summary

Here is a review of the **key concepts** covered in this chapter. We learned that people's incomes are limited by the willingness of firms to pay them for using the factors of production they own. This is the essence of the **marginal productivity theory** of **income distribution**. Incomes can be redistributed by using either **general** or **specific taxes**, and we learned that the general approach can avoid many unintended outcomes. For example, when their effects are combined, our welfare and income tax programs lead to large **disincentives to work**. We learned that a **guaranteed annual income** plan, otherwise known as a **negative income tax** system, can reduce this problem.

By accomplishing redistribution through a general income tax, we can avoid relying on such things as minimum wage laws and import tariffs to protect people's incomes. We saw the inefficiencies involved with minimum wage laws in Chapter 1, and we will appreciate the costs of import tariffs after studying free trade in the next chapter. Taken as a group, these several chapters make a strong case for focusing on a reformed income tax system as the most effective mechanism for helping those on lower incomes.

Chapter 9

Free Trade

Free trade involves dropping all import tariffs and quotas, so that our companies (and those operating in other countries) compete directly with each other. Many people are suspicious of free trade because they are worried about layoffs in industries that were previously protected from foreign competition by tariffs. But economic analysis suggests that we should not reject free trade if what concerns us are layoffs and unfair income redistributions. It indicates that the layoffs are most often temporary, and that other policies can be much more effective for redistributing income and for ending recessions than is a permanent rejection of free trade.

The Benefits of Free Trade

There are three main benefits of free trade. First, the competition provided by firms from outside forces domestic monopolists to behave more competitively. As consumers, we get more goods at lower prices since free trade is a substitute for what many people think has been an ineffective competition policy. Second, free trade opens up markets that are very much larger than Canada's, so that our firms can achieve large scale economies of production and are therefore able to produce more goods at lower costs per unit. Over the years, much of Canadian industry has operated at a size that simply has not allowed it to achieve full economies to scale. The third benefit is simply that when we trade with other countries, people in each country benefit from the fact that worker productivity varies from industry to industry and country to country.

Most of this chapter's analysis is focused on this third benefit. We investigate what economists call the principle of **comparative advantage**. This principle is perhaps most easily explained with an example used by David Ricardo, a famous economist who wrote nearly 200 years ago. He was an economist advising the British government as to whether it should embark on a free trade arrangement with other countries. The example concerns potential trade between England and Portugal. To keep his numerical example simple, Ricardo made several assumptions which we follow.

To simplify, we assume that each country has just 100 workers in their labour force. There are no diminishing returns or economies of large scale - no matter how big or small each industry is. And to simplify the graphing, we consider just two industries: cloth and wine.

NUMBER OF WORKERS NEEDED TO PRODUCE:

	PORTUGAL	ENGLAND
ONE BARREL OF WINE	2	10
ONE BOLT OF CLOTH	1	2

OPPORTUNITY COST:

	PORTUGAL	ENGLAND
ONE BARREL OF WINE	2 BOLTS OF CLOTH	5 BOLTS OF CLOTH
ONE BOLT OF CLOTH	1/2 BARREL OF WINE	1/5 BARREL OF WINE

The top half of the accompanying table shows how much labour is needed to produce one unit of each good in our example. To produce one barrel of wine, it takes 10 of the workers in England but it takes only 2 of the 100 workers in Portugal. So Portugal is better than England at producing wine in Ricardo's example. In the cloth industry, producing one bolt of cloth takes 2 workers in England and only one worker in Portugal. So once again the Portuguese get more output per worker than the English, this time in producing cloth.

These differences in productivity are displayed differently in the bottom half of the table. We see there that one worker in England can produce one bolt of cloth. Similarly, since it takes 10 workers in England to produce one barrel of wine, each worker there can produce 1/10 of a barrel of wine. In Portugal, each worker can produce 1/2 a barrel of wine or five times as much as an English worker. In this example, Portuguese workers can produce twice as much cloth and five times as much wine.

In Ricardo's example, Portugal is better at everything in absolute terms. This is the kind of situation where people doubt there are going to be benefits from free trade. How could Portugal get anything beneficial from trading with such a loser as England, as she is portrayed in this example? When a country is less efficient at producing everything, it has lower living standards. One would think that Portugal would fear having free trade with a country that has such "cheap wages." Similarly, one would expect the English to be very suspicious of free trade. Since they are uncompetitive in both industries, they would fear they could not sell anything to Portugal, and so they would fear mass unemployment if tariff protection were dropped. We shall see that these fears are unfounded since they are based on a confusion between a country's **absolute advantage** and its **comparative advantage**.

Comparative Advantage

We say that England is at an absolute disadvantage in the production of both commodities because English workers are less efficient at everything. But since they are only half as efficient in cloth production and two tenths, or one fifth, as efficient in the wine industry, we say they actually have a comparative advantage in the production of cloth. England is said to have a comparative advantage in cloth production because that is the activity in which she is least bad. And Portugal has a comparative advantage in wine because, while Portuguese workers are more efficient in absolute terms at producing both wine and cloth, the margin of their extra efficiency is greater in the wine industry. As a result of these differences, both countries can benefit if they each specialize in that area in which they have the comparative advantage, and then trade with each other.

Most readers will be able to think of a similar example from their personal lives. Perhaps you have a neighbour who is an excellent auto mechanic, but she finds it more valuable to specialize in practising law. She trades with other people and hires someone else to work on her car. She has an absolute advantage in both providing legal services and repairing automobiles, but she specializes in the activity for which she has a comparative advantage - practising law.

Returning to Ricardo's example, we define comparative advantage according to which country's industry involves the lowest opportunity costs. In Portugal, it takes 2 workers to produce 1 barrel of wine. The same 2 workers could also be producing 2 bolts of cloth, so the opportunity cost of using the 2 workers to produce a barrel of wine is that then they are not available to produce 2 bolts of cloth. And since one worker in Portugal can produce one half of a barrel of wine, this means that the opportunity cost of producing one bolt of cloth is one half of a barrel of wine.

Now we proceed through the similar reasoning for England. In that country, it takes 10 workers to produce one barrel of wine, but the same workers could also be producing 5 bolts of cloth, so the opportunity cost of a barrel of wine in England is 5 bolts of cloth. Similarly, since the 2 workers it takes to produce a bolt of cloth could also produce 1/5 of a barrel of wine, the opportunity cost of a bolt of cloth in England is 1/5 of a barrel of wine.

Which country has the lowest opportunity cost in each industry? Clearly, the opportunity cost of producing wine is lower in Portugal, so we say that Portugal has a comparative advantage in wine. Also, the opportunity cost of cloth is lower in England, so it has a comparative advantage in the production of cloth. It is cheaper to buy wine in Portugal, but it is cheaper (in terms of the amount of wine that must be given up) to buy cloth in England.

Suppose that without free trade, England uses its 100 workers to produce 25 bolts of cloth and 5 barrels of wine, while Portugal uses its 100 workers to produce 10 bolts of cloth and 45 barrels of wine. In that case, world production is 25 + 10 = 35 bolts of cloth, and 5 + 45 = 50 barrels of wine:

World Production With No Trade
Cloth = 25 + 10 = 35 Bolts
Wine = 5 + 45 = 50 Barrels.

Now let us see what would happen if these countries specialized in the industry in which each has a comparative advantage and then traded. If the English produce nothing but cloth, they will create 50 bolts of cloth. They can then trade some of the cloth to Portugal for wine. If the Portuguese specialized totally in wine, they would produce 50 barrels of wine and no cloth. They can trade some of the wine to England to get cloth in exchange. In that case, world production is as follows:

World Production With Free Trade
Cloth = 50 + 0 = 50 Bolts
Wine = 0 + 50 = 50 Barrels

After specialization, there are still 50 barrels of wine in total, but now it is all being produced in Portugal. And now there are 50 bolts of cloth, not just 35. So there are 15 more bolts of cloth in this example - that is a 43 percent increase in the availability of one of the two goods with no loss of the other good. Thus, overall, there is an unambiguous gain to the citizens in both countries, taken as a group.

This gain follows from specialization. International trade does not represent a win-lose situation. One country does not gain because the other loses. Both countries can share the benefits of using their scarce resources in the most efficient way by having each economy concentrate on producing what it is, comparatively speaking, better at producing.

Economists regard it to be a shame if countries cannot get together to enjoy these benefits. This lack of co-ordination often happens for two reasons. For one thing, there is a lack of knowledge concerning the principle of comparative advantage. Another problem is that usually, at the individual level, there are both winners and losers. There is an overall net gain. But some individuals in both countries must switch jobs, and that can be very disruptive.

To look at how gains and losses are distributed, we turn to supply and demand, and we focus on just one industry as our example - the wine industry. We proceed in three stages. First, we examine how market equilibrium is determined when international trade is involved.

Supply and Demand With Free Trade

Figure 1 shows the demand and supply curves for wine in both Portugal and England. As a base for comparison, we first consider the equilibrium in each country that would exist if there is no foreign trade.

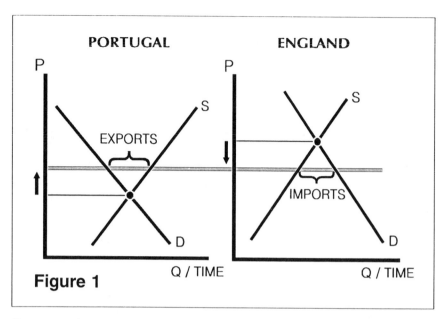

Figure 1

Because wine production is costly in England, the price of wine would be high in the right-hand panel of Figure 1. Portugal has a relatively low price because the opportunity costs of producing wine there are lower.

Now consider free trade. For simplicity, we abstract from transportation costs and assume them to be negligible. Given this assumption, a free-trade equilibrium will emerge with just one world price, and at that price the world quantity demanded must equal the world quantity supplied. Put another way, at the world price, the excess quantity of wine demanded in the importing country must equal the excess quantity supplied in the exporting country.

The equilibrium price is given by the height of the horizontal line running across both panels in Figure 1. At this price, consumers in England demand more wine than is produced domestically, so there is a shortage that is just being covered by what they are receiving from Portugal as imports. Portugal is willing to export this amount, since at this higher price (than obtained before trade) Portuguese producers want to sell more than Portuguese consumers want to buy. An equilibrium exists because there is a common price ruling in both countries, with the excess supply in Portugal (its exports) just balancing the excess demand in England (its imports).

Of course, in reality, the transportation costs involved in taking goods from one country to another affect these conclusions somewhat. But even with transportation costs, free trade provides competition which forces the price of traded items to differ across two locations by only a precise amount. To return to Ricardo's example, as long as the gap in prices is greater than the transport costs, it would still pay someone to buy more wine in the low-price location (Portugal) and sell it in the high-price location (England). Just as before, this process makes wine more scarce

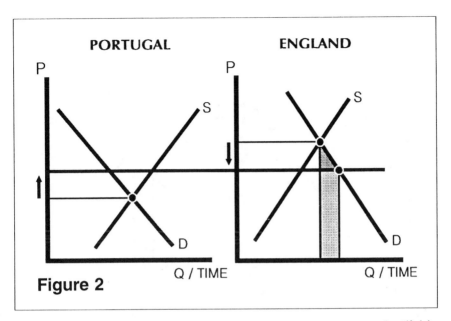

Figure 2

in Portugal so the price rises there, and it makes wine more plentiful in England so the price falls there. Thus, the price differential is narrowed by these competitive forces until it just equals transportation costs. By ignoring transportation costs, then, our analysis of free trade will overstate slightly how much convergence to a common price takes place. But to understand who are the winners and who are the losers following a move to free trade, it is convenient to simplify by ignoring transportation costs.

The Effects of Free Trade in the Importing Country

We can now use the supply and demand graphs for the wine industry to analyze who gains and who loses, and what are the net benefits for both the countries, following a move to free trade. First, we consider which individuals in England gain and lose from a policy of free trade.

We assess free trade by comparing the no-trade outcome with what occurs after a free trade equilibrium is reached, and by focusing on a particular range of output at each stage of the analysis. We begin in England, the importing country. With the falling price of wine there, households slide down their demand curve and consume a greater quantity - an amount given by the width of the shaded area in the right-hand panel of Figure 2. The extra satisfaction these English wine drinkers receive from this extra consumption is given by this area under their demand curve over this range of output - the shaded trapezoid in Figure 2. To get that extra satisfaction, the English just have to pay Portugal the going world price times that number of units consumed - in other words, the lightly shaded rectangle in Figure 2. So the surplus - the excess of additional benefits over what must be paid - is the small dark triangle in

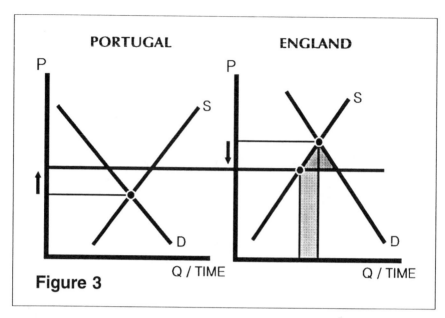

Figure 3

Figure 2. This is the net benefit to the wine drinkers in England. It is a gain for the wine drinkers and not a loss to anyone else in England.

The next range of output we consider is indicated by the shaded trapezoid in Figure 3. This range of output is the amount that used to be produced by wine producers in England before free trade. This domestic wine has now been replaced by imports from Portugal. The domestic producers have reacted to the falling price by sliding down their supply curve. Before trade, the cost to England of producing this wine domestically was the area under the supply curve - the shaded trapezoid in Figure 3. But, after free trade is established, the cost to England of getting that wine from Portugal is just the lightly shaded rectangle (since this area is defined by world per unit price times this number of units). So the cost with free trade is less than the cost the English used to incur by getting this amount of wine from domestic producers. The cost saving is the difference in area between the trapezoid and the rectangle, so the dark shaded triangle is another part of the net gain to the English that follows from free trade. Resources that were previously used to produce wine at a high cost have been freed up to produce cloth.

The final range of output to be discussed is indicated by the width of the shaded rectangle in Figure 4. This quantity of wine is the amount that the English produce domestically and consume, both before and after free trade. For this range of output, the only change is that English wine drinkers used to pay a high price per unit, and now they have to pay only the lower world price. The per-unit saving is given by the height of the shaded rectangle in Figure 4, and the total saving for consumers is the area of the rectangle. But this saving is a straight transfer from wine producers to wine drinkers. What consumers gain, domestic producers lose. So this area is not a net gain or loss for the country as a whole.

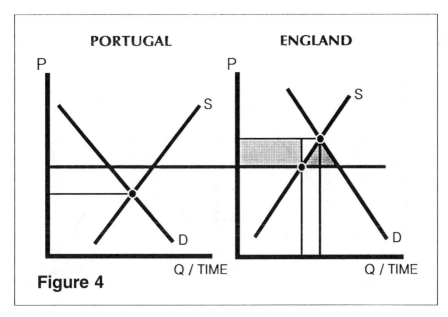

Figure 4

This transfer from domestic producers to domestic consumers can certainly explain why the producers of wine in England would lobby hard to keep their government from allowing this move to free trade, even though there is a net gain to England as a whole (given by the area of the two dark shaded triangles in Figure 4).

All moves toward free trade create gains and losses like those of the English consumers and producers in our example. This is because the opening up of free trade changes prices, and buyers like price decreases while suppliers do not. The distribution of the gains and losses (between buyers and sellers) displays the opposite pattern in the exporting country, as we see in the next section. But it is important to remember that the gains outweigh the losses by an amount equal to the dark grey triangles. Furthermore, the graph represents what goes on every period, so the present value of a move to free trade is a whole series of net benefits, with each one item in this sum equal to the area of the shaded triangles in Figure 4.

The Effects of Free Trade in the Exporting Country

The output of wine in Portugal increases with free trade by an amount equal to the width of the shaded trapezoid in Figure 5. The value of resources involved in producing this much extra wine is equal to the area under the marginal cost curve over this range of expanded output - that is, the area of the shaded trapezoid. But the English are paying the Portuguese a larger amount than this for that extra wine - a rectangle with the same width as the trapezoid and a height given by the world price line. (The world price times that many barrels of wine is what the English have to pay.) So the payment from England exceeds the amount that Portugal

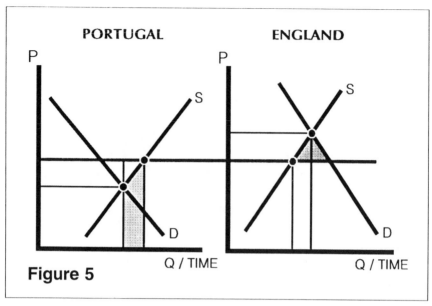

Figure 5

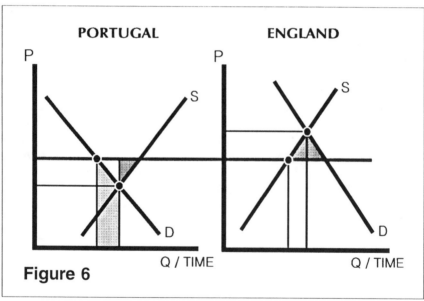

Figure 6

had to incur in terms of actual resources used to get the payment, by an amount equal to the dark shaded triangle shown in the left-hand panel of Figure 6. This area represents a net gain for Portugal.

The next range of output to be analyzed is defined by the width of the shaded trapezoid in Figure 6. This amount was, and still is, produced within Portugal. It used to be consumed by Portuguese wine drinkers, and their benefits equalled the corresponding area under their demand curve - the shaded trapezoid. With free trade, the Portuguese consumers lose that benefit, but Portuguese producers receive the entire

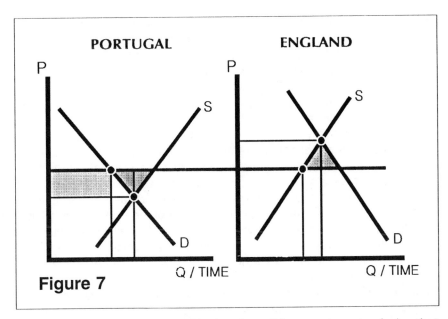

Figure 7

rectangle indicated by the world price times this many barrels of wine that they are now exporting to England. So total compensation to the Portugese for the loss of that amount of wine is the entire rectangle, and this compensation is bigger than what they had to give up to get it (just the trapezoid portion of the rectangle). So there is another triangle of net gain for Portugal, and it is shaded in dark grey in Figure 7.

The rest of the wine production is the amount indicated by the width of the lightly shaded rectangle in Figure 7. This rectangle represents a redistribution within Portugal. Domestic wine drinkers have lost at the expense of the wine producers, since they must pay the higher world price on each of these units purchased. But, just as in the case of England, where the transfer went in the opposite direction, it is important to remember that this transfer does not represent any net gain or loss for Portugal. Transfer payments cancel off from the whole nation's point of view. Overall, gains exceed losses in Portugal by the sum of the two dark shaded triangles in the left-hand panel of Figure 7. And this net gain is received every period.

Comparing the Benefits and Costs of Free Trade

Economists have estimated the elasticities of supply and demand for all the major commodities that are traded, so they have estimated the size of the shaded triangles in Figure 7. In the Canada-US case, economists estimated that the total benefits to Canada from the Free Trade Agreement in 1989 would equal an annual flow of increased Canadian income equal to roughly 3 percent of the total output of the Canadian economy. This increase in income exists for every year into the indefinite future, once the expansion of our exporting industries and the contraction of our import-competing industries is completed.

To calculate the present value of this entire stream of benefits, we must divide its annual size (3 percent of national output) by the appropriate discount rate. That discount rate is the excess of the average rate of interest over the average rate of growth of the economy's overall output. With an interest rate of 7 percent and real growth of 4 percent being representative values, that gap is also about 3 percent. Thus, the present value of an ongoing stream of benefits equal to 3 percent of national output is [.03/(.07-.04)] times today's level of national output. Thus, the benefits stemming from the Canada-US free trade agreement are estimated to be equivalent to a once-for-all increase in the material welfare of Canadians equal to the entire output of the Canadian economy in one year. The actual benefit comes as a flow of small increments over many years, but even after discounting the future, that flow has a present value equal to one year's entire output.

So the overall gains from free trade can be very large. The problem is that these benefits do not come immediately; as just noted, they come in relatively small amounts over many years. And the dislocation costs of moving toward free trade do come immediately. The question Canada faced back in the late 1980s was "Should we give up an entire year's output of our economy to avoid the costs that are imposed on the subset of the population that must relocate and retrain when previously protected industries are exposed to foreign competition?"

One way of answering that question is to ask another. We could ask those individuals who would be forced to relocate and retrain "How much would you need to receive to feel fully compensated for this income loss and dislocation?" Economists have considered the amount of compensation that might be required, and their reasoning can be summarized as follows.

Even when very pessimistic assumptions are made concerning how many people are adversely affected in the short run, the costs of free trade are dominated by the benefits. For example, suppose the Canada-US free trade agreement raised unemployment by 10 percentage points for five full years (which it clearly did not do). Even assuming the corresponding 10 percent loss of national output for five years, and even without discounting this estimated cost (which is 50 percent of one year's output) it is still smaller than the benefits of free trade (which we just estimated at 100 percent of one year's output). Even paying those who lose this big a compensation payment leaves a large net gain. This calculation means that those who gain from trade receive far more than enough to compensate those who lose. For this reason, economists favour free trade.

Many Canadians were less than impressed with the actual free trade arrangement we achieved with the United States and later with Mexico. Economists can understand this reaction because these agreements are just one part of the suggested two-part package that is advocated by economists. The actual FTA and NAFTA deals embraced free trade, but offered very little **adjustment assistance** beyond current policies already in place, to people who were hurt by the need to retrain and relocate.

We can all benefit by gearing our trade-policy decisions to providing higher incomes over the longer term (that is, by embracing free trade) if we actually use our other policy instruments to redistribute income and cushion the blows from big changes in the economy. The cost of failure in using these other policies is that there remains only limited political acceptance for free trade. Over the longer run, then, living standards will be noticeably lower if we do a poor job of managing economic change through adjustment assistance.

The key word here is managing change. This is very different from resisting change. The whole point of removing tariffs is to force people to move out of industries in which Canada does not have a comparative advantage, and to get jobs in industries in which we do have a comparative advantage. In the long run, once that adjustment is complete, people receive higher wages because they are employed in an industry in which they are truly productive. So it is an issue of long-term gain with short-term pain. This change can be managed if tariff reductions are accomplished very gradually, with a clear schedule that is well announced and adhered to over the years. When this strategy is adopted, workers can plan their careers sensibly. As long as young people enter a declining industry at a slower rate than the older workers are retiring, the workforce can contract gradually without any layoffs. By following a gradual plan of this sort, it is possible for us to achieve the longer-term benefits of free trade, while at the same time limiting the government's need to offer adjustment assistance.

The inequitable income-distribution effects that follow from free trade do not indicate that free trade is bad on balance. Instead, these problems are an indication that it is our distribution policy, not our trade policy, that deserves our attention.

Economists have a similar reaction to people's concerns about the layoffs that occur in those industries that were previously protected by tariffs before a free trade arrangement is in place. We devote the remaining chapters of this book to a detailed discussion of what is called stabilization policy. If used properly, the tools of stabilization policy can limit the size and duration of recessions.

Assigning Policy Instruments To Economic Goals

The general issue just raised is that we have several objectives in conducting economic policy, and the government has several instruments with which to pursue those goals. There is more than one way to allocate the policy instruments across the various objectives, and experience suggests that there is one preferred assignment.

We have three broad goals of economic policy:

    A. Efficiency
    B. Equity
    C. Stabilization

We will certainly face many trade-offs if we do not consider at least three independent tools of economic policy, such as:

    1. Market regulations, such as tariffs
    2. The tax system
    3. Monetary, fiscal, and exchange-rate policy.

Economists generally favour the following assignment of instruments to goals. Market regulations like tariffs should be phased out to maximize efficiency, and so raise the standard of living for the average person. Then, the progressivity of a general income tax (including a negative income tax) should be adjusted to ensure that this higher standard of living is distributed in a fair manner. Finally, monetary, fiscal, and exchange-rate policy should be set so that the severity of recessions and inflationary episodes are lessened. In short, economists favour pairing policy instrument 1 with policy goal A, instrument 2 with goal B, and instrument 3 with goal C. Any other assignment fails to exploit the comparative advantage of each policy instrument.

Summary

Here is a review of the **key concepts** covered in this chapter. We have learned that **free trade** brings several benefits: it forces domestic monopolists to behave **more competitively**; it allows firms to operate at a scale that is larger than the domestic market (and so achieve the lower unit costs that stem from **scale economies**); and it permits all countries to take advantage of **comparative advantage**.

Every country must have a comparative advantage in something, since there must be some industry in which the extent of their low productivity problem is the least. A country's standard of living depends on its **absolute advantage**, but no matter how low that standard is, it can be raised because of comparative advantage.

There are individual winners and losers when a country enters a free trade agreement, but the present value of the net benefits exceeds the short-run costs by a wide margin. Also, the costs can be spread more evenly by embracing free trade gradually (as Canada has done over the postwar period), and by offering **adjustment assistance**. Finally, short-run adjustment costs can be lessened if recessions can be limited by **stabilization policy** - an issue we pursue in the remaining chapters.

Chapter 10

Unemployment, Inflation, and National Output

Over the years, the total output of the Canadian economy grows. For example, by the mid 1990s, output per person was two and one half times its 1950 value. But this large increase in material living standards has not been steady; the economy has gone through a series of cycles. Sometimes we have a recession - a period during which the total output of the economy is shrinking, and the unemployment rises. At other times our economy is what analysts call "over-heated" - when we are trying for a level of total output that is beyond the economy's long-run capacity. Inflation is the problem that occurs in this case. In the next several chapters, we work toward understanding how these cycles in our economy develop. We consider these problems from a country-wide point of view - often examining the question as if we were the federal minister of finance or the governor of the Bank of Canada. Economists call this part of their subject that deals with the whole economy at once - **macroeconomics**.

Unemployment

We measure unemployment by interviewing a representative survey of the population each month. Those interviewed fall into one of the following three categories:

1. Employed
2. Unemployed
3. Not in the Labour Force

People are listed as employed, if they had a job or were working in a family business like a farm. If people did not have a job and wanted one, they are listed as unemployed. The sum of the people in these two categories is called the labour force. Not everyone is in the labour force because some people are happy without a job. Retired people and full-time students are among those classified in the third group called simply "not in the labour force."

The **unemployment rate** is the total number of unemployed as a proportion of the labour force. In terms of numbers of people in the groups just listed, the unemployment rate is [2/(1+2)]x100%. As we have already noted, the unemployment rate goes up during recessions, but the amount that it goes up is understated because of what is known as the **discouraged worker effect**. Consider a recession. The fall-off in demand for firms' products means that firms lay off some workers. That involves some people moving from group 1 to group 2. But at the same time, with the chance of getting a job so much reduced, a number of people stop looking for work. These discouraged workers are then listed as not in the labour force. Surveys show that sometimes almost as many people move from group 2 to group 3 as are getting laid off from group 1 to group 2, so the measured unemployment rate understates economic hardship. It does not rise as much as it should during a recession. We can check on the magnitude of this measurement problem by watching how much the **participation rate** falls below trend during recessions. The participation rate is the ratio of the labour force to the population (that is, in terms of numbers in the labour force survey groups, $[(1+2)/(1+2+3)] \times 100\%$).

Inflation

As with unemployment, we measure inflation by conducting a survey. About every five years the Government surveys people, and they use this information to decide the basket of goods and services which is intended to represent the typical purchases of a Canadian household. Then they trace the changing cost of that fixed basket of items for the next several years. As time passes, people change their expenditure patterns and so the longer we focus on a particular basket of goods, the less relevant it is to know how much that set of goods is costing. As a result, many regard the resulting index, the **consumer price index** or **CPI**, as somewhat arbitrary. For example, we know that people shift to less expensive items (at least partially) when prices increase, thereby decreasing to some extent the increase in their cost of living. Since the CPI traces the cost of living without allowing for this substitution away from more costly items, its increase tends to overstate the true escalation in the cost of living by about one-half of one percentage point per year. In any event, the inflation rate is simply the percentage change in this surveyed price index from one period to the next.

Why Unemployment and Inflation are Undesirable

Everyone has read about some of the hardships of the Great Depression in the 1930s - a period in which our unemployment rate reached 25 percent. It seems obvious that high levels of unemployment are undesirable. Material living standards fall when our available resources are not used, and people's sense of self-worth suffers when they are not wanted. There is much evidence that both physical and mental health problems, and criminal activites, rise with unemployment.

But the costs of inflation are less apparent. What is so bad about just a few percentage points of inflation each year? One problem is that inflation redistributes income in an arbitrary way, and we can see this by considering a simple example. At a 6 percent inflation, it takes only twelve years for prices to double. A pensioner who saves all through her working life is fundamentally hurt by an inflation that occurs after she retires. When prices double, and her income is fixed in dollar terms after her retirement, her real welfare is very much reduced. Indeed, the real value of her pension is cut in half after twelve years.

Inflation also affects the amount society is willing to invest in new equipment that workers can use to make them more productive, and so allow them to earn higher incomes. A society will not have any newly produced output to be used in this investment process if its citizens are not willing to save - that is, to abstain from current consumption so that the new machines can be built. In short, lower household saving makes less investment by firms possible, and inflation reduces the incentive to save.

Suppose you do some saving by lending money to someone during a period during which prices double. Suppose that someone buys a house. When she repays, you receive an amount of money that will only buy half a house. So inflation makes saving less appealing, unless inflation makes the interest you earn on your savings go up enough to compensate.

Savings depend on what economists call the **real after-tax rate of interest**. We can calculate this yield by using this formula:

real after-tax yield on savings = i(1-t) - p.

To calculate the true yield on savings, we first take the market rate of interest, denoted by i, and scale it down by the factor (1-t), which is one minus the saver's income tax rate, denoted by t. The proportion of interest that the lender actually gets to keep is (1-t). But even that yield overstates the lender's real yield. We also have to subtract the inflation rate over the lending period, denoted by p, to find out what her after-tax return is in terms of real purchasing power.

Let us substitute some representative numbers into this real-yield formula, so that we can realize the implications of inflation. Consider a lender who faces a 50 percent tax rate and assume that initially the market interest rate is 6 percent and that there is no inflation. The lender's after-tax nominal return is 3 percent. With no inflation, the real rate of return is also 3 percent. Now suppose inflation rises to 6 percent. Let us assume that the market interest rate rises by the same 6 percentage points (to 12 percent) so that without considering taxes, the lender would be fully compensated for the decreased purchasing power of money that is occurring while her money is loaned out. The lender is left with a 6 percent nominal return on an after-tax basis. But then she still has to subtract the inflation rate of 6 percent to get her real yield, and this is now down to zero. So in this instance, even when the market rate of interest rises by the full amount of the inflation, the real return to lending has fallen from 3 percent to zero.

This example makes clear that when inflation interacts with a tax system that was designed for there being no inflation, the return to saving is decreased. As noted earlier, only when a society saves does it make available some of its newly produced output to be kept in the form of new machines and factories. So with lower levels of saving, there is less new equipment for the future labour force to use. As a result, we have lower standards of living in the future, compared to what we could have with no inflation. So even mild inflations interacting with our tax system mean quite significant income losses in the future.

Since both unemployment and inflation are costly, many individuals expect their government to "do something" to solve these problems. But we cannot assess the potential of government policies to be effective in preventing unemployment and inflation unless we have a detailed idea of what causes them to vary. It will take several chapters for us to develop this understanding fully, but we begin that task here. It turns out to be most helpful if we focus our attention on what determines the country's total output, what economists call the **Gross Domestic Product** or **GDP**. We proceed now with three tasks: we see how the GDP is measured; how it has varied; and how economists analyze those movements.

Gross Domestic Product

What we are trying to measure with the GDP is job-creating activity. The Gross Domestic Product is the sum of all currently produced final goods and services that are created in the country in a particular period, say one year. Some sales do not involve current production. For example, if Brian sells David his old car, that transaction would not enter this year's GDP calculation. Brian's old car is a pre-existing object; no production activity takes place in the swapping of existing assets such as dollars for the car. So workers at Statistics Canada cannot simply add up all transactions.

Another reason why our statisticians must take care when calculating GDP is that they must be sure to avoid counting the same economic activity more than once. For instance, wheat production would get counted when statisticians added in the sales of wheat farmers. Then, when they include the sales of finished bread, the wheat production activity gets counted again, since the price of finished bread includes what bakers have to pay to farmers for the wheat. One way of avoiding this double-counting problem is for statisticians to make sure they only include final goods and services. One problem with this approach, however, is that it is hard to know when something is a final good. For example, natural gas that is sold to heat a private home is a final good, but that sold to heat a factory represents an intermediate product.

Luckily, there are several methods of calculating GDP. When all measures give similar totals, our confidence in the data is increased. Here we mention just one of the other methods. It does not involve statisticians looking at the financial records of firms (as does the tallying up of the sales figures of the producers of final goods). Instead, this second method involves adding up all the pre-tax incomes earned by households (not including capital gains or losses on pre-existing assets). The reason this method works is that every time some value is created in the production process, it means that there was some income earned - either paid out as wages, rents or interest payments, or kept as profits for the owners of the firms. Thus, the sum of all income (including profits) must equal the GDP.

Of course some of the income that is generated by the economic activity taking place within Canada does not represent income for Canadians. To the extent that foreigners own some of the capital equipment that is employed in Canada, and to the extent that Canadians are in debt to foreigners, the income of domestic nationals is less than domestic production. Thus, what is known as the **Gross National Product** or **GNP** is less than Gross Domestic Product. Since the cyclical swings in GDP and GNP are almost identical, we ignore the difference between them in our analysis.

As noted earlier, with more than one method to calculate GDP, our statisticians can develop some confidence that they are measuring variations in the overall level of job-creating activity with a fair degree of accuracy. But we cannot forget something we all learned back in school - that we cannot add apples and oranges. Instead of adding up baskets of apples and crates of oranges, our statisticians add up the dollars worth of sales in each industry. Our statisticians solve the adding-up problem by measuring everything in dollar terms, not in physical quantities.

However, there is a problem with this method - we have created a measure that can stretch with inflation. Suppose that from one year to the next, the price of every product doubles and that no new jobs are created. In this case, our GDP measure will say that the level of overall production has doubled. But of course there are no more real goods and services being produced in this case. The only thing that has occurred is that everything is carrying twice the price tag.

So measuring the GDP by using the current market values for all the newly produced final goods and services each year is not such a good idea after all. But this total, called **Nominal GDP**, serves as a useful stepping stone to get to a better statistic. Statisticians take the appropriate price index and divide nominal GDP by this average level of prices to get what we call **Real GDP**. If all prices double, both nominal GDP and the

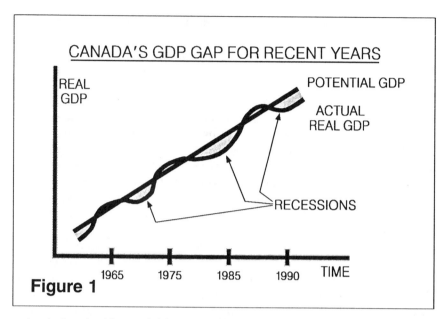

Figure 1

price index double, and this general increase in prices cancels out in the calculation of real GDP, so this measure is unaffected.

Thus real GDP is the sum of all currently produced final goods and services measured in constant prices, and it is what we should focus on when we hear news reports about the economy. It is the variation in this measure that indicates the swings in the overall amount of job-creating activity. Economists call these swings business cycles.

Business Cycles

Figure 1 shows Canadian real GDP for just over three decades - 1960 until the early 1990s. You can see the typical pattern for essentially all economies. GDP follows a rather wavy line. Analysts refer to this wavy line as a series of business cycles. The periods involving a downswing, when real GDP is falling, are referred to as recessions. The upswings are often called periods in which the economy is becoming "overheated." We can appreciate why this term is used by focusing on the other line in Figure 1, which shows the country's potential GDP. Potential GDP refers to that level of overall output that the economy could have produced in each year if all the available resources - machines, factories, and workers - were utilized.

Two facts are evident in the graph. First, the potential GDP path has very few wiggles; this reflects the simple fact that in short periods of time, there are very few drastic changes in the size of the population or in the quantity of capital equipment and technical knowledge that are available. The second point to note is that the actual GDP line has often been below the potential GDP, indicating periods involving excess capacity, and that the actual GDP line is sometimes above potential.

You might well wonder how we sometimes did better than our potential. It is because we define potential not as the maximum output that is possible in the short run, but as the maximum possible on a sustainable basis - assuming that workers are receiving adequate time to rest and that machines are being properly maintained. With heavy doses of overtime labour and by running machines without adequate downtimes for proper repair, we can produce more than is possible on a longer-run sustainable basis. This is what is reflected at several points in Figure 1, when Actual GDP exceeds Potential GDP.

The shading in Figure 1 highlights those periods when Actual GDP fell significantly short of Potential GDP - the recessions when our unemployment rate was much higher than at other times. If we add up all the areas between the Actual GDP time path and the potential line, we get some idea of the total value of goods and services that we could have produced had Canada not had any business cycles. For the period shown in Figure 1, when this calculation is done, we find that the total is equal to about two-thirds of the final year's GDP, so there's a lot of material welfare lost when we have recessions and high unemployment.

Aggregate Supply and Demand Curves

Many of the remaining chapters in this book are devoted to developing a detailed understanding of why these cycles in overall economic activity occur. Once this is understood, we will have a mechanism through which we can evaluate the government's ability to limit unemployment and inflation. The remainder of this chapter introduces the basic tools of macroeconomic analysis - aggregate supply and demand curves.

The overall demand for goods produced within our economy depends on many things, and several of the more important influences are listed in the table on the next page. The first three items affect aggregate demand in a positive way; for example, the higher are people's incomes, the higher are government expenditures, and the more export sales we make with the rest of the world, then the higher is the demand for our products. Other things affect aggregate demand in a negative way; for example, the higher is the price of the products that we are trying to sell, the more taxes people have to pay, and the higher are interest rates that people must pay when borrowing, then the less there is demand for our products. The aggregate demand curve shows the effect on the quantity demanded of just one of these many influences. The inverse dependence of demand on the price of goods is shown by the negative slope of the aggregate demand curves shown in Figure 2.

SOME DETERMINANTS OF AGGREGATE DEMAND

PEOPLES' INCOMES

GOVERNMENT EXPENDITURES　　　} POSITIVE

AMOUNT OF EXPORTS　　　　　　　　INFLUENCES

PRICE OF GOODS

LEVEL OF TAXES　　　　　　　　　　} NEGATIVE

BORROWING COSTS　　　　　　　　　INFLUENCES

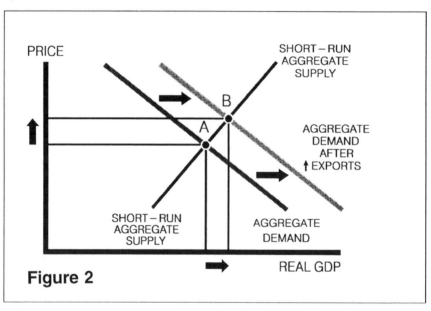

Figure 2

The way we show the influence of all the other determinants of demand is to shift the entire position of the demand curve. For instance, to pick just one of the influences listed in the table, an increase in export sales would stimulate spending and so be shown as a move to the right of the demand curve, as shown in Figure 2. While not shown in the graph, a cut in government spending, an increase in taxes, or an increase in borrowing costs would decrease spending and shift the demand curve to the left. So variations in price involve a movement along the aggregate

SOME DETERMINANTS OF AGGREGATE SUPPLY

PRICE OF GOODS

STATE OF
TECHNICAL ABILITY
} POSITIVE
INFLUENCES

LEVEL OF INPUT PRICES

PRICE OF FOREIGN EXCHANGE

LEVEL OF TAXES
} NEGATIVE
INFLUENCES

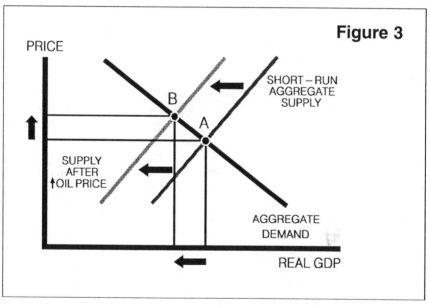

Figure 3

demand curve, while variations in the other determinants of demand cause a shift of that curve.

On the supply side, there are many influences as well (as indicated in the table above). Again, the price of goods matters but this time a higher price makes it possible for firms to profitably produce more output, so price is one of the positive influences. Another positive influence is the state of technical knowledge. The higher is the level of worker productivity, the more goods and services we can produce at any price. Negative influences on the quantity supplied are things like higher input prices; for example, the higher are the wages firms must pay for labour, and the more expensive are the foreign currencies that are needed to pay for imported raw materials and other intermediate products, then the less quantity supplied there will be.

The dependence of aggregate supply on the price of the product itself is shown as a positively sloped line in both Figures 2 and 3. The entire position of this aggregate supply curve is moved whenever we consider a change in any of those other determinants of the supply of goods. For instance, an increase in productivity, a cut in sales taxes, a decrease in wage rates, a decrease in the world price of oil - all are things that shift the supply curve out to the right (to show an increased ability or willingness of firms to produce goods) or down (to show a decrease in costs). The opposite case is shown in Figure 3. An increase in the price of raw materials, such as oil, raises firms' unit costs, and so it shifts up the short-run aggregate supply curve. As with the demand curve, variations in price involve a movement along the supply curve, while variations in the other determinants of aggregate supply cause a shift of that curve.

Armed with these basic tools, we can understand how real GDP is determined and why variations in its level occur. Real GDP is determined by the intersection of the aggregate demand and supply curves, so let us think of the economy being initially at point A in either Figures 2 or 3, before a shock hits the economy. Business cycles are caused by either demand shifts or supply shifts. For example, suppose other countries drop their tariffs and, as a result, we manage to sell many more exports to the rest of the world. That increase in the demand for our products is shown by the shift to the right of the aggregate demand curve in Figure 2, and the new outcome is point B. Projecting the location of points A and B on to both axes to show the results of this shift, we see that one is rising prices, which is inflation, and the other is rising levels of real output. With more goods being produced, more workers get jobs (so there is a decrease in unemployment associated with the increase in output shown on the real GDP axis in Figure 2).

So we see from Figure 2 that there is a **trade-off between unemployment and inflation** when demand shocks hit the economy. Unemployment goes down when inflation goes up. But this outcome only occurs with shifts in demand. Business cycles can also be caused by shifts on the supply side. One instance occurred during the 1970s, when the Organization of Petroleum Exporting Countries (OPEC) formed a cartel and quadrupled the world price of oil. This increase in input prices meant a major shift to the left in Canada's aggregate supply curve, so we moved from an initial observation point A in Figure 3, to the new outcome point B. Again, projections over to the axes show the effects of that development - higher prices but also a lower level of real goods and services produced. Of course, with less produced there are fewer jobs

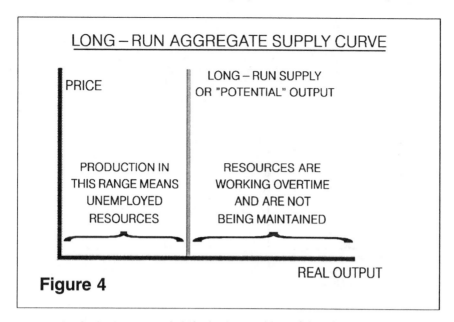

Figure 4

available. So in the case of shifts in the position of the short-run aggregate supply curve there is not a trade-off between unemployment and inflation. We see in Figure 3, that we experience rising inflation and rising unemployment at the same time.

A Self-Correction Mechanism

At several points in this chapter, we have acknowledged that many people expect the government to "do something" about unemployment or inflation. But in the earlier chapters on microeconomics, we stressed the existence of the invisible hand, and noted that often intervention by government was not needed. Is there an analogue to the invisible hand in macroeconomics? The answer is "yes." While it sometimes works very slowly, the economy does possess a self-correction mechanism which can eliminate unemployment and inflation automatically. We now use aggregate supply and demand curves to explain how this self-correction mechanism operates.

We have been using the term **short-run** aggregate supply curve. It is now time to clarify the difference between the short-run and the long-run capacity of the economy, which is our potential GDP. We impose a long-run capacity constraint in our graphs by drawing in a vertical line, positioned along the Real GDP axis at the level of potential GDP, as in Figure 4. Recall that by potential we mean that level of production that can be sustained over a long period. When the aggregate demand and short-run supply curves intersect to the left of the long-run potential line, we know that we have a level of output that is not big enough to generate

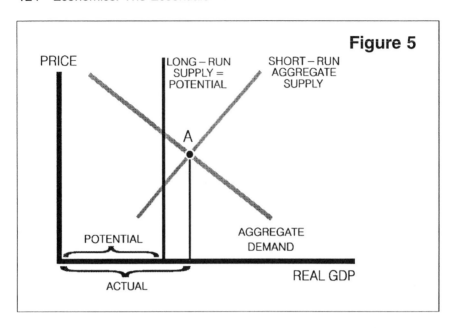

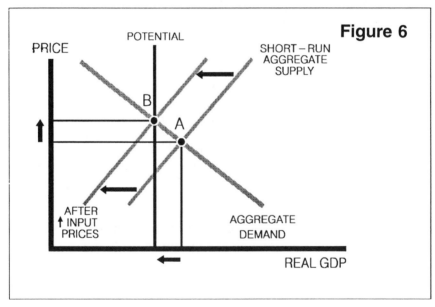

jobs for everyone. On the other hand, if the intersection of the demand and the short-run supply curves occur over to the right of the long-run potential line, then that means we are producing more than we can maintain on a sustainable basis.

The situation just mentioned is shown in Figure 5. There we see that the economy is experiencing what economists call an **inflationary**

gap - with Actual GDP exceeding its long-run potential. This is a situation in which factors of production are in scarce supply. Everyone is working overtime so that the wages people are able to command will rise. Firms are competing with one another to acquire these scarce factors. As wages and other input prices rise, firms' unit costs rise. Since the short-run aggregate supply curve is the entire economy's marginal cost curve, it shifts up (as shown in Figure 6) as wages and other input prices rise. So we gradually move from the starting point A to the final point B.

To summarize: whenever the economy starts off at a point that is beyond its long-run supply potential, the process of wage and price inflation pulls us back to the long-run sustainable level of output. In short, a bout of inflation will cure an inflationary gap. As already emphasized, this happens automatically. We do not need a policy maker to fix an inflationary gap.

Now let us consider the other kind of imbalance we could start with. The aggregate demand and short-run supply curves could intersect to the left of the long-run potential line. This situation, called a **recessionary gap**, is shown in Figure 7. In this case there are men and women who want jobs but cannot find them, and machines are idle as well. We certainly do not observe large wage increases in this case; indeed, in trying to get jobs, workers typically accept concessions and there are lower input prices. Lower input prices mean a shift down and to the right of the short-run supply curve. So gradually, even without any policy maker doing anything, the short-run supply curve drifts out to the right, causing the economy to move from initial point A to final point B, as shown in Figure 8. Prices fall as competition among firms forces them to pass on part of the decrease in input prices, and as a result, output increases. So a recessionary gap can be automatically cured through a process of deflation, that is falling wages and prices. As before, economists describe this process as the economy's self-correcting mechanism.

Some economists believe that the self-correction mechanism works too slowly, especially in the case of recessionary gaps when workers resist wage cuts. These economists want the government to step in by shifting the position of the aggregate demand curve whenever the actual and potential values of GDP do not coincide, rather than waiting for the position of the aggregate supply curve to adjust on its own. But other economists believe that the self-correction mechanism works fine as long as individuals are confident that government will not intervene. They argue that the main reason why workers resist wage cuts during a recession is that they expect the government to solve the unemployment problem for them. In the next several chapters we examine how successful these job-creation initiatives can be expected to be.

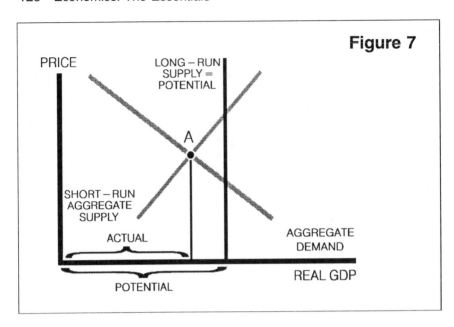

Figure 7

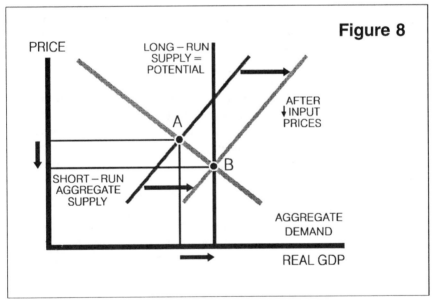

Figure 8

Summary

Here is a review of **key concepts** covered in this program. We have learned how **unemployment**, **inflation** and **GDP** are measured, and why these items are important. We introduced the tools of **aggregate supply** and **demand** to explain why **business cycles** occur, and how those swings in real output, which cause inflationary and recessionary gaps, can be eliminated automatically through the **self-correction mechanism**. Finally, we acknowledged that there is controversy concerning the speed with which the self-correction mechanism works. Should the government be engaged in an ongoing attempt to stabilize the economy? The analysis of most of the remainder of this book is designed to help you develop your own opinion on this central question.

Chapter 11

GDP and the Multiplier Process

Each year, our governments table a budget in parliament. The budget is a detailed statement of what the government will spend money on, and how they will raise tax revenue. Sometimes governments adjust their overall level of spending or taxation with a view to lowering unemployment or inflation. For example, the government might increase how much it spends in an attempt to create jobs or it might lower expenditures to lessen the overall demand for goods and services, so that firms are less likely to increase prices. This whole range of policies - the varying of government spending and taxes to stabilize the economy - is called **fiscal policy**. The purpose of this and the following chapter is to understand fiscal policy. This is accomplished by taking a major "behind the scenes" look at the aggregate demand curve.

A Simple Scale-Model Economy

To examine the logic behind aggregate demand, we consider a simplified model economy whose main features are highlighted in Figure 1. Notice that there are only households and firms in this flowchart. Nowhere in the chart is there any reference to the government, the rest of the world, or a financial sector, since all of these complications are assumed away for now.

Production takes place where firms are located in the flowchart. Firms use the labour time and the machines that are owned by the households to produce goods and services. We have learned that the value of all these goods produced (that is, firms' total sales of final goods and services) equals the value of all the income that is earned by all households. After all, what do firms do with all the revenue they collect when they sell their commodities? They pay some as wages, some as rent payments, and some as interest on borrowed items. The amount left over is profits. In this simple economy, we assume no retained earnings, so all the profits are distributed as dividend income to the shareholders. The arrow at the bottom of the flowchart indicates that all the income that is earned in the production process is sent over to households to do with as they wish.

Households can either spend the income (an amount we call **consumption**), or save it, and the two arrows indicating funds leaving the households in the flowchart show these two possibilites. The funds that are spent travel directly back to the firms. If savings were zero, the total

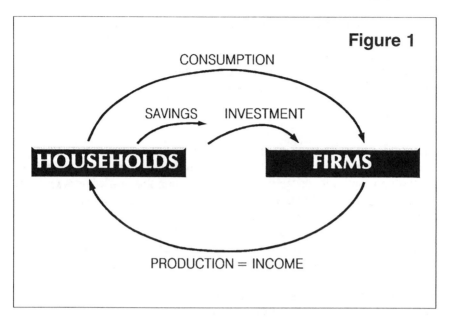

Figure 1

CONSUMPTION

SAVINGS   INVESTMENT

HOUSEHOLDS   **FIRMS**

PRODUCTION = INCOME

amount of consumption expenditures by households would just equal their income. Since this total also represents the value of goods produced, there could be no accumulating inventory problem for the firms in this case. But since households do save, consumption is less than the total value of production. So, if there is not some other component of demand (in addition to the consumption spending by households), there will not be enough purchases to justify the level of production that the firms undertook to create the income in the first place.

There is a second component of demand, since (as a group) firms buy some of their own output. Some of the currently produced output is new machines and new factories. We call this category of expenditures on new plant and equipment - **investment** spending. The system will be in equilibrium (that is, firms will be happy to go on producing whatever level of output they have been producing) if the sum of the household consumption purchases plus firms' investment expenditure equals the amount of goods that were actually produced in that period. In other words, demand equals supply.

Equilibrium in the Circular Flow of Income and Spending

As just noted, equilibrium exists when supply equals demand. Since supply is the value of GDP, and demand is the sum of the intended consumption spending by households (abbreviated as C) and the intended investment spending by firms (abbreviated as I), the equilibrium condition is:

GDP = C + I.

There is another way of stating the equilibrium condition for this simple economy, and it follows from the fact that household saving is all income that is not consumed. Saving (abbreviated as S) equals GDP - C. Combining this definition with the equilibrium condition given above (to eliminate GDP by substitution) yields:

$$I = S.$$

This alternative statement of the equilibrium condition says that the injection of funds on the part of the firms' **investment** spending has to just be the same magnitude as the amount of funds that are withdrawn from the circular flow of income and spending by the households' **saving**. Only if there is this balance will overall demand equal supply.

Notice that we are using the term investment rather differently from its everyday interpretation. When an individual household buys a Canada Savings Bond, most people refer to that as an investment in government bonds. Economists call it an act of saving, not investment. The term investment is reserved for the purchases of new capital equipment by firms. Economists use terms in this way to stress the fact that household saving decisions and firms' investment decisions are quite separate. As a result, there is no reason to presume that intended saving and intended investment will automatically be equal to each other. After all, households make their decision about how much to save without having any knowledge of what firms may need in terms of new plant and equipment. Similarly, firms make their investment decision without any reference to whether households want to do very much saving that period.

Let us examine what happens when households get worried about the future, perhaps fearing that they might lose their jobs. In this situation, households decrease consumption and increase saving. This throws out of balance the initial equilibrium. With the decreased household spending, there is not enough demand to justify the pre-existing level of production, so firms will have to lay some people off. And these job losses do not constitute the whole story. Those laid off will earn less so there will be a smaller amount of income flowing over to households along the bottom arrow in Figure 1. The result is yet another decrease in household consumption expenditures, and firms will have to lay off even more people.

We see that when households react to their fears that they might be laid off, they set in motion a chain of events that causes the very layoffs that were feared. The anticipation of a recession can cause a recession. Many people find this fact quite discouraging. They become even more concerned when they realize that the recession can feed on itself, with each round of layoffs leading to less household spending and so to still more layoffs. Does this vicious circle of lower income and lost jobs keep feeding on itself forever?

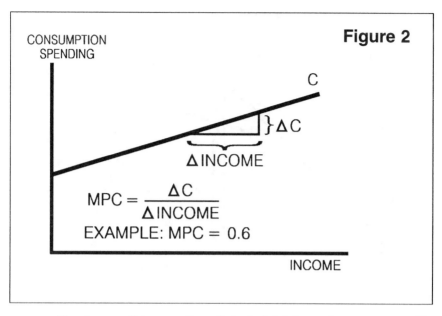

CONSUMPTION SPENDING

Figure 2

C

$$MPC = \frac{\Delta C}{\Delta INCOME}$$

EXAMPLE: MPC = 0.6

INCOME

To answer this question, it is helpful to make more specific assumptions about how households behave. Let us assume that household spending depends on household income in the way that is summarized in Figure 2. We see from this graph that consumption spending goes up when income goes up. When we take annual data for any country, data on total consumption and total income, and plot it, the result is a set of observations that looks just like this straight line. Economists call this relationship the consumption function, and they call the slope of this line the **marginal propensity to consume** or **MPC**. The marginal propensity to consume is positive, but it has a value that is less than one. The consumption function has this slope because we have observed that when people get an extra dollar of income, the increase in consumption is always some fraction of that dollar - such as 90 cents, with the remainder, 10 cents in this example, being saved.

We can emphasize the fact that the marginal propensity to consume is a fraction by adding a 45-degree line to the graph, as in Figure 3. A 45-degree line shows all those points at which consumption would be equal to income (that is, where saving is zero). When people's incomes vary, they spend more than their current income during low-income periods (perhaps by drawing down bank balances), and they spend less than current income during high-income periods (using leftover funds to build up bank balances). Saving is negative in the first case, and positive in the second. The second case is shown in Figure 3.

What we wish to show graphically is that level of total income and production that will just be bought by households and firms, assuming households make their spending decision according to this consumption

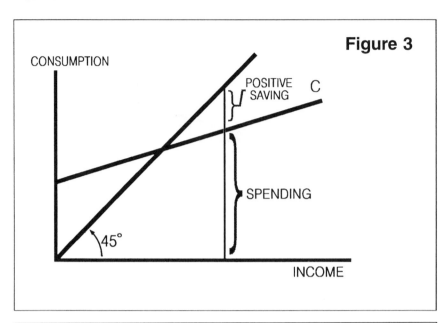

Figure 3

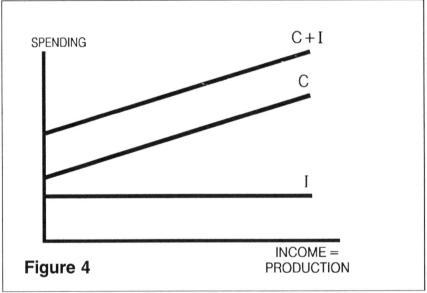

Figure 4

relationship. To obtain an answer to this question, we simplify at this stage by assuming that firms have fixed investment plans. We assume that firms want to spend an amount on new equipment equal to the height of the line labelled I in Figure 4.

Figure 4 involves two schedules of spending intentions: one for each of the two groups in our model economy - households and firms. It contains the upward sloping consumption line (which is the household decision rule showing that spending increases with income) and the

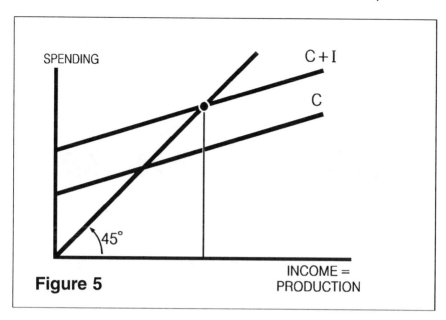

SPENDING

C + I

C

45°

Figure 5

INCOME =
PRODUCTION

horizontal investment line (which is the firms' decision rule showing their fixed investment plans). Figure 4 also shows these two plans combined (labelled as the C+I line). By adding the C and I lines together vertically, we get an overall intentions-to-buy schedule that shows how much total spending will be at all possible levels of national income.

We can use Figure 4 to illustrate the equilibrium level of GDP. For any level of total output that is measured along the horizontal axis, we can read off the corresponding height of the total spending line to see what the total demand for goods is. Equilibrium occurs where supply (the distance along the production axis) is just equal to demand (the height up to C+I line). But it is difficult to compare a horizontal distance to a vertical one. We solve this problem by again adding a 45-degree line, as in Figure 5. The 45-degree line transfers horizontal measures into vertical measures of the same distance.

Consider the intersection of the total spending line with the 45-degree line. At this point, the height of the total spending line (demand) is just equal to the value of goods and services produced and the income that this production generates (supply) since the right-angled triangle in Figure 5 involves sides of equal length. This point determines equilibrium.

The Multiplier Process

Earlier in this chapter, we considered a situation in which households were worried that they might lose their jobs. That concern led to households becoming more cautious and so they increased their savings. This decreased spending led to the very recession that people

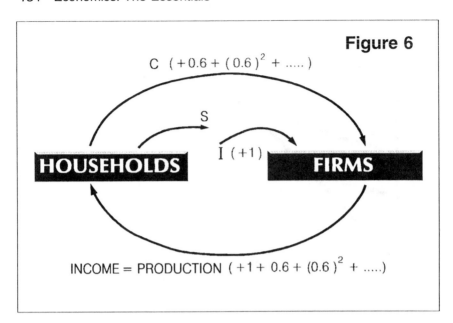

Figure 6

$C\ (+0.6+(0.6)^2+\ ......)$

S

I (+1)

HOUSEHOLDS   FIRMS

INCOME = PRODUCTION $(+1+0.6+(0.6)^2+\ ......)$

feared. We now have the tools that allow us to understand this process in more detail.

A multiplier process is set in motion whenever there is a change in any component of total spending, and the same process unfolds whichever direction the change in spending pushes the economy. Let us consider an increase in investment spending by firms, and you can consider a decrease in spending by households on your own for review.

Suppose firms spend an additional one billion dollars on new equipment. We are interested in determining how much this event will change the nation's GDP. It turns out that the resulting change in GDP is a multiple of the original one billion dollar change in investment spending. We call this ratio of changes the **multiplier**, and writing this ratio of changes in compact form, we have:

multiplier = $\Delta GDP/\Delta I$.

We now derive a formula for this multiplier. Once producers respond to the extra investment demand of one billion dollars by creating that additional amount of new machines and equipment, they will have to have employed some additional workers, and an additional one billion dollars of income will have been created. This fact is shown in Figure 6 by the "plus 1" entry by the investment and production components of the flowchart. Once this extra income reaches the households, they do some additional spending. To have a specific numerical example, we take the marginal propensity to consume to be 0.6. In other words, 60 cents of every additional dollar gets spent, and 40 cents is saved. Given this assumption, there is an induced increase in consumption demand, because there has been the additional one billion dollars of income earned. Thus there is a second round of increased expenditure equal to $600 million. This fact is indicated by the "plus 0.6" entry by the consumption component of the flowchart.

Firms have to increase the level of production again. They have met the new investment demand but they have not yet met the new $600 million of extra demand on the part of households. So once firms create some more jobs for that, they will have created $600 million more income, and so six-tenths of that $600 million will get spent by the next group of people who get hired. This fact is indicated by the "plus $(0.6)^2$" entry by the production and consumption components of the flowchart.

We can see that when all these bits of extra income are added together, the overall increase in production is:

($1 billion) times $(1 + 0.6 + (0.6)^2 + ...)$.

Thus, the multiplier, $\Delta GDP/\Delta I$ is $(1 + 0.6 + (0.6)^2 + ...)$. It turns out that this infinite sum has a finite total equal to $1/(1 - 0.6)$ or 2.5. For this numerical example, then, the expenditure multiplier is 2.5.

The easiest way to see that the multiplier is 2.5 is to multiply both sides of the multiplier equation by 0.6:

multiplier = $(1 + 0.6 + (0.6)^2 + ...)$

(0.6)(multiplier) = $(0.6 + (0.6)^2 + ...)$

Subtracting the second line from the first yields:

$(1 - 0.6)$(multiplier) = 1, or

multiplier = $1/(1 - 0.6)$.

It must be remembered, of course, that we picked the marginal propensity to consume value of 0.6 just as an arbitrary example. It should also be remembered that each additional dollar of income must be either consumed or saved. Thus, if we define the marginal propensity to save (MPS) to be the change in saving divided by the change in income, we have:

MPC + MPS = 1, and

multiplier = $1/(1-MPC) = 1/MPS$.

Do not let all these formal expressions for calculating the multiplier distract you from the basic intuition behind why there is a multiplier in the

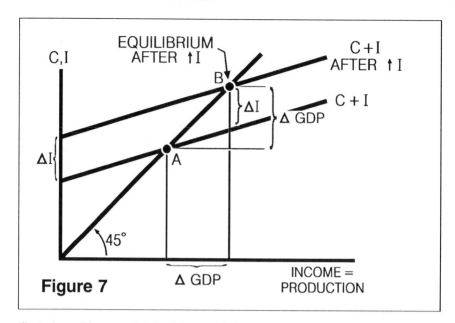

Figure 7

first place. You can think of the multiplier working like a ripple effect - what happens when you throw a pebble into a pond. The ripples in the water go out all across the pond well beyond the point at which the pebble was dropped. In the same way, somebody getting a new job means there is more income to be spent. That creates another job and so on, but in ever smaller amounts. In like fashion, the ripples across the pond eventually die down.

We now illustrate the multiplier in terms of an income-expenditure diagram in Figure 7. The initial equilibrium is point A. Now assume that investment increases by an amount equal to ΔI. The higher level of investment spending raises the I line, and therefore the position of the C+I line by ΔI. The new equilibrium point is where the now-relevant C+I line intersects the 45-degree line - point B. Figure 7 makes very clear that the overall increase in GDP exceeds the initial change in investment spending that causes the expansion, so a multiplier effect does indeed exist. The multiplier is the ratio of the GDP change distance to the investment change distance.

A More Realistic Model Economy

Now that we understand the basic principles, let us make our model economy more realistic by adding a government and a foreign sector. These additional features are included in Figure 8. As before, we start our discussion of how the economy works with firms. Production takes place there, and the total value of production creates the nation's pre-tax income (GDP) which starts on its way over to households near the bottom of the

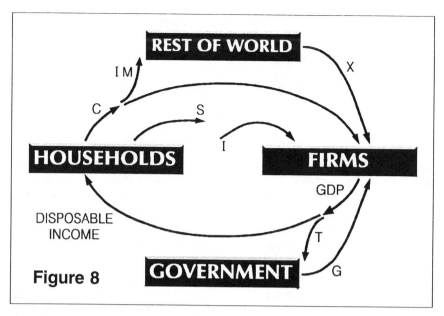

Figure 8

flowchart. But the government takes some of this income in the form of taxes (abbreviated as T), so there is a withdrawal of funds at that point. What is left to make it all the way over to the households is called disposable income; it is that part of pre-tax income that households can dispose of as they wish. Thus, the existence of government means an additional withdrawal of funds (taxes) from the circular flow.

As before, some more funds are withdrawn at the household stage because they save something. Consumption is noticeably smaller than total production in this case, since households only consume a fraction of their disposable income, and disposable income is only a fraction of pre-tax income. It is pre-tax income that equals the value of production. Furthermore, some of the household expenditures are not for our products at all. They are for imports (abbreviated as IM - products coming from the rest of the world) and so yet another withdrawal of funds from the circular flow occurs at the top of the flowchart, as funds are sent to the rest of the world. Funds come the other way too - the rest of the world buys some of our products and those incoming funds are shown in Figure 8 by the arrow labelled exports (abbreviated as X). Firms still do some investment spending on new machines and equipment, and the government buys some goods and services (government spending is abbreviated as G) by building roads and many other things. All these arrows pointing toward the firms in Figure 8 show that there are many more components to aggregate demand in this more complicated and realistic model economy.

But despite this extra detail, the same reasoning that we used before still applies. The equilibrium level of national product is reached when the sum total of all the demands is just balanced by the level of production, that is GDP. Things are a bit more complicated here solely because total demand is no longer just consumption plus investment. In this more general setting, total demand is:

consumption + investment + government spending + net exports, or

total demand = C + I + G + (X - IM).

This fact means that when we draw an income-expenditure diagram to show the determination of equilibrium graphically, we do not just add up the C-line and the I-line. We now have to draw in three more lines: an export line, a government expenditure line, and an import line. And we must do some adding and subtracting to derive the total spending line. So while there is more complicated adding and subtracting, the economic reasoning is the same. Equilibrium occurs where the total spending line intersects the 45-degree line.

   Two points are worth emphasizing. First, since both taxes and imports rise when people's incomes are higher, the subtraction of these components makes the slope of the total spending line (which is labelled C + I + G + X - IM from now on) much flatter than in our previous discussion. Remember, the taxes that are levied on high-income individuals are greater than those levied on low-income individuals. As a result, when the consumption line gets pulled down because of the existence of taxes, it gets pulled down more at the high-income end of the graph than at the low-income end, and this flattens the total spending line.

   This flatter total spending line means that when we consider a change in total expenditure, like a change in investment or government expenditure or exports, it will involve a smaller multiplier effect. Try drawing two income-expenditure diagrams on your own - one with a very flat total spending line, and one with a very steep total spending line. A change in government spending shifts both lines vertically by the same distance, but the multiplied change along the GDP axis is much smaller when the total spending line is flatter. Since Canadians have a high propensity to import, and we face high marginal tax rates, it should not be surprising to learn that Canada's multiplier has been estimated to be less than two. We must appreciate, therefore, that it is misleading to give a lot of emphasis to the multiplied effects that follow expenditure changes. Once a realistic slope for the total spending line is considered, it must be admitted that the very term "multiplier" has a misleading connotation.

   This fact means that we must have rather modest expectations about how much fiscal policy can actually do to reduce a recession. With a small multiplier it takes a large increase in government spending or a large tax cut to significantly raise GDP. Since it is difficult for governments to contemplate big spending increases or big tax cuts when they already have a large budget deficit, the fact that the expenditure multiplier is very small means that it is difficult for the government to create many jobs.

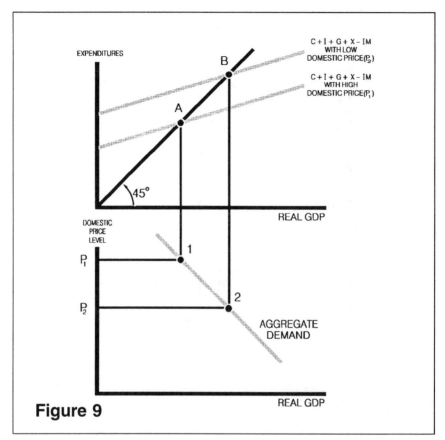

Figure 9

Inflation and the Multiplier

We started our study of macroeconomics by noting that we would focus on the twin problems of unemployment and inflation. But so far in this chapter, we have simplified the analysis by assuming that all increases in demand lead to more workers being hired. There has been no mention of firms raising prices in response to the higher demand for their products. We now fill in this gap.

Variations in domestic prices affect our country's international competitive position. The more expensive are our products, the less successful we are in selling goods to the rest of the world. Also, the higher are prices, the less our holdings of money and other financial assets are worth. To allow for these facts, we must draw a whole family of total spending lines, one for every possible level of domestic prices. In Figure 9, we see two members of this family of total spending lines. The lower one is the total spending line for price level P_1, which stands for a high price level. Expensive domestic goods mean low export demand and a high level of imports, so the result is a low position for the total spending

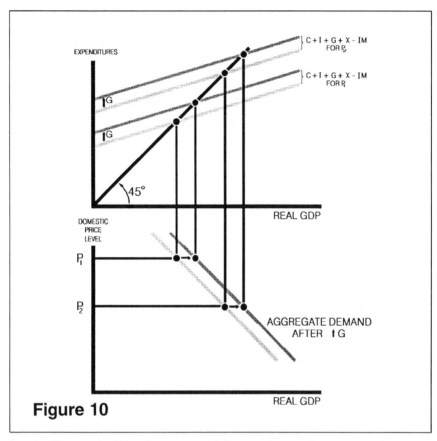

Figure 10

line in the graph. We also see a higher total spending line in Figure 9, corresponding to price level P_2, which stands for a lower level of domestic prices. These lower prices lead to high export sales, a smaller amount of imports, and a higher real value of financial assets. The result is a higher position for the total spending line.

The lower quadrant in Figure 9 summarizes this relationship. If the price level is very high, at P_1, then the lower spending line is relevant and GDP is given by point A. This combination of values for price and real GDP are recorded in the lower quadrant by Point 1. If the price level is lower, at P_2, there is higher spending, and GDP is given by point B. This second combination of values for price and real GDP are recorded in the lower panel of Figure 9 by Point 2. So we have two points in the summary quadrant of the graph which show combinations of domestic price and output for which firms just manage to sell all their current output. We join up all such dots and call the resulting summary line the aggregate demand curve.

In the preceding chapter, we introduced the aggregate demand curve, and in this chapter we have provided the detailed explanation behind it. Now we can understand more precisely how government policy

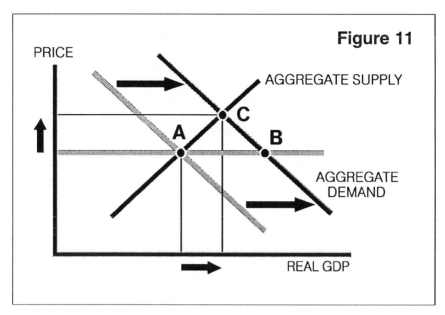

Figure 11

changes affect the position of the aggregate demand curve.

The effect of an increase in government spending is shown in Figure 10. Higher government expenditures shift up the entire family of total spending lines, so this policy moves the position of the summary line, the aggregate demand curve, to the right. Now that we are summarizing the whole multiplier process in terms of the position of the aggregate demand curve, we see that the multiplier represents how much the aggregate demand curve moves horizontally per unit of vertical shift in the family of total spending lines.

So the multiplier summarizes what would happen if prices stayed constant. As is illustrated in Figure 11, prices would stay constant only if the aggregate supply curve were horizontal. In that case, an expansion in government spending (for example) would shift the economy from point A to point B. However, as a matter of fact, the aggregate supply curve is not horizontal. It has a positive slope. Thus, the actual intersection point that the economy moves to following a policy that is intended to create jobs is not point B. The basic multiplier formula yields an over-estimate of the true outcome. In fact, we obtain a smaller increase in real output, such as that given by point C. Some of the effect of the policy is dissipated in the form of higher prices.

Thus, there are two broad categories of reasons why government demand-management policy does not work quite as well as some would like. First, when the government raises its expenditure, it cannot move the aggregate demand curve very far to the right. With high tax rates and a high propensity to import goods and services as our incomes increase, the multiplier is simply too small. Thus, the first stumbling block is that it takes a very major policy initiative to move the demand curve very far to the right. Then there is the second constraint on government policy. Even if the government does engineers a noticeable movement of the demand curve to the right, it has to confront the fact that the aggregate supply curve can be fairly steep. This forces the increase in demand to result mostly in inflation, with the policy having only very limited effect on real output and therefore on job creation. Putting these two considerations together, there is ample justification for us to have rather modest expectations about how well the government can create jobs. Fiscal policy can be used to ward off a major collapse in aggregate demand, but the government cannot fine-tune the economy.

Summary

Here is a review of **key concepts** covered in this chapter. We have understood how **equilibrium GDP** gets determined, and we have used this understanding to follow through how the **expenditure multiplier** process works. By deriving both the multiplier formula, and how the position of the aggregate demand curve depends on the multiplier, we were able to appreciate why Canada's multiplier is quite small. In the next chapter, we will use this set of tools to examine the government's **fiscal policy** in more detail, and to determine the effect of this policy on the government's deficit and our national debt.

Chapter 12

Fiscal Policy and the Deficit

In the last chapter, we learned how the overall level of economic activity is determined and how a change in one component of the demand for goods and services - such as a change in the level of government expenditure - can have a multiplier effect on the level of total output. Fiscal policy refers to the government's attempts to vary its expenditures and taxes, with a view to promoting stability. The purpose of this chapter is to use that analysis to assess the effectiveness of fiscal policy. One of the problems that confronts an active government policy is that the budget deficit can get out of control. If the government tries to both raise its expenditure and cut its taxes to stimulate spending and create jobs, it will go ever more into debt. One of the tasks of this chapter is to assess whether, and to what extent, this national debt represents a problem.

The Basic Rationale of Fiscal Policy

In the last chapter, we focused on the total spending line. Recall that there are four components of total spending: the purchases by households, called consumption spending; purchases by firms, called investment spending on new plant and equipment; purchases by government called government spending on goods and services; and net purchases by foreigners, that is exports minus imports. We saw that equilibrium GDP occurred where the total spending line crossed the 45-degree line. That level of output creates just enough income to have that quantity of goods bought, with no unintended inventory accumulation or decumulation. Thus, the income-expenditure diagram only determines equilibrium from the point of view that the output is willingly purchased.

But having this amount of output does not mean that the economy's labour markets are in equilibrium. We saw in Chapter 10 that the equilibrium GDP can be less than the economy's potential, and in that case the level of economic activity is not enough to create full employment. If the government feels that the self-correction mechanism is too slow and weak to eliminate recessionary gaps, what can it do? In an attempt to create jobs, the government can try to alter the position of the total spending line. One of the ways the government can stimulate spending is to raise its component of aggregate demand - government expenditure. Clearly, if the government builds new highways or does anything of that sort, it can move the entire position of the total spending line up. One of the results is a higher level of economic activity.

There are other government policies that can have the same result. For example, the government can cut taxes. We do not see taxes in the definition of aggregate demand (C + I + G + X - IM), but taxes are in the background. For instance, if the government cuts personal income taxes, it leaves households with a higher level of disposable income so that they can afford to raise consumption spending. So by this method of fiscal policy, the government raises GDP indirectly, by raising the consumption component rather than the government expenditure component of the total spending line.

Other taxes can be used as well. For example, the government can cut corporate profit taxes which may leave firms with more income to spend (and so the investment component of aggregate demand can go up). Foreign developments also affect the position of our total spending line. A lower value of the Canadian dollar makes our exports cheaper for foreigners to buy. Thus, a cheaper domestic currency raises the net exports component of the total spending line and so creates a higher level of economic activity and more jobs. Similarly, foreign tariffs reduce our net exports and so lead to a lower level of economic activity.

At the most general level, there are three possible strategies that the government can use to try to stimulate total spending and therefore job creation. Using our abbreviations (G for government spending and T for taxes), these options are:

1. Raise G while leaving T constant;
2. Cut T while leaving G constant;
3. Raise G and T by the same amount.

Option 1 raises the total spending line by working on the government spending component. Higher economic activity comes with a larger government sector. Option 2 shifts the total spending line up by raising either the consumption or the investment component. Higher economic activity comes with a larger private sector. If you are like most students of economics, you will be puzzled that option 3 is included in the list. It would seem that if the government raises its own spending and takes away dollars from households and firms by exactly the same amount, these two initiatives would just nullify each other's effect on total spending. Why would the increase in the government's injection of funds not simply cancel off the increase in the government's withdrawal of funds from the circular flow? We can use our theoretical tools to answer this question, and to understand why this third policy is, in fact, expansionary.

It is instructive to break the third policy option down into its two component parts. First, an increase in government spending of $1 billion raises the total spending line by precisely $1 billion. This is because government spending is a direct component of total spending. An increase in personal taxes of $1 billion lowers the total spending line because the increase in taxes lowers the disposable income that households have to spend. But the households pay for some of the extra taxes by cutting savings, so they pay for only a fraction of the taxes by cutting consumption. In the last chapter, we used the term marginal propensity to consume to indicate that fraction of changes in income that households take out of consumption as opposed to saving. Thus, if the households lose $1 billion of income through higher taxes, they will cut their consumption by the MPC times $1 billion. So higher taxes lower the total spending line, but by just a fraction of that increase in taxes.

Taking the increase in government spending and taxes together, we have competing effects on the position of the total spending line. It goes up by $1 billion and it goes down by a fraction, MPC times $1 billion. On the balance, the total spending line moves up by (1-MPC) times $1 billion. The resulting equilibrium point is further out to the right; so there is more economic activity and more jobs created.

Many people think that the government must either raise expenditures or cut taxes to create jobs, so that the government must increase its deficit to reduce unemployment. The analysis which we have just discussed is a counter example to this view. A balanced increase in spending and taxes provides some job creation without any increase in the deficit. The intuition behind this counter example is that it involves a shift in some of the economy's spending power away from the private sector and to the government sector. The private sector has a marginal propensity to consume that is less than 100 percent; while under this policy, the government spends every dollar of new tax revenue it gets (so it has a marginal propensity to spend of one). So it is not surprising that a redistribution of income away from the private sector and toward the government sector raises total spending.

The Budget Deficit as an Indicator of Fiscal Policy

The budget deficit is the excess of the government's spending over its tax revenue. Most commentators interpret an increase or decrease in the deficit as an indicator of whether the government has been trying to expand or contract the economy. One dramatic way to see that this presumption can be wrong is to consider a situation in which a recession occurs, and the government makes absolutely no change in its policies - a situation we examine in Figure 1.

Before the recession occurs, equilibrium GDP is determined at point A in the top part of Figure 1. The implications for the deficit are seen in the lower part of the graph. The positively sloped tax function reflects the fact people must pay higher taxes at higher income levels. The horizontal government spending line indicates that the government has fixed expenditure commitments. The budget deficit equals the amount by which the height of the government spending line exceeds the height up

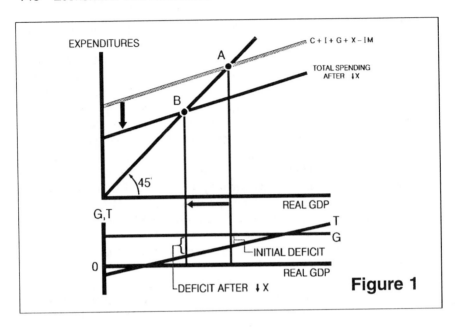

EXPENDITURES

C + I + G + X − IM

A

TOTAL SPENDING
AFTER ↓X

B

45˚

REAL GDP

G,T

T

G

INITIAL DEFICIT

0

REAL GDP

DEFICIT AFTER ↓X

Figure 1

to the tax function, at the equilibrium level of national income - as labelled in Figure 1. Now suppose that we lose a major part of our export sales. That loss in demand causes a drop in the total spending line, so the equilibrium point moves from point A to point B. A recession (a leftward move along the real GDP axis) occurs. Suppose the government does absolutely nothing to try to counteract this recession. This lack of action is evident in the graphs by the fact that the height of both the government spending line and the tax function is unaltered. Despite this lack of action, however, because GDP has shrunk, the government collects less taxes. The height up to the spending line is still the same but the height up to the tax line is much smaller. With people losing their jobs, they are earning lower incomes and paying less taxes. Since the tax base has shrunk, the budget deficit has increased.

So a recession has occurred and the deficit has increased. On the surface, the bigger deficit makes it appear that the government has tried to counteract the recession. But that is an incorrect interpretation, since by assumption in this example, the government has done absolutely nothing. The key point is that the deficit is affected both by government policy (which determines government spending and the tax rates), and by everything else that determines GDP (because that overall level of income is the tax base to which the government's tax rates apply).

The moral of the story is: when you read about the annual budget, do not just focus on the deficit. Consider also the announced changes in both government spending and taxes separately.

The Scope for Fiscal Policy
in Quantitative Terms

To form an independent opinion about the government's fiscal policy, we must have some idea concerning what can be reasonably expected in terms of job creation (when policy is expansionary) and job losses (when policy is contractionary). To establish that benchmark, we must understand the magnitude of the connection between the instrument that the government controls (the level of its own expenditure) and the item that people care about, such as the unemployment rate. Knowledge of the multiplier process lets us make part of this connection - that between the government's instrument and overall GDP. But to predict the effects of policy on the number of jobs, we need to know the precise link between overall output and the labour input in the production process, in quantitative terms. We now discuss each of these connections.

The multiplier is a small number - even ignoring inflation, about 1.67. To see why, consider our basic equilibrium condition: supply equals demand. Supply is the real GDP of the country, and demand is the (by now) familiar sum of the expenditures by households, firms, the government and foreigners. As we have stressed earlier, GDP is not just the value of production. Since the production process is what creates income, real GDP is also total income earned. That income must go in one of three places: it is either taxed away by the government, or households save it or spend it.

We can recast our equilibrium condition by simply substituting this definition of the uses of income into the supply equals demand condition, as is shown in the chart on the next page. Since the left-hand sides of both the first two lines in the chart equal real GDP, we can equate the right-hand sides. The result is an alternative version of the equilibrium condition (the bottom row in the chart) which stipulates that the injection of funds in the circular flow (investment spending, government spending and exports), must be just big enough to make up for the withdrawal of funds (savings, taxes, and imports).

It is important to realize that the magnitude of all these withdrawals depends on the overall amount of income earned in the country. The higher is the level of our incomes, the more saving we do, the more importing we do from the rest of the world, and the more tax the government collects from us. The numbers involved are roughly as follows. We tend to save about one-tenth of any increase in income. The tax rate that is relevant for the average citizen is about 25 percent. And as a society, whenever we get a dollar's worth of extra income, we seem to import about 25 cents more. So if we add up these three propensities to have funds withdrawn out of the circular flow of income and expenditure, we get 0.6. We can conclude that the change in withdrawals in Canada equals roughly 0.6 times any change in GDP.

EQUILIBRIUM:

$$\underbrace{\text{REAL GDP}}_{\text{SUPPLY}} = \underbrace{C + I + G + X - IM}_{\text{DEMAND}}$$

DEFINITION:

$$\underbrace{\text{REAL GDP}}_{\text{INCOME}} = T + S + C$$

EQUILIBRIUM:

$$\underbrace{S + T + IM}_{\text{WITHDRAWALS}} = \underbrace{I + G + X}_{\text{INJECTIONS}}$$

$$(0.6)(\Delta \text{GDP}) = \Delta \text{WITHDRAWALS}$$

EQUILIBRIUM:

$$\Delta \text{WITHDRAWALS} = \Delta \text{INJECTIONS}$$

$$(0.6)(\Delta \text{GDP}) = \Delta \text{INJECTIONS}$$

MULTIPLIER:

$$\frac{\Delta \text{GDP}}{\Delta \text{INJECTIONS}} = \frac{1}{0.6} = 1.67$$

To maintain equilibrium both before and after an expenditure change, it must be the case that the change in withdrawals is precisely equal to the change in injections. Both this equilibrium requirement, and the rate at which withdrawals respond to national income are summarized in the chart above. If we combine the two expressions by substitution, we obtain the relationship between the changes in GDP and injections. After cross-dividing, we see that the multiplier is indeed 1.67.

As noted in the last chapter, however, these calculations ignore the fact that part of any shift in aggregate demand ends up affecting the price level, not real GDP. On average, this fact means that the multiplier formula overstates the true effect on real output by about a factor of two. Thus, a more relevant multiplier coefficient is 1.67/2 or 0.83.

We must now focus on the link between output (GDP) and input (labour). This link can be summarized by simply comparing the percentage increases in real GDP that have occurred over the years to the corresponding changes in the unemployment rate. The typical pattern for most Western countries, including Canada, is that a one percentage point increase in the level of real economic activity translates into only about a one-half of one percentage point decrease in the unemployment rate.

There are two reasons for this lack of a one-for-one response. One is the discouraged worker effect which we discussed in Chapter 10, and the other is the simple fact that firms can vary their labour input by adjusting hours per worker, without making any variation in the number of people hired.

Now we can complete our quantitative analysis of a typical budget. In 1994, the federal government budget introduced expenditure cuts of $10 billion dollars, in an attempt to reduce its deficit. With a multiplier of 0.83, this contractionary policy can be expected to reduce real GDP by about $8.3 billion - that is, by about 1.2 percent. Since the unemployment rate only responds with a coefficient of one-half to any GDP change, it can be expected that the budget pushed the unemployment rate above what it otherwise would have been by about six-tenths of one percentage point.

When the purpose of fiscal contraction is to lower the budget deficit (as was the case in 1994), government officials are pleased that the unemployment effects that follow policy changes are not too large. At other times, however, when the government is trying to create jobs with an expansionary fiscal policy, many people are discouraged by how impotent policy appears to be. One must remember, too, that six-tenths of one percent of Canada's labour force represented 84,000 jobs in 1994, and these individuals and their families did not regard fiscal policy as unimportant. Perhaps a balanced view is that we should have only modest expectations about how fiscal policy can contribute to stabilizing the economy.

Which Taxes are Best for Stabilization

Thus far in discussions of fiscal policy, we have focused primarily on changes in government expenditure. Now we analyze tax changes, with a view to establishing which taxes represent effective instruments for short-run stabilization policy.

For many years, the Canadian government has favoured using the corporate profit tax for stabilization purposes. The idea is that by cutting the corporate profit tax, firms have more income and they can use that income to spend on new plant and equipment. This raises the investment component of total spending. But what is often overlooked is that many of the firms operating in Canada are foreign-owned. They are subsidiaries of multinationals. The parent companies get credit for taxes already paid in Canada when calculating the taxes they owe to the government of the country in which the parent company resides. Thus, a tax cut by the Canadian government turns out to be nothing but a reduction in that foreign tax credit, and so it is a straight transfer from the Canadian government to the foreign government. Since the firm gets no more disposable income, it does not increase investment spending. The Canadian government suffers a big revenue loss, and we obtain no stimulation of aggregate demand. So corporate tax concessions are not recommended.

A favourite instrument for stabilization policy in the United States has been variations in personal income tax rates. Sometimes these tax cuts stimulated the economy; sometimes they did not. When the tax cuts were announced to be very temporary, say just lasting for the worst part of a recession, they did not stimulate spending significantly. But when they were permanent tax cuts, and announced to be so, consumption spending by households was significantly raised. Economists were not surprised by this mixed record, since basic theory has long suggested that the more frequent are personal income tax changes, the less effective they are for stabilizing aggregate demand.

People do not make their consumption-savings decision solely on the basis of their current disposable income. Many people gear their consumption spending to the longer-run average level of income they expect to receive. When they have short-run variations in their income, especially those that are caused by tax changes that are known (by announcement) to be temporary, they let their level of savings be the buffer, so that consumption can remain insulated from these temporary disturbances. The more frequently the government tries using tax changes for stabilization purposes, the more certain people can become that the increases and decreases in their taxes are temporary. Thus, the more ineffective this stabilization strategy becomes.

Is there any tax for which the more temporary the change is, the bigger is the impact? The answer is "yes" - the more temporary a sales tax change is, the more it causes people to react and to change the timing of their expenditure on big-ticket items. Suppose your refrigerator is wearing out and you are going to replace it fairly soon anyway. Suppose the government offers a temporary reduction in sales taxes. You know you can get a major price decrease by buying the new refrigerator now, rather than waiting until next year (since the temporary sales tax cut will be a matter of history by then). Many people choose to bring forward their replacement purchases in this situation. And the more temporary is the sales tax change, the better an instrument it is for getting people to shift the timing of their expenditures to the period when the economy most needs stimulation.

Until the late 1980s, our federal government did not have a general retail sales tax. Whatever else you may think of the GST it does give the federal government access to the one tax that it could use to conduct a sensible fiscal policy. Of course, as a practical matter, we cannot expect the government to make significant, even temporary, sales tax cuts. The reason is the size of the budget deficit. By the mid 1990s, the government was compelled to regard fiscal policy as a luxury it could no longer afford. Instead, cutting government spending and raising taxes, even during recessions, had become standard fare - all because the government needed to bring down its deficit.

The National Debt

The national debt is the sum of all the annual deficits run by our federal government for the entire history of our country. By 1994, the federal debt had passed the $500 billion mark. Just 25 years earlier, the debt was about $25 billion. So the debt has increased 20 times more in Canada's fifth quarter century, than it did in the entire first century following Confederation.

Government debt would not have accumulated if the government had taken the advice that follows from our theory of fiscal policy. That advice is to run a deficit (by raising expenditure and/or cutting taxes) during the recession phase of each business cycle, and to run a surplus (by cutting government expenditures and/or raising taxes) during the boom half of each business cycle. This policy would balance the economy over the cycle, and it would balance the budget over the time interval of each full cycle. This would be sufficient to keep the debt from increasing over the longer term.

Governments have followed this advice during recessions - indeed they have appreciated the fact that economists condone deficit spending during these periods. But governments have chosen to disregard the other half of the advice from economists, since they have not run surplus budgets half the time. Indeed, the federal government has not run a surplus since the early 1970s, and for much of the 1980s and 1990s, the deficit in any one year (which is the annual increase in the debt) has exceeded the entire national debt that we incurred during the country's first century. By the 1990s, our governments had become so preoccupied with stopping the growth in debt by balancing their budgets, that they could no longer give any attention to trying to help balance the economy.

Governments pay for each annual deficit by selling a large quantity of government bonds each year. When those bonds are sold domestically, they compete for the limited quantity of household saving. That competition makes it harder for firms to obtain funds to finance their investment expenditures in new plant and equipment. Canadian workers are left with less equipment (and outdated equipment) to work with, so our standard of living does not rise as much in the future, as it would have without the government borrowing "crowding out" the firms' attempts to obtain funds. Thus, the buildup of debt has meant a major transfer across generations. Current generations have "spent beyond their means" and bequeathed a lower living standard to future generations.

Many individuals are concerned about the fact that many of the government bonds have been sold to foreigners. By relying on foreign lenders, governments have not competed so much with domestic firms for domestic savings. As a result, investment spending by firms is not reduced as much. But our children and grandchildren are stuck with high taxes just to make interest payments to the rest of the world. Since foreign debt pushes GNP below GDP, future living standards are lowered just the same. As of 1994, foreign interest payments alone were lowering each four-person Canadian family's income by $4000 every year.

It is figures like these that convince many Canadians that it is important to eliminate the deficit. After all, getting the deficit to zero just stops the accumulated debt from continuing to rise. Eventually, many years with budget surpluses are needed to bring the debt down, and therefore to start reversing the intergenerational transfer.

So there is a substantial long-term gain to be had from deficit reduction. But the short-term pain is significant as well. Contractionary policy raises unemployment, and the more our tax dollars go to cover interest payment obligations, the less they can be used on social policies and other programs that have come to be regarded as part of the Canadian identity.

Confronted by such large up-front costs involved with deficit reduction, it is not surprising that many politicians have hoped that we can simply grow our way out of our debt problems. This hope is based on the proposition that if the debt becomes an ever smaller proportion of our income, it will represent an ever smaller burden. According to this view, then, we should only be concerned with the ratio of the debt to our GNP. While not quite as appropriate, many commentators (and government documents) focus on the debt-to-GDP ratio.

It is easy to appreciate why it is not possible for growth to eliminate our debt problem. If the government covers each year's interest payment obligations by issuing that many more government bonds, the debt must grow at an annual rate equal to the rate of interest. Thus, the numerator of the debt-to-GDP ratio must grow faster than the denominator as long as the rate of interest exceeds the economy's growth rate. Since this has been true for many years, it is simply unreasonable to expect an "automatic" cure to the debt crisis. Direct government action is needed over a prolonged period. Painful budget cuts in the short run and/or lower living standards in the long run are the legacies of our imprudent fiscal policies of the past.

Summary

Here is a review of the **key concepts** covered in this chapter. Aggregate demand is affected by any of its components, so **fiscal policy** can work through several channels: changes in **income** or **sales taxes** to alter consumption, changes in **corporate profit taxes** to alter firms' investment spending, or changes in **government spending**. Further, government policy can change tariffs or our foreign exchange rate to alter net exports.

The government's **budget deficit** is the excess of its expenditure over its tax revenue. A well-designed fiscal policy involves stimulating aggregate demand during recessions by running a deficit, and contracting aggregate demand when the economy is overheated, by running a surplus. In recent decades, however, Western governments have run deficits through all phases of each business cycle, forcing high taxes, painful government cutbacks, and high levels of **debt** to be part of the Canadian landscape for many years.

Because the servicing of high debt levels will constrain fiscal policy for so long, some commentators argue that increased emphasis should be given to another instrument that they feel can be used to help regulate the business cycle. This other instrument is monetary policy - and it is the subject of our next several chapters.

Chapter 13

Money and Banking

In the last two chapters we have discussed fiscal policy - the attempt by government to vary its expenditures and taxes with a view to influencing the overall level of economic activity. In this chapter, we continue our focus on the government's attempts to stabilize the economy, but we turn our attention to what is called monetary policy.

Most of us have borrowed money to finance some purchase like a new car or our university education. We are quite familiar with the fact that the interest rate we are charged on that loan is an important determinant of how much we can spend. Monetary policy concerns how the government tries to affect the level of interest rates, and to understand this process we must become acquainted with Canada's financial system.

In the circular flowchart back on page 129, there was no mention of the financial system. The household saving arrow just went off to an unspecified area of the flowchart, and no details were offered concerning how firms finance their investment spending. We fill in those details now, since these are some of the questions which are addressed in this chapter.

There are four ways in which firms can finance investment expenditures. They can simply retain some earnings and not pay out all the profits as dividends. They can sell shares on the stock market. They can borrow money by selling a bond or they can take out a loan from banks. Whichever of these four financing methods firms rely on, they acquire cash that can be used to pay for investment expenditures. It turns out that the macroeconomic implications are the same, whichever option is chosen. Thus, to keep things simple and to avoid repetition, we focus on just one of the financing options. We assume that the firms take out bank loans. But before we talk about money and banking in detail, consider the flowchart on the next page. It highlights the role of money in our economy.

The Bank of Canada is the institution through which government prints money. Suppose the Bank prints more money. What is that going to do? Since most individuals deposit the bulk of their money in their chartered bank or trust company, most of the new currency will find its way into what we call the reserves of the chartered banks. Banks earn no interest on reserves, since these are just units of currency held in their vault. Since banks want to make profits, they try to hold no more reserves than is necessary to facilitate the withdrawals made by their customers. Banks loan out the rest of these funds, and they make money when

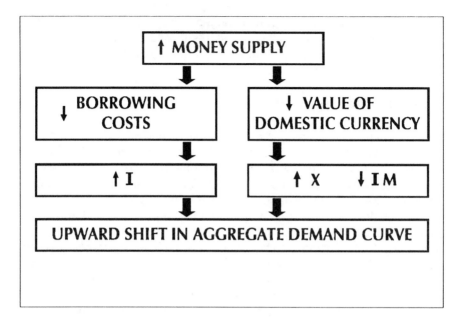

↑ MONEY SUPPLY

↓ BORROWING COSTS

↓ VALUE OF DOMESTIC CURRENCY

↑ I

↑ X   ↓ IM

UPWARD SHIFT IN AGGREGATE DEMAND CURVE

borrowers pay interest on these loans. Thus, when the Bank of Canada prints up more currency, chartered banks get extra reserves, and this means an increased capacity to make loans.

But the only way banks can get more people to take out those loans is to have lower interest rates. When they charge lower interest rates, it means that more people can afford to buy large items and that more firms can afford to expand plant and equipment. So the consumption and investment components of total spending increase, and aggregate demand expands. Thus, jobs can be created and prices are increased when there is a significant increase in the nation's money supply. This chain reaction is summarized on the left hand side of the chart above.

We have already discussed the latter stages of the chain reaction (how higher investment spending has a multiplied effect on aggregate demand) in earlier chapters. The job for this chapter is to develop the details of the early part of the causal sequence.

What we have just sketched is the domestic route showing what happens following an increase in the money supply. If some of the extra money is used in foreign transactions, then the avenue of effect is a little different but the net result is the same. An increased supply of Canadian dollars in the world's currency markets causes a fall in the international value of our currency. This makes it cheaper for foreigners to buy our goods and more expensive for us to buy imports. In this case, then, it is the net export component of aggregate demand that increases to create jobs and put upward pressure on prices. This transmission mechanism for money supply changes is summarized on the right hand side of the chart above.

Whether money supply changes affect interest rates or the exchange rate, the end result is the same. It will be helpful to keep this flowchart in mind (as a general "road map") while we delve into the details of the financial system.

Historical Background

We have just sketched how monetary policy works. But to discuss policy in more detail, we must also talk about institutions. Sometimes banks and trust companies go bankrupt, and there are crises of confidence in the financial community. To appreciate the origin of these problems, we must understand the history of money.

Money was invented many centuries ago as a mechanism for people to avoid what economists call "the double coincidence of wants". This difficulty in finding trading partners is necessarily involved when people simply barter one good for another. All kinds of commodities have served as money, but a commodity needs to satisfy several criteria before it can last as a useful money. It must be storable; it has to be easy to carry around; and it has to be hard to counterfeit. Precious metal coins satisfied all these needs and so were widely used. But coins can still be stolen, so many years ago enterprising individuals set up warehouses where people could deposit their gold coins. They were given receipts for their gold deposits. These receipts were I.O.U. slips which depositors could use to retrieve their gold whenever they wanted to make an expenditure.

After a while people realized that they could just trade the I.O.U. slips. If Brian wanted to buy something from David, he crossed out his own name on the slip and wrote in David's name. As a result, the warehouse then owed David the gold instead of Brian. So with this practice of financing trades by exchanging the warehouse receipts, societies moved away from using a commodity money (that had its own intrinsic usefulness) to paper money (a system in which the medium of exchange, paper currency, had no intrinsic value). Despite having no real value on the used paper market, this kind of money was accepted because it was regarded "as good as gold." After all, if people started to lose confidence in the paper currency, they could cash it in for gold at their warehouse.

After a while, the gold warehouse managers realized that they were hardly ever asked for the gold. They realized that a profit could be made by loaning out the gold. Every time they loaned some of the gold, someone would receive it as payment for the goods and services that someone sold to the borrower. That someone then deposited the gold in her warehouse, receiving another I.O.U. slip as a receipt. Considering the entire group of gold warehouses, there soon came to be many more I.O.U. slips than there was gold in storage. When depositors realized this fact, some feared that when they took in their I.O.U. slips there might not be any gold left. In that case, the warehouse company would go bankrupt and the depositors would lose their wealth.

As you have probably guessed, the warehouses eventually became banks and trust companies, and government regulations were introduced. The regulations were designed to avoid crises of public confidence by keeping these institutions solvent. One arrangement we now have is deposit insurance. Even if a financial institution goes bankrupt, so long as your deposit is less than $60,000, the government will pay you back. So now there's no reason to have a run against a bank (unless your account is very big).

What serves as most of our money today, then, is not even paper currency. Since we often pay by cheque, it is mostly the passbook entries in our deposit accounts at banks that represent the nation's money supply. So if we are to understand how the quantity of money varies, we have to understand chartered banking.

Chartered Banks and the Money Multiplier

The easiest way to understand banking is by considering the balance sheet of a typical bank - as shown in the chart on the next page. The balance sheet keeps a record of all the **assets** and **liabilities** of the bank. An asset is anything an individual or an institution owns, and a liability is anything that that individual or institution owes someone else.

As can be seen in the chart, one of the things a chartered bank owns is its reserves (currency kept in the vault), and the second important asset is the stock of loans that the bank extends to its customers. Loans allow households and firms to buy many items such as houses and factories. From the bank's point of view, each loan is an asset because it represents an income stream of interest payments coming into the bank. The loan is a liability from the household's or the firm's point of view, but it is the bank's balance we are considering here. Finally, there are other assets like the bank building, but these other assets do not figure into our discussion of monetary policy.

Over on the liabilities side, the main entry is deposits. These deposits are the customers' assets, but since the deposits represent an obligation to its customers, they are liabilities from the bank's point of view. Banks make money by charging a higher rate of interest on loans than they pay on deposits and, if successful over the years, the accumulation of profits is reflected in the fact that the company's assets exceed its liabilities. Accountants call the amount by which assets exceed liabilities the company's net worth. They record net worth on the liabilities side of the balance sheet, so that the sum on both sides reaches the same number.

BALANCE SHEET FOR A PRIVATE BANK

ASSETS	LIABILITIES & NET WORTH
RESERVES	DEPOSITS
LOANS	
BUILDINGS	NET WORTH

The most common definition of the nation's money supply (called M1) is the total of the public's chequing deposits at chartered banks plus any currency circulating outside banks. Other definitions include all deposits in banks and some of our deposits in trust companies and the caisses populaires. However, since it is not necessary to consider this wider set of deposits to understand monetary policy, we focus on just the chartered banks and M1.

Since most of the money supply is the level of bank deposits, we must understand how much the total quantity of deposits rises when any given amount of new currency is printed up. We now consider a specific example to illustrate what economists call the money multiplier.

For simplicity, we consider a situation in which no one holds any money in the form of currency. Thus, initially we assume that everyone who receives money puts it all on deposit at banks. Also, we assume that banks choose to hold on reserve an amount equal to 10% of whatever their deposit obligations are. Actually banks hold a much lower reserves-to-deposit ratio than 10% since very little is needed to satisfy the withdrawal habits of the banks' customers. But we just want a simple numerical example to illustrate the principles involved.

Suppose a brand new $100 bill is sent to you, as part of your student loan. Given our first assumption, you will either deposit it in your bank, or you will pay for something - say the services of a typist for your economics essay. In that case, the typist is the one who puts the $100 into his bank, say Bank Number 1 (see the accompanying chart). After this initial deposit, there is $100 more in that chartered bank vault (because the $100 bill is now there), and that bank will record an additional $100 obligation to the typist for having deposited the money there.

BANK 1 :   AFTER INITIAL DEPOSIT

ASSETS	LIABILITIES
RESERVES + 100 LOANS	DEPOSITS + 100

BANK 1 :   AFTER MAKING NEW LOAN

ASSETS	LIABILITIES
RESERVES + 10 LOANS + 90	DEPOSITS + 100

But Bank Number 1 will not be comfortable with this outcome. This is because the bank is holding reserves on a one-for-one basis for this new deposit of $100. The bank cannot make a profit by paying interest on the deposit while earning none on the reserves. We have assumed that banks only want to hold reserves on a one-for-ten ratio, compared to deposit obligations. Thus, the bank will loan out $90 of that $100.

The second step in this process is that Bank Number 1 shuffles its portfolio of assets - drawing the new reserves down to just $10, and

---

BANK 2 : AFTER MAKING NEW LOAN

ASSETS	LIABILITIES
RESERVES + 9	DEPOSITS + 90
LOANS + 81	

---

loaning out $90 to some other customer. That person buys something with the funds. Whoever receives that payment deposits it in her bank, say Bank Number 2. So in Bank Number 2, there will be $90 more in both reserves and deposits. But just like Bank Number 1, this bank cannot make money holding a full dollar more of reserves for every new dollar on deposit. Given the one-for-ten desired reserve-to-deposit ratio, Bank Number 2 will pull its extra reserves down to just $9, and it will make an additional loan equal to $81.

Of course, just as before, that new loan will get spent and somebody else will deposit $81 in yet another bank. You can see what is happening - it is another multiplier process.

Our goal is to determine the total quantity of bank deposits that gets created as a result of the extra $100 of new currency that was introduced into the system. To determine this total, we add up all the extra deposits that are created round after round:

$100 + $90 + $81 + ...

A more fruitful way of writing this sum is:

$100 x (1 + .9 = (.9)^2 + ...).

This sum is similar to the expenditure multiplier formula we calculated in Chapter 11. The sum equals:

$100 x (1 /(1 - .9)) = $100 x (1/0.1) = $1000.

Thus, there is a money multiplier as well as an expenditure multiplier, and in this numerical example, because the reserve-to-deposit ratio of the banks is one-tenth, the money multiplier is the inverse of that, or 10.

How does the actual value of the money multiplier compare to this example value of 10? In fact, our simplifications involve both an upward and a downward bias. For one thing, people do not hold all their money as deposits; they hold some of their money as cash. To that extent the banks do not get to loan out as much as they did in our example, so the actual money multiplier is smaller. But more important is the fact that modern banks can satisfy the day-to-day needs of their depositors with a reserve-to-deposit ratio of much less than one-tenth. By June 1994, all laws stipulating that a certain fraction of deposits must be kept on reserve were phased out in Canada. Now all that induces banks to keep some reserves is to service the withdrawals of their customers. A very small stock of reserves (relative to deposits) is sufficient for this purpose. Thus, the nation's money supply is a large multiple of the quantity of currency that the government prints. As a result, it is important that the government not print up an inappropriate quantity of currency.

Bank of Canada Operations

The last step in understanding the mechanics of money and banking is to appreciate how the initial $100 of new currency actually gets introduced in the first place. To facilitate this understanding, we must learn a few things about Canada's central bank, the Bank of Canada.

The Bank of Canada came into existence with the passage of an act of parliament in 1935. Some of the provisions in this act put regulations on our chartered banks to make sure that they do not take part in such risky ventures that people lose confidence in the stability of the financial system. The act established The Bank of Canada as a kind of lender of last resort, that can loan out reserves to any chartered bank that is running short in any particular period, again to provide stability to the financial system.

The governor of the Bank of Canada is appointed for seven years, and while he or she normally works very closely with the federal minister of finance, the governor is able to be somewhat independent. Central bankers take it as one of their fundamental purposes to preserve the purchasing power of money and that means keeping inflation under control. Since ultimately inflation results from "too much money chasing too few goods," central bankers often find themselves serving as an independent check on a government's temptation to print a lot of new currency as a method of financing government expenditures that are in excess of the government's willingness to raise taxes.

We can better understand the Bank of Canada if we focus on a simplified version of its balance sheet (presented on the next page). The

BANK OF CANADA'S BALANCE SHEET

ASSETS	LIABILITIES AND NET WORTH
GOLD	CURRENCY IN EXISTENCE
FOREIGN EXCHANGE	DEPOSITS
GOVERNMENT BONDS	OF CHARTERED BANKS
	OF FEDERAL GOVERNMENT

main items which our central bank owns, or controls, are: gold, the country's foreign exchange reserves, and government bonds. Gold used to be the international medium of exchange, and that is why this item appears in the list of things that the Bank of Canada has purchased over the years. On the liabilities side of the Bank of Canada balance sheet, the major item is the total number of dollar bills that have been issued - the currency in existence. Paper currency is a rather unique liability; it is an I.O.U. slip from an accountant's point of view, but of course, you cannot get anything if you present your dollar bill to the Bank of Canada (other than a crisp new dollar bill in exchange). The other liabilities are the deposit obligations of the Bank of Canada. The general public is not allowed to hold deposit accounts at the Bank of Canada. The only institutions that do are the chartered banks (and similar institutions) and the Government of Canada.

We are now in a position to see the main way in which the Bank of Canada changes the overall reserves of the chartered banking system. At the intuitive level, it is very simple. To increase the supply of currency, all the central bank has to do is to buy something and pay for it with the new currency. Since the Bank of Canada usually does this through a purchase of government bonds on the open market, called **open market operations**, we follow through the recording of that transaction in the balance sheets. Refer now to the chart which contains both the Bank of Canada's balance sheet and a balance sheet for the chartered banks.

The chart contains numbered arrows, 1 through 4, that summarize the Bank of Canada's purchasing some government bonds. As the Bank of Canada buys the bonds (that were previously held by some member of

OPEN MARKET OPERATIONS BY THE BANK OF CANADA

BANK OF CANADA		CHARTERED BANKS	
ASSETS	LIABILITIES	ASSETS	LIABILITIES
GOLD	CURRENCY	RESERVES	DEPOSITS
FOR. EXCHANGE	DEPOSITS	CASH	GOV'T
GOV'T BONDS ↑1	GOV'T	DEPOSITS ↑4	PUBLIC ↑2
	BANKS ↑3	AT BANK	
		OF CANADA	
		LOANS	

the public), we show the central bank's acquiring the bonds by Arrow 1 in the chart. The Bank of Canada pays for these additional bond holdings by writing a cheque to the member of the public who sold the government bond. That individual deposits the cheque in her account, at whichever chartered bank she does her banking, and that is why Arrow 2 is included in the chart. This individual now has a larger bank deposit.

But this is not the end of the story because the cheque has to be cleared through the banking system. After all, why should the chartered bank go more in debt to this individual when this bank has done nothing to warrant its being further in debt. The chartered bank gets compensated (for honouring the cheque on behalf of the Bank of Canada) by sending the cheque back to the Bank of Canada, which credits the chartered bank's account there by the same amount. This final settling up of the transaction is recorded in the chart by Arrows 3 and 4.

So the chartered bank's deposit at the Bank of Canada goes up by the same amount as the original purchase of bonds. That fact represents both an increase in the Bank of Canada's liabilities (Arrow 3) and an increase in chartered bank assets (Arrow 4). The complete set of four arrows are needed to fully record the open market operation. But while the description of that transaction is now complete, what follows from it is just about to begin.

The chartered banks are just at the first stage of the money multiplier process that was described earlier. The reserves of the chartered banks can be held either as cash in their vaults, or as funds on deposit at the central bank. So, as a result of the open market purchase of bonds by the Bank of Canada, chartered bank reserves have gone up dollar-for-dollar with their deposit obligations. Banks want to hold only a very small fraction of this amount as additional reserves. We do not need to pursue events any further, since we have already seen how new loans and further deposits get created when the banks are in an excess reserve situation of this sort. The point of this discussion was just to explain how the additional reserves are created in the first place.

There is one additional point worth emphasizing. We could move Arrow 1 from the government bonds entry to the foreign exchange entry (among the list of Bank of Canada assets) and the other three arrows would stay exactly the same. This implies that, as far as what happens to the reserves of the chartered banks is concerned, it does not matter what the central bank buys. Central bank purchases of foreign exchange have the same effect on the nation's money supply as do purchases of government bonds. Either of these actions is referred to as an "expansionary" monetary policy.

The Bank of Canada often buys or sells foreign exchange, with a view to affecting the international value of the Canadian dollar (that is, our exchange rate). What the balance sheet analysis makes clear is that an exchange-rate policy of this sort and monetary policy are the same thing. Our central bank can try to control the international value of our currency by standing ready to buy or sell large quantities of foreign exchange. For example, to keep the value of the Canadian dollar from rising, the Bank of Canada must make more Canadian dollars available by buying foreign exchange. But if the Bank does that, it has performed an expansionary monetary policy. By controlling the exchange rate, then, monetary policy is dictated by whatever develops in the foreign markets. The central bank gives up its freedom to have an independent monetary policy if it fixes the value of our exchange rate.

In addition to conducting open market operations involving bonds and foreign exchange, the Bank of Canada is also involved in **deposit switching**. On a day-to-day basis, there is a great deal of shuffling around of deposits from one chartered bank to another (as people and firms settle their accounts). This can cause short-run variations in the overall quantity of reserves and so lead to some instability in financial markets. The central bank can iron out these fluctuations. All the Bank of Canada has to do is to write a cheque from the government to the government. That may seem like a pointless thing to do, but by consulting the balance sheets, we see that it does matter for the nation's money supply.

For instance, suppose the Bank of Canada writes a cheque against the Government of Canada's deposits that are held at the central bank. This action draws down that account, as shown by Arrow 1 in the chart on the next page. The cheque is made payable to the Government of Canada, so the cheque is deposited in one of the government's accounts at a chartered bank (raising the balance in that account by the same amount - Arrow 2). The government neither gains nor loses, but it is important to see what happens when the cheque clearing process goes

DEPOSIT SWITCHING OPERATIONS BY THE BANK OF CANADA

BANK OF CANADA		CHARTERED BANKS	
ASSETS	LIABILITIES	ASSETS	LIABILITIES
GOLD	CURRENCY	RESERVES	DEPOSITS
FOR. EXCHANGE	DEPOSITS	CASH	GOV'T ↑2
GOV'T BONDS	GOV'T ↓1	DEPOSITS ↑4	PUBLIC
	BANKS ↑3	AT BANK	
		OF CANADA	
		LOANS	

through. The chartered bank sends the cheque back to The Bank of Canada and, for honouring the cheque, they get compensated by having their deposit account up at the Bank of Canada (that is, their reserves) credited by that same amount (Arrows 3 and 4). Once again we have a situation in which chartered bank reserves and deposits have gone up one-for-one. But in a fractional reserve system, banks do not need or want reserves to go up anything like this much. So once again, by this simple shuffling of government funds, the Bank of Canada has arranged it so that the chartered banks are in a position to start a multiple expansion of loans and deposits.

So the day-to-day operations of monetary policy are deposit switching and open market operations in either the bond or foreign exchange markets. Deposit switches toward chartered banks and open market purchases are "expansionary" monetary policies, while deposit switches toward the central bank and open market sales are "contractionary" monetary policies. But these sorts of transactions are fairly hard for people to understand. What we need, and luckily what we have, is a single indicator that many people look at to see whether the central bank is trying to expand or contract the country's money supply. That indicator is the bank rate.

The Bank Rate

Every Tuesday afternoon, a number of short-term government bonds, called treasury bills, are auctioned off. Whatever rate of interest that auction brings is called the treasury bill yield for that week. The bank rate is that interest rate which the Bank of Canada charges the chartered banks for any loans the chartered banks ever need to take out to replenish their reserves on a short-term basis. Bank rate is always set at precisely one quarter of one percent above the weekly treasury bill auction yield. The chartered banks virtually never have to borrow any reserves, so the bank rate is a loan rate that almost never matters in that direct sense. But it is still watched by a great many firms and individuals as an indicator of what the central bank has been doing.

For instance, if the central bank has been either deposit-switching toward chartered banks or making open market purchases of bonds and foreign exchange, then they have been raising the reserves of the chartered banking system. The only way the chartered banks can make all the additional loans that the new reserves make possible is by lowering the interest rate they charge on those loans. Thus, in the short run, lower interest rates must accompany increases in the money supply. Thus a lower bank rate means that the central bank has been expanding the money supply that week, and a higher bank rate means that the central bank has been contracting the money supply.

When discussing consumer loan and mortgage rates, the news media often refer to the bank rate as "trend-setting." This is somewhat misleading. As just explained, changes in the bank rate follow changes in the market-determined interest rates, since the bank rate change is always the one-quarter of one percent add-on. Nevertheless, it is not worth our while to get too involved in the precise day-to-day timing of which interest rates change just before or after others. The main point is that, in the short run, the general level of all interest rates is reduced by money supply increases, and that the general level of interest rates is pushed up when the money supply is decreased.

Summary

Here is a review of the **key concepts** covered in this chapter. We learned how our system of **fractional reserve banking** evolved. The total quantity of the public's deposits at chartered banks is a major component of the country's **money supply**, and that total is equal to the **money multiplier** times the quantity of bank reserves. In a simplified setting, the money multiplier is the inverse of the chartered banks' reserves-to-deposit ratio. Chartered bank reserves can be increased by **open market purchases of bonds or foreign exchange**, and by **switching government deposits** into chartered banks. Expansionary monetary policies of this sort put downward pressure on interest rates, which we can monitor by observing the weekly exchanges in the **bank rate**.

Throughout this chapter, we have discussed Bank of Canada operations as if the Bank knows what the "appropriate" value of the money supply is. We have focused on how the central bank regulates the reserves available to the private banking system, but we have not explained in any detail why this is necessary. Our job in the next chapter is to determine what the "appropriate" level for the money supply is. With that in mind, we will switch our attention from the mechanics of monetary policy to the purpose of monetary policy.

Chapter 14

Interest Rates
and Exchange Rates

In the last chapter, we discussed the history of money and the basic tools that the Bank of Canada can use to control the reserves of the banking system. This chapter's task is to connect these developments in money and banking to the earlier analysis of aggregate supply and demand. Understanding this connection involves learning how both interest rates and exchange rates are determined. Once these analyses are complete, we will understand how developments in the financial markets affect the rest of the economy, and how changes in output and the price level affect financial markets.

First we review the basic logic behind monetary policy, at least how it operates through domestic financial markets. You may wish to refer back to the left side of Figure 1 in the last chapter (page 155). Suppose the central bank increases the reserves of the banking system. The result is an increase in the money supply. With extra reserves available, chartered banks try to earn more profits by making more loans. To find the additional customers to take these loans, banks must lower interest rates. The lower borrowing rates lead to more spending, particularly the investment component of aggregate demand, and that means a shift to the right in the aggregate demand curve. The result is higher real output, higher prices, or both.

The only stage of this chain of reasoning that we have not discussed fully in earlier chapters is the connection between changes in the money supply and interest rates. To make this connection clear, we develop a supply and demand analysis of the nation's money market.

The Money Market

On the quantity axis of our money market graph (see Figure 1), we measure the quantity of money, denoted by M, and on the price axis, we measure the rate of interest, denoted by r. By the interest rate, we mean the rate of return that can be earned on assets other than money; that is, the yield available on things like bonds and stocks. First we consider the money supply curve, for which we use the label MS. The higher is the interest rate that people can earn on their deposits at banks, the more they forgo the convenience of carrying a lot of currency, and deposit their funds at their bank. The result is that the banks acquire more reserves, and so they can make more loans. The money multiplier then applies to a bigger quantity of reserves. The result is a larger money supply when interest rates are high, as shown in Figure 1 by the positive slope of the money supply curve.

If the central bank purchases treasury bills on the open market, this action increases chartered bank reserves, and moves the entire position of the money supply curve to the right. But before we can demonstrate what will happen to the interest rate, we must derive a money demand curve. To develop the money demand curve, we embark on a fairly extended consideration of the decisions households face in their financial affairs.

Broadly speaking, households have two decisions to make. First, they have to decide the rate at which they want to add to their accumulated wealth. So there is an additions-to-wealth decision and that is just another name for the consumption-savings choice. Whenever we save, our wealth goes up by that amount. The consumption line we drew in the income-expenditure graph is the decision rule which households in our model of the economy use to solve their additions-to-wealth decision.

But households also have to decide the form in which they want to hold the wealth that they already have. So they must make an allocation-of-wealth decision as well. Assume that households have only two ways they can hold wealth. Either they can hold money, in the form of cash or on deposit at their bank, or they can hold what we call "bonds" - a label which stands for all assets that earn higher interest rates than bank deposits, such as government bonds and corporate stocks.

Holding money has both advantages and disadvantages, in comparison with holding bonds. The main advantage of holding money is that it is convenient; you can easily use it to buy things. In contrast, if your wealth is in the form of a bond, you have to incur delays and brokerage charges to sell your bond before making payment for a purchase. But people do not hold all their wealth in the form of money, because doing so has some disadvantages too. The main disadvantage is that holding money involves an opportunity cost - the forgone interest that you could have earned had you held a bond instead.

We can summarize how households react to these good and bad features of money and bonds as follows. The more transactions people make, the more they need to hold their wealth in the form of money to facilitate all those purchases. One convenient measure of the total value of purchases is the nominal value of the Gross Domestic Product. Thus, we summarize by saying that the amount of money people would like to hold varies positively with nominal GDP. It will be convenient to use abbreviations in our graphs, so we use MD to stand for money demand, and the letters Y and P to stand for real GDP and the price level, respectively. Given these definitions, we denote nominal GDP as the product PY, and the summary we just gave can be abbreviated as MD increases when PY increases. Remember, by the amount of money

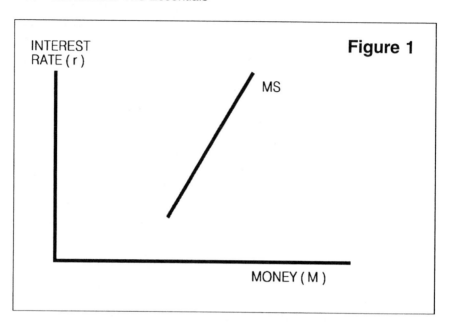

INTEREST
RATE (r)

Figure 1

MS

MONEY (M)

demanded, we mean the amount of people's wealth that they want to hold in the form of money, not bonds.

The second determinant of money people demand is the rate of interest that can be earned on the alternative - bonds. The higher is that interest rate, the less people want to hold their wealth as money. Overall, then, the amount of money demanded depends on two things; it increases when nominal GDP is higher, and it decreases when interest rates are higher. As usual with two-dimensional graphs, we show the dependence of money demand on one influence as the slope of a curve, and we show its dependence on the other influence as a shift in the entire position of that curve. The money demand curve is shown in Figure 2 (on page 172); the negative slope indicates that the lower is the interest rate that can be earned on bonds, the more money people will want to hold. The other determinant of money demand is the level of transactions. We show that influence by shifting the curve; for instance, the money demand curve shifts to the right when there is a higher level of transactions in the country (that is, when PY is higher).

A summary of our abbreviations is provided in the accompanying charts. P stands for the price level, and we care about it because a rising P is inflation. Y stands for the level of real GDP, and one of the reasons we care about it is that an increase in Y means job creation. The product P times Y stands for the level of nominal GDP, and we care about it because changes in that measure cause shifts in the position of the money demand curve. We are now able to understand the determination of interest rates by putting the supply and demand curves for money together in the same graph, as shown in Figure 3 (on page 173).

MD   MONEY DEMAND

Y   REAL GDP

P   PRICE LEVEL

PY   NOMINAL GDP

MD↑ WHEN   PY↑

MD↓ WHEN   r↑

P   PRICE LEVEL
      ↑ P IS INFLATION

Y   REAL GDP
      ↑ Y MEANS MORE JOBS

PY   NOMINAL GDP
      ↑ PY MEANS MD CURVE
      SHIFTS TO THE RIGHT

Equilibrium in the money market is determined by the intersection of supply and demand. But to fully understand why this is so, it is instructive to consider what happens if the market is not at this point. Thus, to see how the money market operates, suppose the interest rate happens to be 10 percent, as in Figure 3. At this high rate of interest, bonds are appealing, so people do not want much of their wealth in the form of money. The amount of money demanded is given by distance AB, and it is much smaller than the available money supply, given by distance

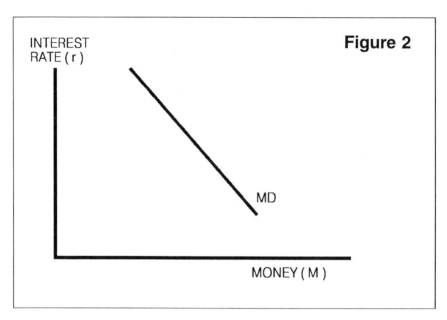

Figure 2

INTEREST RATE (r)

MD

MONEY (M)

AC. So there is more money in existence than people want to hold. Consequently, they use these excess money holdings to start buying bonds. As individuals begin switching over their portfolios toward more bonds, they bid up the price of bonds.

What does a higher bond price mean for the yield that can be earned on bonds? It must be remembered that a bond is simply a piece of paper that says whoever owns the piece of paper will receive whatever payments are stipulated on the contract. For example, consider a bond that stipulates that the owner will receive $10 a year for five years and then she will get $100 when the bond matures (that is, when the contract expires). If you pay precisely $100 to buy this bond, then you will receive a 10 percent annual interest yield. You receive $10 every year on an investment of $100. However, if you have to pay $110 for the bond, your percentage yield is lower. You still receive $10 a year, but that return would be for a larger initial investment of $110. Dividing 10 by 110 yields less than 10 percent. Thus, the more we have to pay for bonds, the lower is the effective interest rate we earn on those bonds.

Now that we understand that effective bond yields vary inversely with bond prices, we can return to Figure 3. At a bond yield of 10 percent, individuals start off with too much money in their portfolios, and so they try to buy bonds with their excess money holdings. This activity bids up the price of bonds, and we now know that this is just another way of saying that it will bid down the effective yield on bonds - what we are measuring as r on the vertical axis in the graph. This process of falling interest rates continues until the money supply and demand imbalance is completely eliminated. The equlibrium is given by point E in Figure 4, and in this example, the interest rate settles at 7 percent.

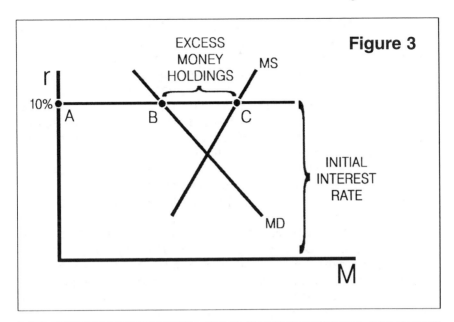

Figure 3

EXCESS MONEY HOLDINGS

MS

MD

A   B   C

10%

r

M

INITIAL INTEREST RATE

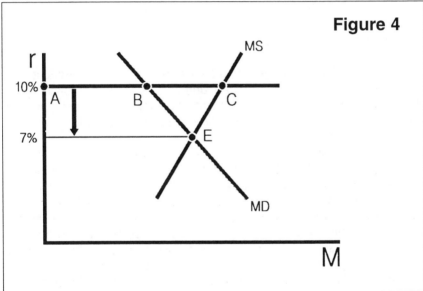

Figure 4

MS

MD

r

10%

7%

A   B   C

E

M

Now we can explain precisely how central bank policy affects interest rates in the short run. If the central bank buys some government bonds and pays by issuing some new currency, the position of the money supply curve shifts to the right, as shown in Figure 5. As a result, the equilibrium point moves down from E to F, and interest rates decline. Contractionary money policy works the same way - just in reverse. By shifting the money supply curve to the left, the contractionary policy makes loans more scarce and so interest rates rise.

In the next two chapters, we will use this analysis of interest rate determination in two ways. First, it is all we need to know to discuss interest rates in a large economy, like the United States, whose financial markets represent a significant part of the entire world's financial system. Since economic developments in Canada depend so much on those in the United States, the analysis has this indirect, though important, relevance for Canada. The second use of this analysis is that it serves as a stepping stone for understanding small economies like Canada, whose financial markets are only a tiny fraction of world markets.

Financial markets are highly integrated throughout the world. No one will hold a Canadian issued bond if the yield is not as high as can be obtained elsewhere. Since competition in world markets forces Canadian interest rates to settle at levels that are roughly equal to foreign yields, Canadian policies can affect interest rates only temporarily. As a result, the lasting effects of Canadian monetary policy come from our ability to change our exchange rate, not our interest rate. But to appreciate how exchange rates are affected, we must understand the temporary interest rate changes, and that is the second reason we must understand the domestic money market analysis that we have just completed. But now we must explain how exchange rates are determined.

Foreign Exchange Rates

By foreign exchange we mean the currencies of other countries - such as US dollars, German marks and Japanese yen. To simplify our discussion, we just refer to US dollars. We now develop a supply and demand analysis which can determine how much a US dollar is worth in terms of Canadian dollars.

On the quantity axis in Figure 6, we measure the quantity of foreign exchange (US dollars) being traded each period. On the price axis, we measure the Canadian price of a US dollar. The exchange rate can be measured in either of two ways. It can be defined either as the number of Canadian dollars it takes to buy one US dollar, which is the way it is measured in Figure 6, or it can be defined the other way around - the number of US dollars it takes to buy one Canadian dollar. One definition is simply the inverse of the other. To say that the Canadian dollar is worth 80 cents US is just the same thing as saying that the US dollar is worth $1.25 Canadian (since 1/0.8 = 1.25).

Supply and demand curves for foreign exchange are shown in Figure 6. Among the suppliers of foreign exchange is anyone who sells goods or financial assets to the rest of the world. Consider Canadian farmers selling wheat on the world market as an example. The contracts are typically in US dollars. When farmers bring their sales proceeds home, these US dollars must be converted into Canadian dollars, since the farmers are committed to pay labour and other costs in Canadian dollars.

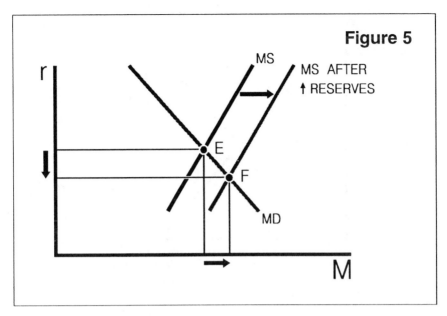

Figure 5

These individuals must then enter the foreign exchange market, as suppliers, to turn their sales proceeds into domestic currency.

Among the demanders of foreign exchange is anyone who buys goods or financial assets from the rest of the world. For example, Canadian importers of Florida oranges need US dollars to pay for the oranges. The importers collect Canadian dollars from Canadian customers, and must convert them into US dollars. The importers must enter the foreign exchange market, as demanders of US dollars, to turn their sales proceeds into the foreign currency that is needed to pay for the imports.

The higher is the Canadian price of the US dollar, the more profitable it is for Canadians to export, because the US dollars that are earned through export sales can be converted into more Canadian dollars. So the higher is the Canadian price of a US dollar, the more exporting we do, and that is why the supply curve of foreign exchange has a positive slope. For Canadian imports, though, a higher Canadian price for the US dollar means imports are more expensive. Thus, we demand fewer imports, and so we demand less foreign exchange to buy these imports when the price of foreign exchange is high. This relationship is shown by the negative slope of the demand curve in Figure 6.

The Canadian-US dollar exchange rate was not allowed to vary during the late 1940s and during the decade of the 1960s, but the authorities have allowed it to vary for the rest of the postwar period. The government's exchange rate policy is conducted by the Bank of Canada. We can now use supply and demand analysis to explain how both fixed and flexible exchange rate regimes operate.

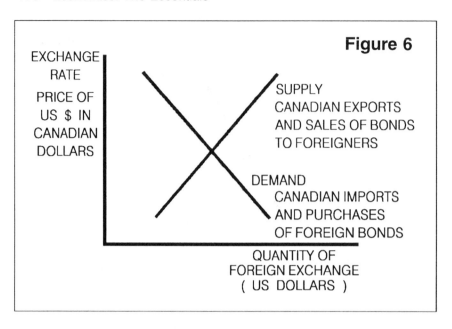

Figure 6

Fixed and Flexible Exchange Rates

With a flexible exchange rate, the Bank of Canada simply takes no action and lets the foreign exchange market operate by free market forces. The exchange rate is determined by the intersection of supply and demand, such as at point E in Figure 7, where in this example it takes $1.25 Canadian to buy one US dollar.

But central bankers sometimes take the view that short-term fluctuations in the exchange rate can be disruptive to international trade decisions. Thus, they sometimes enter the foreign exchange market, and try to keep the price from fluctuating much. The extreme form of this approach is called a fixed exchange rate policy. In the situation shown in Figure 8, the Bank of Canada has decided to keep the Canadian price of US dollars at $1.33, and so keep it from falling to the equilibrium value that is given by point E.

At this high price of foreign exchange, the quantity of US dollars demanded is much smaller than the quantity supplied. Thus, to fix the exchange rate, the Bank of Canada has to act as a residual buyer of the otherwise unwanted foreign exchange that is coming into the country (the amount labelled as excess supply in Figure 8). By adding that additional demand for foreign exchange onto the amount demanded by private traders, the total demand is just balanced by supply at the $1.33 price.

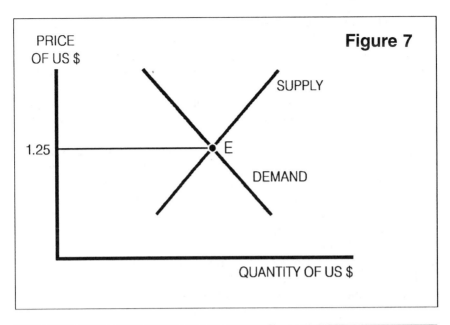

Figure 7

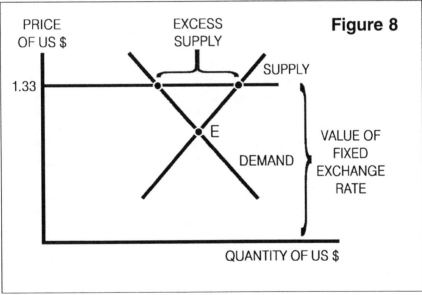

Figure 8

This policy requires that the Bank of Canada buy precisely the amount of US dollars shown as the private excess supply every period. This amount of "official" foreign exchange purchases is called the **balance of payments surplus**. To pay for these foreign exchange purchases, the Bank must issue Canadian dollars. All the Bank does in this case is print up the necessary Canadian dollars.

While fixing the exchange rate is therefore feasible, it is not clear that it is desirable. If the policy is maintained period after period, the Bank will have to keep printing up new domestic currency every period. A large expansion of chartered bank loans and deposits will result. So the real check on fixing the exchange rate in this range is that the resulting expansion in the money supply causes inflation. Central bankers usually try to avoid inflation by abandoning a fixed exchange rate policy in this situation.

What about a fixed exchange rate policy where the central bank tries to maintain an exchange rate on the other side of the free market equilibrium? Suppose the Bank of Canada tries to fix a low Canadian price for the US dollar, such as $1.11 as shown in Figure 9. With a cheap US dollar, Canadians want to do a lot of importing, so we demand a large quantity of US dollars to finance this importing. But at a low Canadian price for the US dollar, the revenues of Canadian exporters are low. As a result, less exporting is done, and there is this small quantity of foreign exchange being supplied to the market. The excess amount demanded is shown in Figure 9, and it is called the **balance of payments deficit**. With a fixed exchange rate policy, the central bank does not allow this excess demand to be eliminated through a bidding up of the price of foreign exchange.

To maintain this low Canadian price for the US dollar, the Bank of Canada must add to the supply of US dollars coming in to the country each period, so that the overall supply curve - that involving both the private traders and the Bank of Canada - shifts over to intersect the demand curve on the fixed exchange rate line. So the Bank must sell foreign exchange every period, and that per-period amount is what is labelled as excess demand in Figure 9. Of course, there is a limit to how long the Bank can intervene in the market, since the Bank will eventually run out of its foreign exchange reserve holdings. The Bank can print Canadian dollars, but it cannot print other currencies.

Market traders get wary in the situation that is depicted in Figure 9, in which foreign exchange is trading at an artificially low price (or equivalently, the domestic currency is overvalued). They know that the central bank cannot maintain this policy indefinitely, since by reading the central bank's published balance sheet each month, they can see how rapidly the Bank's holdings of foreign exchange are running out. They can easily calculate when that supply is likely to be exhausted, and they know that when it is, the Bank can no longer intervene in the market, and so will have to let the domestic currency fall in value (depreciate). Speculators then scramble to ensure that their wealth is not denominated in Canadian dollars, since they see that it is about to lose some of its value. Thus, speculators attack an overvalued currency.

Speculators know that when the Bank of Canada's foreign exchange reserves run out, the US dollar is going to rise in value. This is

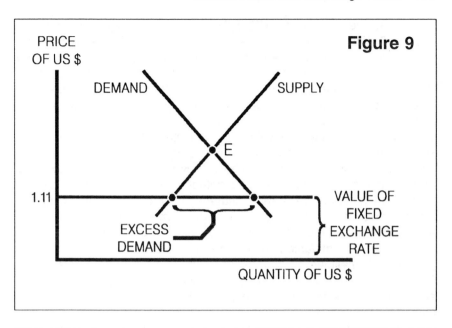

Figure 9

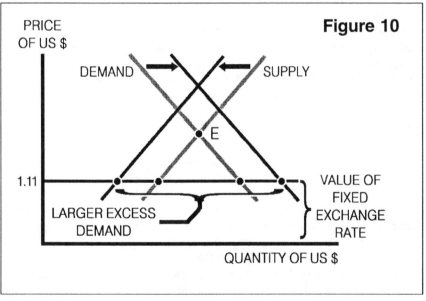

Figure 10

just another way of saying that the Canadian dollar will depreciate. Once they expect this change, they sell off their Canadian-based assets, and use the funds to buy US-based assets. They want to avoid the capital loss that will be involved for those holding Canadian bonds, and they want to benefit from the capital gain that will be enjoyed by holders of American bonds. So all speculators move in this same direction, demanding even more US dollars, so that they can purchase the American bonds.

So the demand for US dollars shifts to the right, as shown in Figure 10. For the same reasons, the supply of US dollars shifts to the left. No one wants to sell the currency that is about to appreciate. So the magnitude of the excess demand for US dollars gets much bigger. If the Bank of Canada was already running short of foreign exchange reserves before this speculation effect set in, it is sure to run out after this has taken place. This analysis exposes a fundamental problem with a fixed exchange rate policy. It involves a large capital gain opportunity for speculators. By simply observing central bank behaviour, speculators know which way the exchange rate will move if it moves, and they know that the moment they act to take advantage of this, they magnify the size of the market imbalance so much that they may force the very change in the exchange rate that they were expecting. Thus, the speculators' own actions can guarantee the outcome from which they can profit.

Two central bank reactions to a speculative attack of this sort are common. Sometimes central banks push domestic interest rates up (temporarily). By making domestically issued bonds more appealing to savers in this way, they try to reverse the shifts in the supply and demand curves for US dollars that are shown in Figure 10. But a more thorough-going solution to the speculation problem is to stop fixing the exchange rate altogether. Thus, as a result of the speculative opportunities that a system of fixed exchange rates creates, many economists favour a flexible exchange rate policy. We discuss other advantages and disadvantages of a flexible exchange rate in Chapter 16. Our task at this stage has been simply to understand how the Bank of Canada fixes the exchange rate, not why it sometimes does so.

Summary

We can now summarize how monetary policy works in both large and small economies. In an economy like the United States, which is big enough that its financial markets are a significant part of the world financial system, monetary policy works through changes in interest rates. A decrease in the money supply raises the interest rate, and so lowers the investment component of aggregate demand.

But a smaller economy like Canada can affect domestic interest rates only temporarily. In full equilibrium, we must accept interest rates as determined in world financial markets. Monetary policy works through changes in the exchange rate. A decrease in the domestic money supply pushes our interest rates up temporarily. Funds flow into the country as savers in the rest of the world acquire the currency they need to buy our high-yield bonds. The result is that the international value of the Canadian dollar rises. This squeezes the profits of Canadian exporters, and it makes imports cheaper for Canadians. Thus, contractionary monetary policy works by reducing the net export component of aggregate demand.

So a reduction in the quantity of money has a contractionary effect in either case. But to understand the process fully, we needed to study both the domestic money market (to determine the interest rate effects even if they are only temporary), and the foreign exchange market (to determine the exchange rate effect).

Here is a review of the **key concepts** covered in this chapter. By combining the **supply and demand for money**, we have realized how **interest rates** are determined. Also, by deriving both the supply and demand curves for **foreign exchange**, we have learned that we have a **flexible exchange rate** if free market forces prevail. The alternative is that the Bank of Canada can **fix the exchange rate**. Finally we have understood that monetary policy works primarily by affecting interest rates in a large economy like the United States, and primarily by affecting the exchange rate in a small economy like Canada.

We are now in a position to discuss both fiscal and monetary policy in a truly integrated fashion. In the next two chapters, we will pull together our analysis of money markets and our analysis of the market for goods and services, so that we can fully examine the effectiveness of stabilization policy.

Chapter 15

Pitfalls in Stabilization Policy

Monetary and fiscal policy are the two tools that can be used to help stabilize the economy. In earlier chapters, we analyzed monetary policy by studying a supply and demand graph depicting the nation's money market, and we analyzed fiscal policy by studying a supply and demand graph depicting the nation's market for goods and services. In this chapter, we pull together these two partial analyses. The result will be a much clearer understanding of what we can reasonably expect from government policy.

Monetary Policy in a Large Economy

We start by reviewing the chain reaction that summarizes how monetary policy works in a country that is large enough to have a lasting effect on its own interest rates (the left side of the flowchart shown on page 155). An increase in the money supply reduces the interest rate; lower borrowing costs raise investment spending; higher total spending raises real GDP (at least temporarily) and the price level. This summary (and flowchart) seems to suggest that cause and effect run in only one direction - from the money market to the goods market. But a careful review of our supply and demand graphs indicates that this analysis is incomplete, since some of the causal mechanisms run in the reverse direction.

Figure 1 summarizes equilibrium in both the money and goods markets. The money-market graph has been used to show the first part of the monetary policy story, while the goods-market graph has been used to show the second half. Recall the major things that can cause a shift in each curve. The level of bank reserves is the key shift influence for the money supply curve. The overall level of transactions (nominal GDP) is the shift influence for the money demand curve. Anything that can affect total expenditure (such as government spending, taxes, investment, and net exports) is a shift influence for the aggregate demand curve for goods. And remember - since investment depends on interest rates, and since net exports depend on the exchange rate, these financial variables are indirect shift influences on the aggregate demand curve. Finally, the position of the short-run aggregate supply curve depends on input prices such as the level of wages.

We can now appreciate that the outcome in each market affects what happens in the other. The interest rate that is determined in the

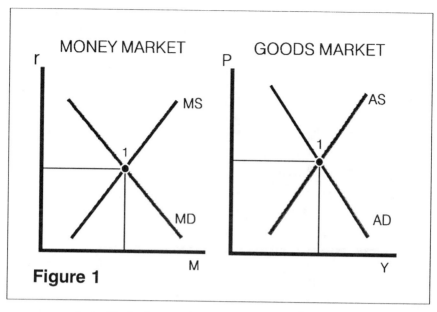

Figure 1

money market affects the position of the aggregate demand curve for goods, and the values for price and output that are determined in the goods market define nominal GDP, and so govern the position of the money demand curve. So the money and goods markets must be considered simultaneously. In this chapter, we accomplish this task for the case of a large economy that can have a lasting effect on its own rate of interest. We provide a similar analysis for a small economy in Chapter 16.

Let us assume that the economy starts out at the points numbered 1 in both markets in Figure 1. Now consider a monetary policy that is intended to expand economic activity. The increase in bank reserves shifts the money supply curve to the right, and the short-run equilibrium in the money market shifts to point 2, as shown in Figure 2. The important result is the lower interest rate. Since investment spending is increased by lower interest rates, the aggregate demand curve shifts to the right, and the outcome in the goods market shifts to point 2 in Figure 3. The important results are a higher level of real economic activity and higher prices.

This cannot be the end of the story. The economy now has higher prices and higher real output - so nominal GDP, which is the price level times real output, must be higher, and nominal GDP is the shift influence for the money demand curve. So there must be some further developments back in the money market. The higher level of transactions means an increased need for the means of payment, and that is shown as a shift to the right of the money demand curve. So the final outcome in the money market is point 3, not point 2 (refer back to Figure 2). By comparing the height of these two points in Figure 2, we see that we were over-estimating the fall in interest rates in our earlier analysis, which just stopped the discussion at point 2. But this secondary move from point 2

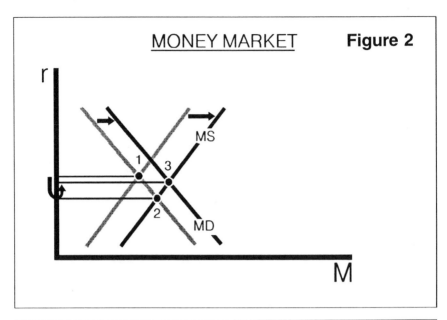

MONEY MARKET   **Figure 2**

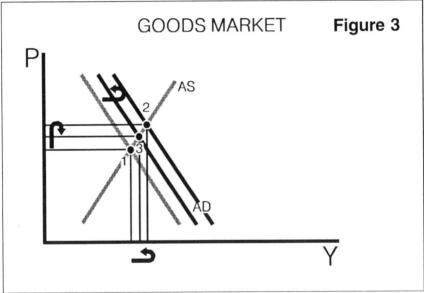

GOODS MARKET   **Figure 3**

to point 3 means that our description of what happens in the goods market has been exaggerated as well. If we previously over-estimated the fall in interest rates, we must have also over-estimated the rise in investment spending. Thus, to be thorough and consistent, we must show the shift in the aggregate demand curve to be less dramatic. Thus, in Figure 3, we see the aggregate demand curve shifted back somewhat, with the final equlibrium being point 3. This feedback between the markets continues in ever decreasing amounts, but (since that further discussion is simply a repeat of what we have now clarified) we take the final equilibrium as point 3 in both markets.

The moral of the story is that while the more simplified explanation of how monetary policy works (which we discussed in earlier chapters) predicts the direction of the effects correctly, it over-estimates the degree to which monetary policy can be used to regulate the economy. And we know from before that even point 3 in Figure 3 exaggerates the effect on real output if it corresponds to a level of production that exceeds the economy's long-run potential. In that case, an inflationary gap has been created, so that rising wages cause the aggregate supply curve to shift up, and the level of output is pulled back down.

A More Complete Analysis of Fiscal Policy

We have just seen that the nation's money and goods markets interact in important ways, and that if we do not appreciate this fact, we will have exaggerated expectations concerning the power of monetary policy to regulate business cycles. We now see that a similar warning applies to fiscal policy.

As before, we consider the economy starting at points numbered 1 in both the money and goods markets (as shown in Figure 1). Suppose the government increases its spending. Government expenditure is a shift influence for the aggregate demand curve in the goods market, so the outcome in that market moves from point 1 to point 2 in Figure 4. The important short-run results are shown along the axes: an increase in real output (so some jobs are created), and an increase in the price level. So there is a short-run trade-off between job creation and inflation.

But this is not the end of the story. With higher prices and real output, nominal GDP must be higher, and this is a shift influence for the money demand curve. So fiscal policy causes indirect effects in the money market - effects that we did not consider adequately in earlier chapters, since we deliberately concentrated on a simpler analysis at that stage. More transactions mean an increased desire to hold money, so the money demand curve shifts to the right. The outcome in the money market moves from point 1 to point 2, as shown in Figure 5. The important result is a higher rate of interest. Remember, with higher interest rates, investment spending is lower, so the aggregate demand curve (in Figure 4) must shift back somewhat to the left.

Initially, the demand for goods shifts out to the right (to position 2) because of the higher government spending component of total demand. But since that policy results in higher interest rates, some investment spending gets choked off, and the aggregate demand curve shifts back to the left (to position 3). For completeness, we should note that since this subsequent shift back in aggregate demand causes a reduction in both price and real output, the money demand curve also shifts back

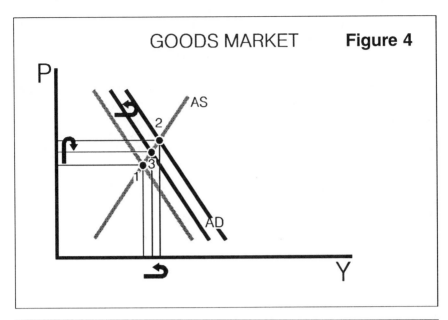

GOODS MARKET   **Figure 4**

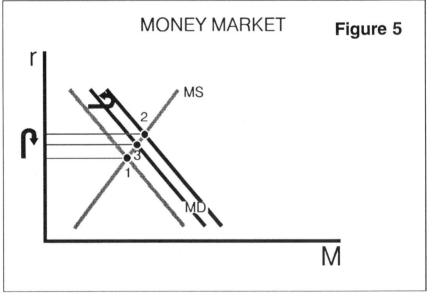

MONEY MARKET   **Figure 5**

somewhat. The final position is at an intermediate point like 3 in both markets (Figures 4 and 5).

Once again, the moral of this more complete story is that even when we ignore the longer-run effects of wage changes, fiscal policy is less powerful than we previously thought. Our introductory analysis that abstracted from the financial market implications of fiscal policy got the direction of effect right, but it exaggerated the job-creation potential of fiscal policy.

$$\begin{array}{c} \uparrow\!\downarrow \\ \uparrow\!\downarrow \\ \text{AGGREGATE} \\ \text{DEMAND} \end{array} = \begin{array}{ccc} \uparrow & \downarrow & \uparrow \\ C + I + G + X - IM \end{array}$$

Economists have called the effect that we have just emphasized - that higher government spending leads to some reduction in private investment spending - the **crowding out effect**. It is often mentioned in the media as one of the major costs of what some regard as excesses in government spending. It is worth appreciating the intuition behind this crowding out effect in more detail.

Aggregate demand is the sum of the several components that are highlighted in the accompanying chart: consumption spending by households, investment spending by firms, government spending, and the net spending by foreigners for our output. When government expenditure is increased, aggregate demand is raised directly. In earlier programs, we placed great emphasis on the fact that the increase in government spending had an indirect effect as well. Higher demand leads to an increase in national income, and consumption spending by households depends positively on how much they earn. Thus, there is an induced increase in consumption that follows the increase in government spending. We called this a multiplier effect since the overall increase in output is the sum of the two component increases. (In the accompanying chart, the overall increase in aggregate demand was estimated to be the sum of both of the upward-pointing arrows.)

But now we know that one of the implications of higher spending is an increased need for money. With money more scarce (relative to demand), interest rates rise and investment spending is reduced. So the downward-pointing arrow must be included in the summary chart to show the crowding out of the investment component of aggregate demand. It is even possible that this reduction in total spending can be as big as the total of the other two. If so, the attempt to add to aggregate demand by increasing government expenditure and creating jobs in the government sector, really just replaces pre-existing demand by destroying jobs in the investment goods sector. When the government borrows more to finance its higher spending, it "uses up" more of the households' savings. With less funds remaining to finance firms' investment spending, firms are "crowded out" of the bond market.

It is important to have some feel for whether this crowding out effect on investment spending by firms is large or small. It turns out that the magnitude of this effect depends on the slope of the money demand curve.

A More Complete Analysis of Money Demand

To keep things simple so far, we have drawn the money demand curve as a straight line. But in actual fact, it is curved as shown in Figure 6, and it is easy to appreciate why. Given any society's institutional arrangements, there is a minimum amount of money that simply must be held to actually carry on any level of spending. Once the rate of interest on bonds has risen to the point that people have cut back on money holdings all the way to that bare minimum, then further increases in the interest rate cannot cause further decreases in the quantity of money demanded. So the demand for money curve becomes vertical at that point (at the upper end of the curve in Figure 6).

Similarly, at the low interest rate end, people become nearly indifferent toward holding bonds. At some point, with very low yields, buying bonds is not worth the brokerage costs. So there is a minimum acceptable rate of interest on bonds. Once the rate of interest has fallen low enough to make people want to hold all their wealth in the form of money, then the further reductions in the rate of interest are not required to increase the demand for money. So that means the demand for money curve flattens out at that minimum acceptable rate of interest.

Now we explore the implications of the resulting curve in the money demand function. This is best done by comparing the 1970s and 1980s with the years of the Great Depression (the 1930s). In the 1970s and 1980s, we had high interest rates, so during those years we know that the money supply and demand curves must have intersected well above the flat region of the money demand curve. When the money supply curve was shifted to the right during these years, interest rates fell noticeably. So monetary policy worked in the 1970s and 1980s because it had a significant effect on interest rates.

But back in the 1930s, we had the lowest rates of interest we have ever observed. The relevant graph for the 1930s shows the supply curve for money intersecting the demand curve down in the flat region, as in Figure 7. In this instance, when the money supply curve is shifted to the

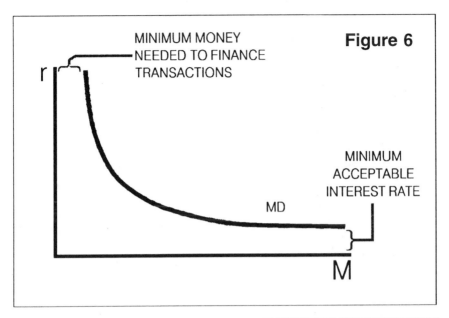

Figure 6

MINIMUM MONEY NEEDED TO FINANCE TRANSACTIONS

r

MINIMUM ACCEPTABLE INTEREST RATE

MD

M

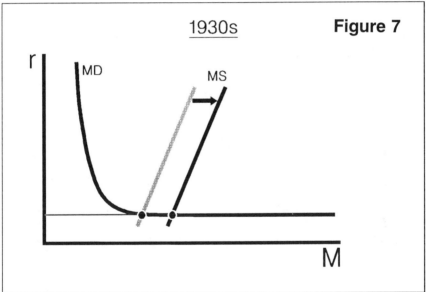

1930s   **Figure 7**

r

MD

MS

M

right, such a policy simply moves the intersection along the flat region, so the interest rate does not fall. As a result, monetary policy has no expansionary effect on the economy. If policy cannot cause interest rates to drop, it cannot stimulate investment spending.

Intuitively, we can understand the Depression as follows. An increase in the money supply gives people more wealth, and all that new wealth is in the form of money. Normally, people want to diversify, and so they want to turn some of that new wealth into bonds. But people do not

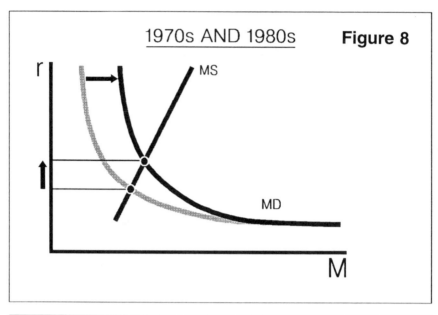

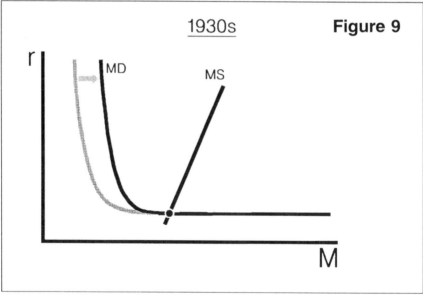

want to invest in the bonds of firms that are about to go bankrupt, and people did think that many firms were in that position in the Great Depression. Thus, people were quite unwilling to buy bonds and to diversify during the 1930s. They preferred keeping all their wealth in the form of money, and they hoarded any new money that was given them. Clearly, when people just hoard the new currency, monetary policy accomplishes very little. So increases in the money supply have been much more important in recent times than they were back in the 1930s.

What about fiscal policy? We can now explain why the crowding out effect is much more important today (and in the 1970s and 1980s) than it was during the Great Depression. As noted already, in recent decades, the money supply and money demand curves have intersected in the higher interest rate region, as shown in Figure 8. Recall that when there is a fiscal expansion, the indirect effect is that people have increased needs for money, so the demand for money curve shifts to the right. When interest rates rise by a significant amount (as we see in Figure 8), there is a noticeable crowding out effect.

Things were different back in the 1930s, as is shown in Figure 9. The same stimulation of demand by higher government spending caused the same shift to the right in the negatively sloped part of the money demand curve. But because the money demand and supply curves were intersecting in the flat region, the shift to the right did not change the interest rate. With borrowing costs not rising, the crowding out effect was minimal. Thus, fiscal policy was at its most powerful back in the Depression of the 1930s.

Pitfalls in Actual Policy Making

As we have just seen, the relative power of fiscal and monetary policy to affect aggregate demand appears to have changed significantly over the decades, and we now understand why. Unfortunately, some of this understanding comes with the benefit of hindsight. Sometimes government officials have applied the lessons learned in one decade to the policy problems of the following decades, without realizing that doing so can be inappropriate. For example, printing a lot of money during the Great Depression would not have stimulated demand to a great extent. Some policy makers reacted to this lesson by simply presuming that printing money would not have much effect in later periods either. This presumption was wrong. But before this fact was widely understood, all Western central banks printed lots of money during the late 1960s and 1970s, and so they created a world-wide inflation.

A similar lag in appreciating the limitations of fiscal policy has also been evident. During much of the 1930s, 1940s, and 1950s, interest rates were low and the crowding out effect was small. As a result, fiscal policy could be counted on to provide a significant stimulus for job creation in the short run. However, policy makers continued to try to use fiscal policy for job creation in later decades, without appreciating that the crowding out effect was much more important then. With interest rates rising appreciably in these later decades, the national debt was driven up to a very great extent, and the policy did not create the number of jobs that had been (unreasonably) expected.

In summary, for quite a long time both fiscal and monetary policy were too expansionary, as the lessons of the 1930s were applied in later

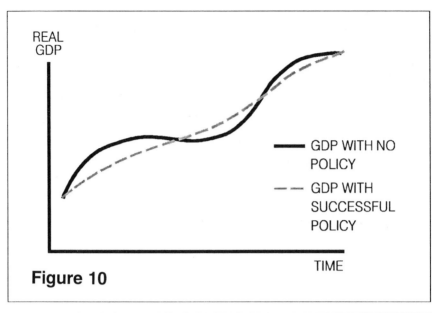

REAL
GDP

GDP WITH NO
POLICY

GDP WITH
SUCCESSFUL
POLICY

TIME

Figure 10

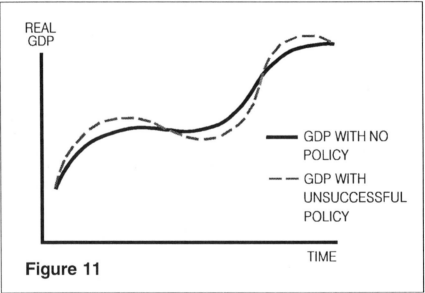

REAL
GDP

GDP WITH NO
POLICY

GDP WITH
UNSUCCESSFUL
POLICY

TIME

Figure 11

decades when the situation had changed. Rising inflation was the result of the inappropriate monetary policy, and rising debt was the result of the inappropriate fiscal policy. Much pain was incurred during the 1980s as monetary policy was thrown in reverse to pull the inflation rate back down. Much pain will be incurred in the 1990s as fiscal policy is reversed to slow down the growth in the national debt.

So stabilization policy has not always worked out as well as government officials had hoped. And even when there is no mismatch between the underlying theory and the characteristics of that decade, there are other problems such as **time lags**.

There are several lags in the process of implementing government policies. One is the recognition lag. It takes government officials quite a while to find out whether the economy needs to be stimulated or pulled back. It takes several months just to estimate what GDP was in the previous quarter. Then there is an implementation lag, because officials cannot raise government spending immediately. They have to decide which category of spending is most needed, and they must allow private firms time to submit tenders (in an attempt to win the government contracts). On average it has taken between 18 months to 2 years after the need for an expansionary fiscal policy was actually recognized, before the higher spending has been implemented. So by the time the stimulative effect on aggregate demand takes hold, the recession could already be over, and the policy might actually worsen inflation in the boom half of the cycle, rather than easing the previous recession.

Implementation lags are shorter with monetary policy. Deposit switching and open market operations can be decided upon quickly. But firms sometimes wait quite a while after a decrease in the interest rate before increasing their investment spending. Firms want to be sure the recession is almost over before expanding their operations. So there are discouragingly long lags involved with both monetary and fiscal policies.

The general problem of time lags is summarized in Figures 10 and 11. In each case, the solid line shows the time path for real GDP. Its wavy nature illustrates the existence of business cycles. If government policy can dampen demand in the boom periods, and fill in the troughs during recessions, it can change the time path of real GDP from being the solid line to being the dashed line in Figure 10. But, unfortunately, the impact of policy is usually so delayed, that the government has sometimes pushed the economy up in the booms and down in the recessions. In this latter case, the government has transformed the real GDP graph from being the solid line to becoming the dashed line in Figure 11. Well-intentioned policy can, and sometimes does, worsen the business cycle.

The Short-Run Trade-Off Between Inflation and Unemployment

Time lags do not represent the only impediment to a successful stabilization policy. Even if government officials could time their interventions perfectly, they must be careful not to overdo things in terms of the size of the government initiative. Too much stimulation in an attempt to create jobs simply drives up the rate of inflation.

To appreciate this trade-off, which is equally relevant for large economies and small open ones like Canada, we must review the economy's self-correction mechanism. Suppose the economy is initially at

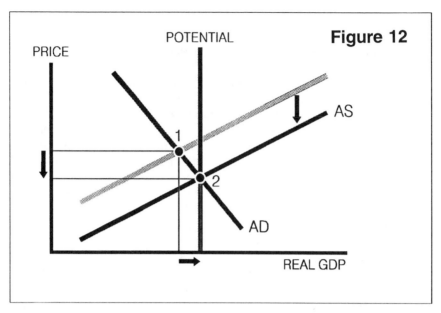

Figure 12

point 1 in Figure 12. A recessionary gap exists since actual real output falls short of potential output. The fact that unemployment is high at this time means that there is downward pressure on wages, and the wage rate is a shift influence for aggregate supply. As wages fall, the aggregate supply curve shifts down, and the economy drifts from point 1 to point 2. This process may take a long time, but it is worth stressing its basic implications: No outcome that is indicated by any point that is off the Potential GDP line can be a long-run equilibrium. The self-correction mechanism forces the economy to move away from any such point. A recession will cure itself if we wait long enough.

Of course, some people are dissatisfied with waiting; they want to use policy to shift aggregate demand to the right, to avoid having to wait for aggregate supply to move automatically. But there is a problem with being impatient, and it is illustrated in Figure 13. The government may stimulate aggregate demand so much that the economy moves from point 1 to point 2 in this graph. Now there is an excess amount of labour demanded, since the economy is trying to maintain a level of production in excess of its long-run potential. In this case, the self-correction mechanism involves rising wages. With just the self-correction mechanism, employment then falls as the aggregate supply curve shifts up and the economy moves from point 2 to point 3 in Figure 14. But an impatient government will stimulate demand whenever employment is falling. Such a government will initiate another expansionary policy, and so push the economy to point 4 in Figure 15.

Consider what happens as this process continues. There is a whole series of wage increases (which shift up aggregate supply), and expansionary policies (which shift up aggregate demand), so that the

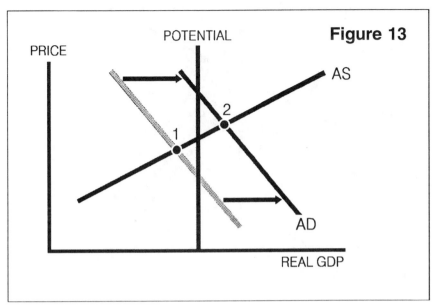

Figure 13

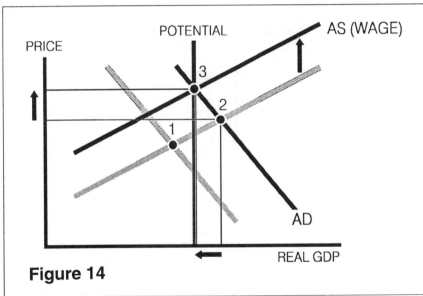

Figure 14

economy traces through a set of observations like points 4, 5 and 6. The overall result is ever-rising prices, and no improvement in employment. This is basically what happened in Canada in the 1960s and 1970s.

By the early 1980s, the government decided to stop inflation by shifting its policy to one of contracting aggregate demand. The result was a shift to point 7 in Figure 16. Broadly speaking, the government maintained this policy into the early 1990s - contracting aggregate demand further every time employment showed much sign of increasing. The result

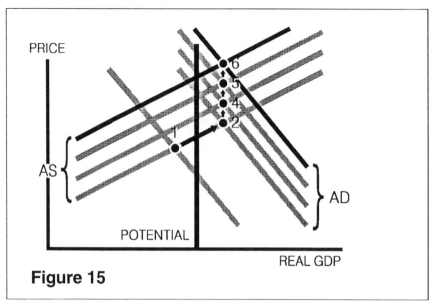

Figure 15

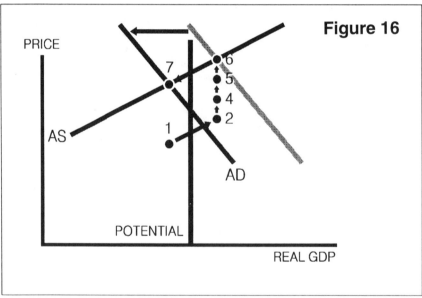

is shown in Figure 17 as a sequence of outcomes such as points 8 and 9. These outcomes are reached by a series of contractionary policies (which shift down aggregate demand), and a set of wage reductions (which shift down aggregate supply). This move from points 7 to 9 took more than a decade, and, at times, it involved significant hardship. That so much time was involved should not be surprising; after all, it took the better part of two decades to travel from point 2 to point 6, and wages tend to be more flexible in the upward direction.

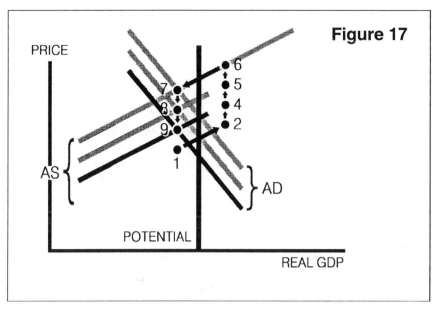

Figure 17

In retrospect, we have incurred a high cost (periods of high unemployment in the 1980s and 1990s, and inflation in the 1960s and 1970s), just to have unemployment temporarily lower in the earlier decades. Many economists have concluded that the costs of going through a several-decade cycle like this are not worth the temporary benefits. Thus, they advocate the following **rules for governing macroeconomic policy**.

According to this view, monetary policy should focus on limiting inflation. Fiscal policy should be used to help stabilize the business cycle, but only in a responsible way. This means balancing the budget over the time involved for each full cycle, so the national debt does not rise over time. And this also means relying primarily on what are called **automatic stabilizers**. Things like our income tax and unemployment insurance systems operate in the same way as would a fiscal policy maker who never makes mistakes. For example, during a business downturn, people earn less, and so they automatically pay less tax and receive more unemployment insurance benefits. These institutional arrangements involve fiscal policy turning expansionary without any recognition or implementation lags, and that is why they are called automatic stabilizers.

The Canadian government appears to have accepted this more passive approach to stabilization policy. The government has published its inflation target - that the annual inflation rate be between 1 and 3 percent for a 5-year period - and it has instructed the Bank of Canada to conduct monetary policy so that this target is achieved. The government has also set a firm target for reducing its budget deficit. With fiscal policy committed to achieving the deficit target, and monetary policy focused on the inflation target, there is no other policy instrument left for addressing high cyclical unemployment. For that problem, then, we must rely on the economy's self-correction mechanism.

Summary

Here is a review of the **key concepts** covered in this chapter. We learned that stabilization policies are **sometimes weak** and **sometimes powerful**. For example, an expansionary monetary policy has no effect on aggregate demand when money is hoarded (as it was when interest rates were low and bonds were risky during the 1930s). Another example is provided by the **crowding out effect**: higher government spending pushes up interest rates and so decreases pre-existing investment spending. This effect is a bigger problem today than it was in the Great Depression.

Stabilization policies operate with **long lags**, and so they can accentuate business cycles instead of lessening their magnitude. Another impediment to implementing stabilization policy is that there can be trade-offs between objectives. Because of the economy's **self-correction mechanism**, there is a **short-run, but not a long-run trade-off between inflation and unemployment**. Ultimately, employment is determined by the economy's potential, not the temporary variations in the position of the short-run aggregate supply and demand curves. Given the long-run capacity constraint, the **benefit of higher inflation** is just a **temporary reduction in unemployment**.

These facts lead many analysts to favour a "hands off" policy in which the central bank has the limited objective of avoiding inflation, and fiscal policy is limited to the provision of **automatic stabilizers** like unemployment insurance and progressive taxes.

Chapter 16

Stabilization Policy for a
Small Open Economy

In the last chapter, we discussed monetary and fiscal policy from the vantage point of a large economy - one whose financial markets are a big enough proportion of the world financial system that the country's policies can affect interest rates. We learned an important message for all economies: we must have modest expectations for stabilization policy because of time lags and the short-run nature of the unemployment-inflation trade-off. In addition, what we learned about stabilization policy in a large economy is needed as a stepping stone for understanding the options for a small open economy, such as Canada's, whose financial markets are very much integrated with world financial markets, especially those in the United States.

Since Canada is such a small part of the North American financial market, it is impossible for us to maintain interest rate levels different from those in the United States for very long periods. Competitive pressure simply forces our effective yields to be in line with those in the United States.

When we look at data for Canadian and US interest rates, there is a slight difference which analysts call the **risk premium**, and this premium does vary through time. For instance, it widened in 1992 when there was uncertainty about the constitutional referendum and whether Quebec would separate. The risk premium has remained substantial during the 1990s, partly because of the continuing uncertainty concerning the future of Quebec, and partly because foreign lenders have become increasingly concerned that Canadian government debt levels are out of control. But in this chapter, we do not analyze variations in this risk premium. Indeed, for convenience, we assume the risk premium to be zero so that we can focus all our attention on short-run stabilization issues, rather than on considerations of longer-run political stability.

For the analysis in this chapter, then, the small open economy constraint is that the Canadian interest rate must equal the US interest rate in full equilibrium. In the graphs, this constraint will involve abbreviations: $r_{can} = r_{us}$. Of course, we do consider temporary gaps between Canadian and American interest rates, and Canadian government policy is one of the things that can cause these gaps to occur for a while. But we always follow through how these interest rate differentials are eventually eliminated by the flow of savings out of the low-interest rate country and into the high-interest rate country.

This flow of funds either changes the exchange rate (if our central bank policy permits that to happen), or this international flow of funds forces our central bank to conduct whatever monetary policy is necessary to keep fixing the exchange rate. In this chapter, we explain how either of these developments eliminates the temporary interest rate differential.

Broadly speaking, there are two tools available for affecting aggregate demand - fiscal and monetary policy; and two possible exchange-rate policies we can follow. So we consider a set of four analyses: fiscal policy undertaken in either a flexible or a fixed exchange rate environment, and monetary policy undertaken in each of those same two exchange rate regimes. Our goal is to determine whether or not there is a lasting effect on aggregate demand in each case.

Fiscal Policy with a Flexible Exchange Rate

We start by assuming that both the economy's money market and goods market are in equilibrium at the points numbered 1 in Figure 1. Recall the major items that can cause a shift in each supply and demand curve. The level of bank reserves is the key shift influence for money supply, and the level of transactions (nominal GDP = PY) is what shifts money demand. Changes in any of the major expenditure components can shift the aggregate demand curve for goods. The exchange rate is particularly important for a country like Canada since it affects our large export and import components of total spending. Finally, the position of the short-run aggregate supply curve depends on input prices, such as wages.

Compared with the Chapter 15 analysis, what is new in Figure 1 is the world interest rate line. Initial point 1 is a full equilibrium since the Canadian rate of interest (which is given by the height of the intersection of the supply and demand for money curves) is equal to the foreign rate of interest (which is given by the height of the US interest rate line). With equal yields, there is no incentive for bond holders to switch their holdings from one country to the other. But keep in mind that our analysis of any government policy will not be complete unless the final equilibrium point in the money market also occurs somewhere on this US interest rate line.

We now consider an increase in government spending, with the economy starting from point 1 in each of the money and goods markets. The first effect is that the demand for goods shifts to the right, and for a short interval, the outcome is point 2 in the goods market in Figure 2. The usual results occur: higher real output and higher prices. These developments mean that nominal GDP (the product of the price level times real output) must have increased, so that people want to hold more money for transaction purposes. We show this effect as a rightward shift of the money demand curve, so that the outcome in the money market moves to point 2 as well.

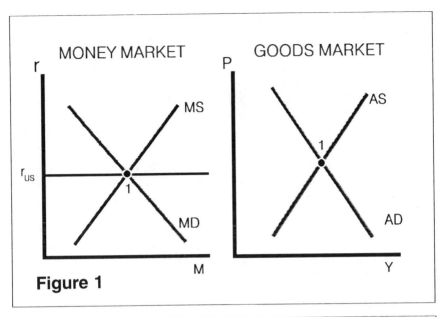

Figure 1

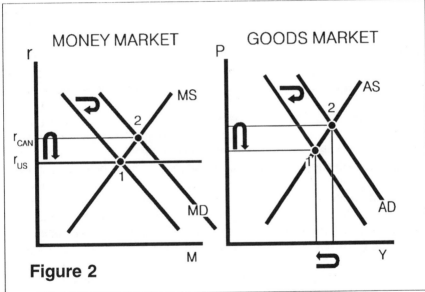

Figure 2

Now comes the new part of the story - the part that is specific to a small open economy. Point 2 in the money market is above the US interest rate line, so the fiscal policy has caused an interest rate differential to open up between Canada and the United States. We must now follow through the implications of this temporary differential.

With our rate of interest higher, savings from the rest of the world flows into Canada, and since we are considering a flexible exchange rate, this means that our currency will be bid up in value. When the Canadian dollar becomes more expensive for foreigners to buy, it makes our exports more expensive. So our exports begin to fall. For the same reason, we find imports cheaper so we do more importing. The combination of lower exports and higher imports pulls the aggregate demand curve in the goods market back to the left. Point 2 slides back down toward point 1.

As the aggregate demand curve drifts back toward its starting position, both the price level and real output decline, so nominal GDP slips back down. In the money market, as nominal GDP declines, people's desire to hold money declines as well, so the money demand curve moves back toward its starting position. But so long as that move back is only partial, the Canadian interest rate remains above the yield available in the United States, so funds continue to flow into the country. Thus, the Canadian dollar continues to appreciate, our exports continue to be crowded out in world markets, and the adjustment process has not been completed. It can end only when the demand curves shift the full distance back, so that point 2 in both markets is all the way back to, and then coincides with, the initial point 1.

So in the end, fiscal policy has no lasting effect on aggregate demand under flexible exchange rates. All an increase in government expenditure does is to push up the value of the Canadian dollar, so that instead of adding to aggregate demand, it simply replaces some pre-existing private demand that was in the form of net export expenditures. Jobs are created in the government sector but they are destroyed in the export and import competing sectors. This process is the open economy version of the **crowding out effect** - it works through the exchange rate, not the interest rate.

Because of the exchange-rate-induced crowding out effect, then, fiscal policy has no lasting effect on aggregate demand when it is undertaken in a flexible exchange rate environment. This has been proved in many episodes in Canadian history, the most famous being one in 1960 when the Diefenbaker government introduced a very large budgetary change in an attempt to lower unemployment. But this fiscal policy did no good, because our central bank governor at the time, James Coyne, was determined to pursue a flexible exchange rate policy. There ensued a crisis: the governor of the Bank was forced to resign, and Canada moved to a fixed exchange rate policy. This crisis was perfectly predictable on the basis of our analysis, and this fact is one of the things that gives economists confidence concerning the applicability of this analysis. We now consider whether an attempt to expand aggregate demand with fiscal policy works any better under a fixed exchange rate environment.

Fiscal Policy with a Fixed Exchange Rate

Once again, we start at point 1 in both markets (as in Figure 1) and once again, the increase in government expenditure shifts the

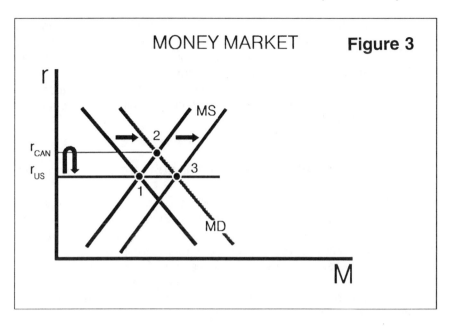

aggregate demand curve to the right and we move to point 2 in the goods market (as in Figure 2). As before, the higher level of nominal GDP means an increased desire to hold money, so the demand for money curve moves to the right (as in both Figures 2 and 3). As we have seen, point 2 is the initial, but not the final, outcome since the Canadian interest rate cannot remain above the American interest rate indefinitely.

Again, funds flow into Canada, but this time the Canadian dollar is not bid up in value because the Bank of Canada simply does not allow that to happen. To keep the exchange rate from changing, the Bank buys the otherwise unwanted US dollars that are coming into the country. (The owners of these funds want to turn them into Canadian dollars, to buy the relatively high yielding Canadian bonds.) But when the Bank of Canada buys incoming foreign exchange, it has to pay with newly issued Canadian money, and this increases the reserves of our chartered banking system. Thus, the money supply curve shifts out to the right, as is shown in Figure 3. As this curve shifts, the Canadian interest rate comes down, and this process must continue so long as any interest rate differential persists.

A full equilibrium is possible only when point 3 is reached and the Canadian interest rate has fallen back to the level of US yields. There is no reason for any shifting back of the demand curve for goods in this case, because there has not been any exchange rate change to alter the competitiveness of our exporters or importers. Thus, the conclusion is that fiscal policy can have a lasting effect on aggregate demand. But we have learned that this conclusion only applies in a fixed exchange rate environment, when that commitment forces the Bank of Canada to alter the money supply in a way that supports the fiscal initiative.

So the first thing you should check when forming an opinion on the government's annual budget policy is whether Canada is currently following a flexible exchange rate policy or not. If so, the budget changes will be largely irrelevant for aggregate demand, and any claims about major job creation simply are not credible. However, if Canada is controlling its exchange rate, the budget changes will have an effect on aggregate demand.

Monetary Policy in a Fixed Exchange Rate Environment

Now we consider the options for monetary policy. As before, the initial equilibrium is point 1 in both markets (in Figure 1), but since we are now considering monetary policy, the first shift occurs in the money market. Let's examine a contractionary monetary policy. This policy involves a decrease in chartered bank reserves, so the initial effect is a leftward shift in the money supply curve. We move from point 1 to point 2 in the money market, as shown in Figure 4. We see that the Canadian interest rate rises above the US interest rate.

We know that this interest rate differential is something that cannot last. As before, with the Canadian rate of interest being higher, foreign funds flow into the country. With a fixed exchange rate, the Bank of Canada is obliged to buy the otherwise unwanted foreign exchange that is entering the country. The issuing of new Canadian money to pay for these purchases simply pushes the money supply curve back out to the right, as shown in Figure 5. The Bank of Canada is forced to keep allowing this to happen so long as the interest rate is higher here than in the United States. In other words, the money supply curve drifts all the way back, so that point 2 recedes back to and becomes point 1.

So this temporary shift in the money market, from point 1 to point 2 and then back again, is all that happens. With competition precluding any lasting interest rate effect, and with the Bank of Canada fixing the exchange rate, there is no mechanism through which the aggregate demand for goods can be affected. All that happens is that the Bank of Canada has performed two open market operations that just cancel each other off. The Bank started off with an open market sale of government bonds. But this just set up a temporary interest rate differential that, given the commitment of the Bank to fix the exchange rate, forced the Bank to make an open market purchase of foreign exchange. So the open market sale of government bonds and the open market purchase of foreign exchange simply offset each other, and there is no net effect on the position of the money supply curve.

In 1970, the Bank of Canada embarked on what was intended to be the most contractionary policy it had tried up to that time during the post-war period. But we had a fixed exchange rate. The attempt to use

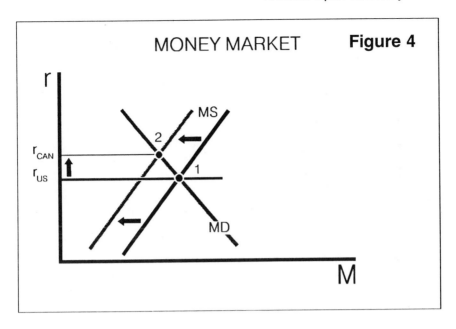

MONEY MARKET **Figure 4**

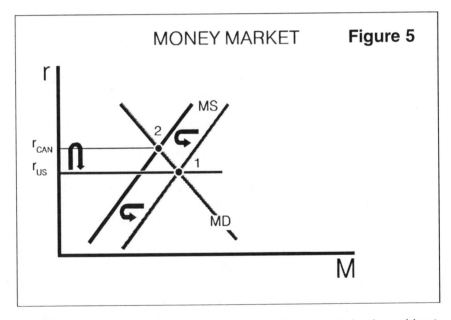

MONEY MARKET **Figure 5**

monetary policy at a time when, as we have just seen, it simply could not work caused an exchange rate crisis. Within a very few months, Canada was forced to give up its fixed exchange rate policy. We now consider the same monetary policy undertaken in a flexible exchange rate environment.

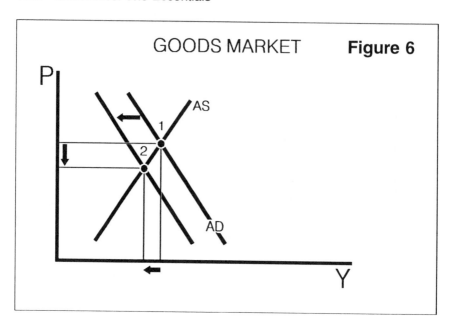

GOODS MARKET   **Figure 6**

Monetary Policy in a Flexible Exchange Rate Environment

As before, the initial equilibrium is point 1 in both markets (see Figure 1) and then the reduction in bank reserves moves the money supply curve to the left. The equilibrium moves from point 1 to point 2 (as in Figure 4) and the now-familiar temporary interest rate differential emerges. With the Canadian interest rate temporarily higher, funds flow into Canada. With the Bank of Canada not bothering to intervene in the foreign exchange market in a flexible exchange rate environment, the Canadian dollar is bid up in value. As this happens, foreigners find it more expensive to buy Canadian goods and so our exports fall. For the same reason, Canadian imports rise. The fall in net exports then causes the aggregate demand curve for goods to shift to the left, and the results are shown along the axes in Figure 6 - lower prices and lower real output.

Both of these developments mean that nominal GDP is lower, and so the demand for money is less. As usual, we show this effect by shifting the money demand curve to the left, and this sequence of events must continue until the shifting demand for money curve moves the observation point from 2 to 3 in Figure 7, and the Canadian interest rate is pulled back down to the point that the interest rate differential is eliminated. So a contractionary monetary policy works under flexible exchange rates, but it works because the exchange rate change affects net exports, not because interest rate changes affect investment.

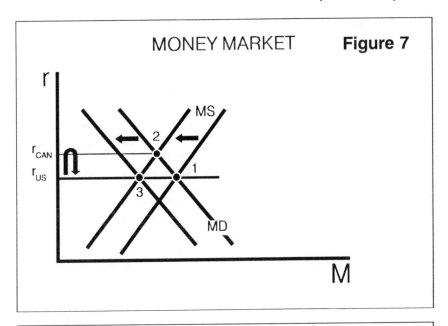

MONEY MARKET   **Figure 7**

LASTING EFFECTS ON AGGREGATE DEMAND

	FISCAL POLICY	MONETARY POLICY
FIXED EXCHANGE RATE	YES	NO
FLEXIBLE EXCHANGE RATE	NO	YES

The accompanying chart summarizes this analysis of domestic policy options for a small open economy. There is an exchange rate environment in which each of fiscal and monetary policy can have a lasting effect on aggregate demand. But each instrument must be used at the appropriate time, if it is to have any chance of meeting its objective of stabilizing the economy. Also, it is important to recall that having a lasting effect on the position of the aggregate demand curve is not enough for policy to have a significant job-creating effect. It is necessary but not sufficient. The impact on jobs will still be limited if the short-run aggregate supply curve is fairly steep and if wage increases cause that supply curve to start shifting up.

Space limitations preclude our using this model of a small economy to analyze the effects on Canada of various foreign developments. But you are now fully equipped to do this, and so can use the formal model on your own to consider such things as increases in foreign interest rates or increases in foreign tariffs. To allow you to check your reasoning, the following intuition is provided. Foreign tariffs are like a decrease in domestic government spending; they both decrease the aggregate demand for Canadian products. We have learned that this effect will only last in a fixed exchange rate environment. Thus, a flexible exchange rate policy is recommended for better insulating the Canadian economy from foreign trade restrictions.

Foreign interest rate increases can be analyzed by shifting up the US interest rate line in the money market graph. This shift results in an initial flow of funds out of Canada. In a fixed exchange rate environment, there is no exchange rate change that can possibly counter the depressing effect of higher interest rates on firms' investment spending, so aggregate demand falls. But in a flexible exchange rate environment, the flow of funds out of the country causes a depreciation of the Canadian dollar, which stimulates net export demand. Thus, there is a mechanism to offset the depressing effect of higher interest rates on aggregate demand, so once again, a flexible exchange rate policy provides better insulation from disruptive foreign events.

The Supply-Side Effect of Exchange Rates

Thus far in our analysis of a small open economy, we have simplified by overlooking one important fact: some of Canada's imports are intermediate products. They are not bought to consume directly; instead, they are things that go into production operations within Canada. If the value of the Canadian dollar falls, these inputs to business operations in Canada become more expensive. These higher costs cause our aggregate supply curve to shift up whenever the value of the Canadian dollar falls. Thus, the exchange rate is a shift influence for both the aggregate supply and demand curves.

Some people think our government should deliberately devalue the Canadian dollar, in an attempt to stimulate jobs in our export industries. Let us consider this suggestion by referring to Figure 8. Those making the devaluation suggestion hope to shift the aggregate demand curve to the right. The devaluation makes foreigners better able to afford our goods, so those in favour of devaluation think of it as moving the equilibrium from point 1 to point 2 in Figure 8. Jobs will be created because real GDP is predicted to increase. Of course, the graph also

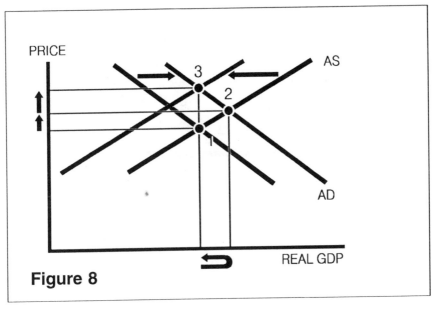

Figure 8

points out the usual short-run trade-off: some inflation.

Those who are skeptical of devaluation argue that this use of the graph exaggerates the intended effect (more jobs), and it underestimates the unintended effect (higher prices), because the graphical analysis has so far ignored the supply-side effect of devaluation. Since devaluation raises business costs directly, it shifts the aggregate supply curve too. The more complete analysis then predicts a move from point 1 to point 3, not from point 1 to point 2. We can immediately see that this more complete analysis is very much less supportive of devaluation. Indeed, as in the example pictured in Figure 8, the supply-side effect of the exchange rate can be large enough to so magnify the unintended effect (more inflation), that the intended effect of higher jobs can be totally eliminated.

Even if the supply-side effect of a depreciating currency is not as big as it is illustrated in Figure 8, there is a problem in terms of retaliation by other countries. Creating jobs in this manner is generally viewed as unfair by our trading partners. Over the years, countries have tried to set up international agreements so that disruptive trade wars and competitive devaluations do not take place too often.

The History of the International Monetary System

We have had three different international monetary systems. The first was called the Gold Standard and it was the method of financing world trade from the earliest days until the Great Depression of the 1930s. Then we shifted to a system that has been called the US dollar standard, and it was in place from World War II until about 1970. Since then, the

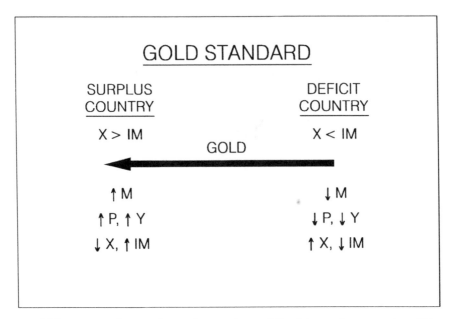

world has moved more toward a system of flexible exchange rates. We now provide a very brief sketch of how the earlier systems worked.

For centuries, precious metal coins served as money within individual countries, so it should be no surprise that gold became the international medium of exchange. The accompanying chart shows how the gold standard worked. Consider a country with a surplus position in its trade with the rest of the world. Such a country was exporting more than it was importing. Also consider a deficit country, with imports exceeding exports. The gold standard eliminated imbalances in trade such as these automatically.

Since the deficit country was spending more than it was earning, it had to ship some of its gold over to the surplus country as payment. Shipments of gold entering the surplus country meant an increased money supply in that country. This raised aggregate demand and so pushed up prices. Higher prices made the country less competitive and so its exports fell. Similarly, in the deficit country, with some of its money supply being shipped over to the other country, it was as if the deficit country had performed a contractionary monetary policy. That caused a recession and decreased prices. Lower prices made this country more competitive and that stimulated its exports.

This automatic adjustment process meant that there were inflations in surplus countries and recessions in deficit countries. Of course, sometimes in world history there were worldwide inflations. These occurred when there were major gold discoveries. At such times, even though deficit countries shipped gold over to the surplus countries, they still had more gold than before, so money supplies in all countries rose, and so did prices.

After World War II, most traders found it convenient to use the currency of the dominant country as the international medium of exchange, so US dollars replaced gold. The system worked exactly the same as before, except that deficit countries shipped US dollars over to the surplus countries instead of gold. (Just envision the word "gold" being replaced by "US dollars" in the accompanying chart. This change in labelling has no effect on the underlying causal mechanisms.) The whole sequence of the adjustment in trade balances was the same - an enforced expansionary monetary policy in surplus countries and an enforced monetary contraction in deficit countries.

Worldwide inflation could still occur in the US dollar system. It occurred whenever we had the equivalent of major discoveries of US dollars, and this happened most dramatically in the late 1960s. President Lyndon Johnson was waging both a war against poverty on the home front and the Vietnam war on the international front. He was paying for this by printing up large quantities of US dollars. By shipping many US dollars to the other countries of the world (who maintained fixed exchange rates with the US dollar), the United States effectively forced all those countries to conduct very expansionary monetary policies, just as the United States was doing. The result was worldwide inflation.

The rest of the countries in the western world did not want this inflation. Since they could not affect US monetary policy, the only remedy they had was to break out of the US dollar system, and so they simply refused to continue trading their currencies for the US dollar at a fixed rate of exchange. Thus, the world moved to the flexible exchange rate system that we have today.

Flexible exchange rates involve a self-correction mechanism as well. When a surplus country is selling more than it is buying from the rest of the world, the price of its currency is bid up. This change makes it less competitive and reduces its trade surplus. Similarly, there is a low demand for the deficit country's currency and so it is bid down, and its firms become more competitive. Thus, eventually trade imbalances are automatically corrected.

Summary

Here is a review of the **key concepts** covered in this chapter. A small open economy must accept that in full equilibrium, its **rate of interest is determined in the rest of the world**. In Canada's case, ignoring variations in risk, the Canadian interest rate always gravitates to the American rate of interest. There are two implications of this fact. First, **monetary policy works by changing the exchange rate**, not the interest rate, so monetary policy cannot be performed once the decision to fix the exchange rate has been taken. Second, since the **crowding out effect** involved with fiscal policy works through the exchange rate, not the interest rate, it can only be **avoided if the exchange rate is fixed.**

Fiscal policy has a lasting effect on aggregate demand only under fixed exchange rates, and an independent monetary policy is possible only under flexible exchange rates.

There is an **automatic correction mechanism** for **eliminating trade imbalances** with all international monetary systems. Under fixed rate systems, like the gold standard and the US dollar system, countries with trade deficits have recessions and surplus countries have inflations. With flexible exchange rates, these effects are tempered: deficit countries have depreciating currencies while surplus countries have appreciating ones.

As we have seen, stabilization policy involves many problems, such as lags, crowding out effects, and trade-offs. As a result, many economists have turned their attention to the longer term issue of how a country can achieve a high rate of growth in its level of potential output. It is to this long-term consideration that we turn in our final chapter.

Chapter 17

Growth and Development

Most people are aware of the desperate poverty that is endured by a large part of the world's population. These countries have not shared in the process of economic growth that the developed economies have enjoyed in the last 300 years. This final chapter considers how growth in the standard of living occurs, and what government policy can do to affect this process.

Thus far, our focus in macroeconomics has been on stabilization policy. The difference between growth policy and stabilization policy can best be appreciated by looking back at the first graph we considered in macroeconomics - Figure 1 in Chapter 10 (on page 118). We saw there that Potential GDP has a very smooth time path, but that the level of Actual GDP is buffeted about, so that we endure a series of business cycles. We have learned that this cyclical time path for Actual GDP is due to major shifts in the aggregate demand and supply curves that occur in the short run.

The whole point of stabilization policy is to try to fill in the troughs and shave off the peaks - to make the Actual GDP time path more closely approximate that for Potential GDP. From a growth point of view, we are interested in the longer-run outcomes of the economy, and in that respect, we tend to ignore the short-run dips and swings of the business cycle. Thus, in this final chapter, we focus only on the time path for Potential GDP. The purpose of growth policy is to pivot the time path up to make the Potential GDP time path steeper, so that people can enjoy a bigger quantity of goods and services in the future.

But growth in real GDP is only necessary for higher living standards; it is not sufficient. After all, if the number of people grows faster than the total quantity of goods, the amount available for each individual actually shrinks. So economists focus on a concept called labour productivity.

Labour Productivity

Labour productivity is defined as the total quantity of goods and services that the economy produces divided by the number of workers that produce that total. This ratio is an important determinant of our standard of living, since it defines the level of real wages that workers can earn. Workers cannot generally have a rising standard of material welfare

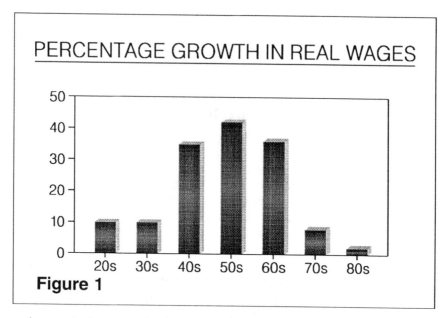

PERCENTAGE GROWTH IN REAL WAGES

Figure 1

unless output grows at a faster rate than does the labour force, so that **output per worker** is rising.

Over the first 125 years following Confederation, Canada had an average rate of growth in labour productivity of just less than 2 percentage points per year. This growth rate has raised our standard of living by a factor of 8 times! Small changes in either the growth rate or the number of years during which growth takes place can make an even more dramatic difference. For instance, a 3 percentage point growth rate in labour productivity operating for 200 years allows the standard of living to go up a staggering 300 times. So a little bit of stimulus to raise the growth in labour productivity even a fraction of a percentage point is important for the growth of real wages.

In recent years, there has been a marked slowdown in the growth in labour productivity and therefore in real wage growth. Figure 1 shows the evidence. For example, income growth fell from 36% in the 1960s, to 8% in the 1970s, to just 2% during the 1980s. There is simply no way we can afford better health care, more thorough-going environmental clean-ups, or other valuable things, if we do not have higher income growth. Many economists regard the productivity growth slowdown during the last 25 years to be one of the most important economic events of this century.

Policies That Can Lead to Higher Economic Growth

Now we know how growth is measured, and that growth can bring large benefits. But many questions remain - such as: Why do some countries grow more rapidly than others? What are the costs associated with higher growth? Can growth proceed when the world has limited amounts of key resources? We now turn to the first of these issues: What policies lead to higher economic growth?

The items that are conducive to higher economic growth are:

1. a high saving rate,
2. education,
3. research,
4. social acceptance of the profit motive,
5. flexibility in the workplace.

First, let us focus on a **high savings rate**. It has been stressed several times in earlier chapters that the only way workers can have more capital equipment to work with is if society chooses not to consume all of the output that it produces in any one year.

The role of savings differs when we shift our focus from short-run to long-run issues. In the short run, our primary focus is on stabilization policy, since many people believe that the economy's self-correction mechanism needs time to fully operate. In that short-run time frame, we focused on the circular flow of income and spending, as shown in Figure 1 of Chapter 11 (on page 129). We noted that an increase in savings meant less spending by households. Since interest rates and prices do not fall sufficiently in the short run, there is not an off-setting increase in firms' investment spending. The result is that aggregate demand falls and a recession occurs. That analysis is relevant for the short run.

But in the longer run, there is no insufficiency of demand problem. After all, if savings become larger than investment, banks can raise their profits by lowering interest rates - both on deposits which will discourage savings, and on loans to encourage investment. Thus, given enough time, the self-correction mechanism of interest rate adjustments in a large economy (or an analogous process involving exchange rate adjustments in a small open economy), solves any aggregate demand problem. In the longer run then, when the focus is on economic growth and not cycles, any temporary dislocation caused by a higher saving rate can be de-emphasized. Instead, we concentrate on the lasting implication of higher savings - a higher ratio of investment to GDP, which means more productive equipment for each labourer to work with, and so higher incomes.

The circular flow chart also points up the opportunity cost of higher growth. To obtain the increased quantity of investment goods, we must save - that is forgo some current consumption. There is a trade-off: to have higher standards of living in the future, we must accept lower standards of living now. This same trade-off is involved when we try to promote growth through **investment in education and research** (items 2 and 3 listed above), instead of through investment in physical equipment. Investment in higher skills can raise productivity, but these investments also mean less current consumption.

Another important factor for growth is that the **profit motive**, and **entrepreneurial activity** in general, not be regarded as anti-social behaviour. In some societies, people who search out profit opportunities are not well accepted, and these countries have low growth rates.

Finally, an important consideration is that labour relations be such that there is **flexibility in the workplace**. When new production methods are invented, management and labour need to embrace the new technology in a constructive fashion, rather than resist it. The countries that have co-operative labour relations, as opposed to confrontational ones, seem to have higher growth performance.

Let us assess how well some of these prerequisites for growth are satisfied in other countries. We consider both the developing countries and the former centrally planned economies. It is easy to see why the developing countries are having a great deal of trouble. They possess very little capital equipment; and they have low levels of education and research activity. Further, some of these societies do not support making profits, so they fall short on essentially all the main criteria for rapid growth. Low growth rates in these countries represent a staggering problem because many of them have high population growth rates. They need a high growth rate in GDP, more than other countries do, just to keep living standards from falling even lower.

One very constructive thing we can do to help solve this problem is to drop the significant **barriers to trade** that the industrialized world has erected against the products from the developing countries. Many of these countries get all their foreign exchange from selling a few primary commodities. While there have been large reductions in tariffs among Western countries, this process has not happened with agricultural commodities. Indeed, restrictions that favour the developed countries at the expense of the less developed ones have become much more prevalent, with the result that income growth in the developing countries has been severely limited.

What about the former centrally planned economies? These countries have little experience with the market mechanism and the profit motive. Decentralized trades between individuals and firms require that there be a system of well established **property rights** and a legal system to enforce those property rights. After all, you will not pay me for something if you are not confident that it is actually mine to sell. But when countries move abruptly from a centrally planned system in which everything is state owned, there simply are not any private property rights. Institutions cannot be created quickly.

Indeed, Western countries took centuries to develop the institutions that support free enterprise. The reliance on markets occurred very gradually, starting in feudal times with just a very small proportion of the economy involving itinerant traders. So the formerly planned countries are trying to develop a market system much more quickly than we ever did, and these countries are trying to assign property rights in some way which can be regarded as fair. We never did that; property rights were distributed through political decision and historical accident centuries ago as the market system gradually evolved. On both fronts, then, the time frame and the emphasis on equity, the Eastern bloc countries are trying to do something that has never been done before.

Considering the plight of other countries provides valuable perspective, but to really examine growth policy within Canada, we must be able to evaluate what has come to be called Trickle-Down Economics.

Trickle-Down Economics

The basic approach to growth policy within Western countries has been to focus on what we have listed as the first item that is important for growth - saving. The general advice is that we should use our tax system to discourage consumption and to stimulate saving. There are various ways of doing this. One option is tax-free registered retirement savings plans. A second is an increased reliance on sales taxes, such as the GST, instead of general income taxes. Sales taxes must be paid only when individuals spend; sales taxes can be avoided by saving.

A number of people oppose these kinds of tax measures on equity grounds; they feel that only the rich have enough income to do much saving and to benefit from these tax breaks. Those who favour these programs argue that this presumption is incorrect. They argue that most of the benefits go to those with lower incomes. But since the process by which these benefits "trickle down" the income scale is indirect, they argue, many people do not understand it, and so reject these tax initiatives inappropriately. We now examine whether this trickle-down view is correct, first in a large economy, and then in a small open economy setting.

Figure 2 is a graph of the market for capital. Recall that in competitive markets, the demand curve for any factor of production like capital is the marginal product curve for that factor. As noted earlier, the supply of capital ultimately comes from the savings done by households. Since people do more saving when the rate of interest is higher, the supply curve has its usual positive slope. So in a free market, both the amount of capital and the return on capital get determined by the intersection of supply and demand (at point E in Figure 2).

The graph also determines the overall level of output and income. Think of the economy having just two factors of production - capital equipment and labour. If we add up all the area under the marginal product of capital curve we get the total product, that is - the country's GDP. Thus, GDP is the entire shaded area in Figure 2. Since each unit

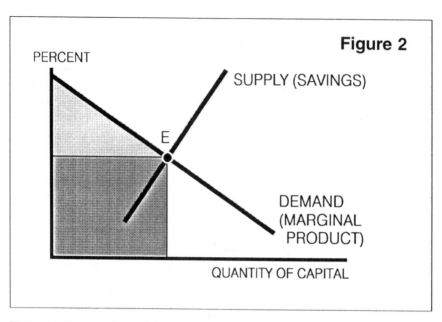

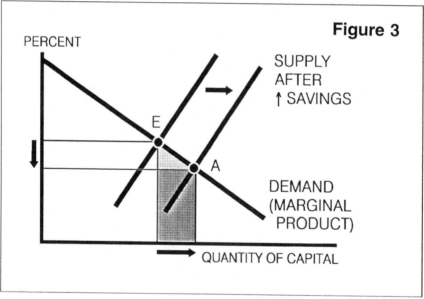

of capital is receiving a rate of return equal to the height of point E, capital's share of national income is the dark grey rectangle. Labour gets the residual - the lighter grey triangle. So the graph shows both the size and the distribution of national income.

Now consider a tax measure designed to stimulate saving. This initiative shifts the supply of capital curve out to the right, as shown in Figure 3. Equilibrium moves from point E to point A. Total production increases by the additional area under the marginal product curve - that is, by an amount equal to the shaded trapezoid in Figure 3. So the growth policy works. By stimulating savings, we get more output. How is this additional material benefit distributed? The owners of capital get the dark grey rectangle, and labour gets the lighter grey triangle. So even if the capitalists do all the saving and so are the apparent beneficiaries of the tax break for saving, and even if labour can afford to do no saving, labour does get something.

Furthermore, labour's benefit is not just the small light grey triangle in Figure 3. With capital being more plentiful, its rate of return has been bid down to a lower level. Since that lower rate of return is being paid on all units of capital, there has been a transfer of the rectangle formed by the horizontal lines running through points E and A to labour. By comparing Figures 2 and 3, we can see that this area used to be earnings of capital, but with the policy that stimulated savings, it is now part of labour's income. So, in the end, capitalists as a group may not win as a result of this stimulation of savings. Capitalists gain the dark grey rectangle in Figure 3, but they lose the unshaded rectangle that we have just discussed. The only group that is a clear winner is labour - they gain both the light grey shaded triangle and the unshaded rectangle. That is, labour gains the entire trapezoid formed by the horizontal lines going through points E and A. Recall that labour is the group that was assumed to be too poor to benefit directly from any tax break that stimulated savings. The reason labour benefits indirectly is that workers become more productive when they have more capital to work with.

We conclude that, in a large economy which can set its own interest rate, tax breaks that stimulate saving do not just benefit high-income capitalists; the benefits trickle down to low-income wage earners. While the term "trickle down" has acquired a kind of pejorative interpretation, we have just seen that this standard analysis supports the trickle-down process. The remaining question is: Can this standard analysis be legitimately applied to a small open economy like Canada?

In earlier chapters, we stressed that domestic policy cannot have a lasting effect on the domestic rate of interest in a small open economy setting. Thus, while the standard analysis just presented (which assumes the contrary) can be used to support the trickle-down approach in a large economy like the United States, it does not apply in Canada. We now modify the trickle-down analysis so that it is applicable to the Canadian case.

In Figure 4, the marginal product of capital curve appears as before; it is the demand for using capital equipment in Canada. Again, as before, the supply of domestic savings is part of the analysis. But Figure 4 contains one additional relationship - a line which shows the supply of savings on behalf of lenders in the rest of the world. These individuals are ready to buy capital equipment that is employed in Canada, should the return be adequate. To satisfy foreign lenders, the return must equal the risk-adjusted rate of return that capital can earn when it is employed in the

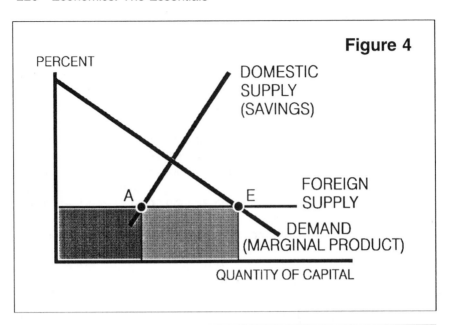

Figure 4

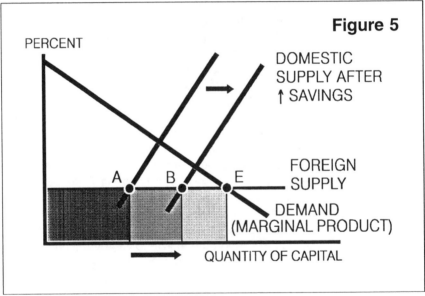

Figure 5

rest of the world. We assume that this alternative yield is given by the height of the foreign supply curve in Figure 4.

Equilibrium occurs at point E, and GDP is the entire trapezoid under the marginal product curve up to point E. The rate of return for each unit of capital is given by the height of the foreign supply curve, so capitalists earn the shaded rectangles under that line, while labour receives the white triangle. The domestic supply of savings curve indicates the proportion of capital's income that goes to Canadian-owned capital (the dark grey rectangle) as well as the proportion that is the income of foreign capitalists (the lighter grey rectangle).

We now consider, as before, the granting of a tax break for domestic capitalists if they save more. This policy shifts the domestic supply curve out to the right, as shown in Figure 5. In this case, equilibrium remains at E. There is no growth in the amount of goods produced. But there is growth in the amount of income that Canadian residents can achieve from that output, because the income of Canadian capitalists increases by the amount of the shaded rectangle between point A and B in Figure 5 (and the income of foreign capitalists decreases by this same amount).

Since labour is still working with the same overall quantity of capital, labour's income - the white triangle - is unaffected. So the entire increase in national income goes to capitalists. This is a very different conclusion than the one we reached when this same tax policy was applied to an economy that is not constrained by international competition. So the critics of trickle-down economics are justified in a small open economy like Canada. The benefits of tax breaks that stimulate savings do not trickle down to labour in any direct fashion. Of course, many workers are indirectly partial capitalists. Their pension funds and insurance companies own capital. Nevertheless, this analysis suggests that investing in better education and training, which directly raises labour's skills and therefore labour's marginal product, may be a more direct way of helping labour while stimulating growth.

Is Continued Economic Growth Sustainable?

The analysis of tax breaks to stimulate higher output through increased saving assumes that continued growth is possible. Many individuals focus on the world's rapidly growing population and the world's limited supply of non-renewable resources, and they doubt this presumption.

To many concerned individuals, it seems a hopeless rat race - all countries trying to keep output growing just to keep pace with their growing populations. If the current rate of world population growth continued for just 650 years, there would be one person on every square foot of the earth's surface (including all the oceans). Since such population density is impossible, however, population growth will be slowed - either painfully through dwindling incomes and death for millions of people, or less painfully through rising income levels and improved education, both of which lead to dramatic declines in birth rates. Perhaps paradoxically, then, one of the most important things that we can do to make economic growth sustainable in the longer term, is to help the developing countries grow more now. Only with higher incomes can the citizens in these countries achieve higher levels of education and lower birth rates.

Population growth is not the only reason to be concerned that the growth process may not be sustainable. What about non-renewable resources? Many people worry that if we run out of some of the key inputs to the production process, the whole economic engine will grind to a halt, so that income standards will plummet. Economists are less worried about the non-renewable resource issue than many others, because they have identified a self-correction mechanism that operates in a free market for resources.

Suppose you are the owner of a non-renewable resource, trying to make the following decision: should you sell off some of your scarce resource now and invest the proceeds? or should you leave it in the ground and sell it at a future date, say next period? If today's price of the resource is P_1, you would get a sum of money equal to P_1 should you sell it today. You could then invest this sum for a period and earn rate of interest r. So if you mined the resource, sold it now, and invested the proceeds, the amount of money you would have by next period would be the selling price P_1 scaled up by the factor $(1+r)$.

Your second option is to leave the resource in the ground for now and then sell it in the second period for price P_2. You would choose this second option if the return, P_2, is bigger than the return of the first option, $P_1(1+r)$. An equilibrium does not exist unless resource owners are indifferent between selling the resource now or keeping it for the future. Thus, in equilibrium,

$$P_1(1+r) = P_2.$$

Consider what happens if this condition is not met. For instance, if P_1 is very high, then the expression on the left is greater than P_2. In this case, resource owners would see this fact, and would therefore mine the resource very quickly, bringing a great quantity to the market. By flooding the market now they would reduce the current price, P_1, reducing the left-hand side and bringing it into line with the right-hand side. Similarly, if the current price P_1 were very low, resource owners would tend to withhold supply today, shifting the supply curve for today dramatically to the left. That shift forces P_1 up; and once again the two sides of the equation are brought into balance.

If we transpose terms, divide by P_1, and re-express the equilibrium condition, it becomes:

$$(P_2 - P_1)/P_1 = r.$$

This version of the equilibrium condition states that in equilibrium, the private incentive for profit among resource owners will ensure that, on average, the price of natural resources will rise at a rate equal to the rate of interest.

Consider the implication of this fact for a graph showing any natural resource price changing through time. In such a graph, we must obtain an exponential growth curve. Eventually, the price of non-renewable natural resources must go to infinity, and at an ever faster pace. This conclusion gives us confidence that there must eventually be tremendous profit incentives for people to invent substitutes for these natural resources. If people are not doing so now, it simply means that we are still on the fairly flat region of the exponential growth path for prices. But once prices really start taking off, we can rest assured that many people will be engaged in activities making sure we find ways to do without these resources.

So the truly daunting issue that follows from natural resource use is not a problem of availability; rather it is the effect on the environment of our using these resources. We can expect the market mechanism to automatically solve the availability issue, but we cannot expect it to cope with pollution problems automatically, because of all the spill-over issues, the property rights issues, and the equity issues (that we discussed in Chapter 7). No one owns the environment, so there is no self-correction mechanism to regulate its use.

The Fundamental Challenge

The problem of world pollution highlights the connection between the developing countries and the developed ones like Canada. Just to stay alive, citizens in the developing countries have strong incentives to cut down rain forests at an alarming rate, and there are spill-over effects for the entire planet. The citizens of the developing countries cannot afford to cease this activity for the general benefit of everyone. In the short run, transfer payments to these developing countries are necessary. In the longer run, we need to foster economic growth (not discourage it) especially in the developing countries, so that transfers do not need to be permanent.

But where are the developed countries going to find the resources to offer this help? Economics is the study of choices. Is there any advice the discipline can offer society about how we might somehow set priorities among the many claims on our governments?

One of the biggest challenges we face is how to increase efficiency within the public sector. With all the competing demands on government funds, and a commitment to compassionate social policy that seems to be part of the Canadian identity, we just cannot afford inefficiency. Because of this, economists advocate the adoption of voucher systems for such things as pollution control, education, and health care. The key feature of voucher programs is that they maintain universal access while harnessing the **efficiency** of **private incentives** in the **provision** of **public services**. Our desire to do so many things through government can then be pursued in a realistic fashion that accepts human nature as we know it.

Perhaps the central theme of this book has been to explain how, by relying on our knowledge of private incentives when designing social and economic policy, we can minimize the trade-off between our equity and efficiency objectives. It is hoped that you are now more equipped to form your own opinion on these important questions.

We have tried to show that it is possible to have both a soft heart and a hard head at the same time. The softness of one's heart concerns equity; the hardness of one's head concerns efficiency. We confront various combinations of hearts and heads everyday in public policy discussions. Some give over-riding emphasis to a hard-head approach. They understand that we cannot spend beyond our means indefinitely, and they advocate deficit reduction even if that involves gutting social policies. Others give over-riding emphasis to a soft-heart approach. They push for the expansion of social policies even when we cannot afford current spending levels. Economics shows that respect for both the principle of scarcity and a policy of compassionate social programs is possible, but only with an increased awareness of, and reliance on, private incentives.

Appendix

Questions and Answers

If you have been reading this book just to increase your literacy in economics, you may not want to work through these practice questions. But if you are enrolled in a course in economics, you will be writing examinations that will involve questions like those that follow. Experience has shown that students can know a lot of the material but still do rather poorly on examinations. This is because most examinations test your ability to solve specific problems, rather than ask you to review what you have learned. Without practice at problem solving, many students have difficulty showing how much they know. This appendix contains 50 questions (with answers provided on pages 236-238). You are strongly advised to struggle with the questions before checking the answers. It is only by struggling that you can identify what parts of the material you need to review.

Chapter 1

1. Which of the following assumptions is not typically made by economists?
a. Rationality is sufficiently prevalent to engender order in observed behaviour.
b. Wants will always exceed the means to satisfy them.
c. People are generally altruistic.
d. Resources are generally more productive in some uses than in others.

2. Asuume that the demand and supply functions for beans are as follows:
   quantity demanded = 12 - P, and
   quantity supplied = 2P,
where P is the price. Suppose that the government is interested in raising the income of bean farmers and thinks it can do this by setting a legal minimum price for beans at 6. Compare the quantity of beans bought and sold, as well as the total expenditure by households on beans, before and after the government policy.

Chapter 2

3. The wine industry is in the doldrums. Taxes on alcohol are rising and pushing up costs. Also, because people have become more health-conscious and more aware of laws against drinking and driving, they are

drinking less. These factors combined imply that (I) the price of wine must have risen, and/or (II) the quantity of wine sold must have declined.
a. I and II.
b. II, but not I.
c. I, but not II.
d. Neither I nor II.

4. Consider the following demand and supply functions for commodity X:
   quantity demanded = 100 - 4P, and
   quantity supplied = 6P,
where P is the price of X.
a. If this market is in equilibrium, what is the price of X and how many units are produced?
b. Suppose the government buys some of good X to stockpile, in case there is an interruption in future supply. Assume that, in addition to the private purchases that follow from the demand function, the government buys 10 units of X each period. What is the increase in the total sales revenue received in each period by the producers of X as a result of this policy?
c. Now consider that the price of X has been set at non-market-clearing levels.
(i) If there is a shortage of 20 units, what must the set price be?
(ii) If there is a surplus of 50 units, what must the set price be?
d. Now suppose this country opens its borders to foreign trade.
(i) If the world price of X is 6, how many units will this country export or import?
(ii) If the world price of X is 12, how many units will this country export or import?

5. The government is considering alternative policies to restrict the consumption of beer. The supply and demand curves are:
   quantity demanded = 300 - P, and
   quantity supplied = (1/2)P,
where P is price expressed in cents and quantity is measured in millions of bottles. What is the equilibrium price and quantity before the imposition of any government policy?
a. The first policy being considered is to impose a quota of 80 million bottles on the production and sale of beer (that is, no more than this amount could be sold). What would be the new equilibrium price if this policy were introduced? If the government auctioned off the quota rights, how much revenue would it receive?
b. The second proposed policy is to impose a per-unit tax on beer. What level of tax would be necessary to restrict beer consumption to 80 million bottles? How much revenue would the government collect?
c. Compare the effects of the two policies.

Chapter 3

6. Assume that Graeme has a demand curve for steaks given by
    Q = 10 - 0.4P,
where Q and P stand for the quantity of steaks and the dollar price of steaks. If the price of a steak is $5, what is Graeme's consumer surplus?

7. Assume that the demand for wheat is given by the following equation:
    Q = 10 - 0.5P,
where Q is the output of wheat and P is the price of wheat in dollars. Assume also that wheat can be produced for a price of $5, no matter how much wheat is produced (that is, there are no diminishing returns in the wheat industry).
a. What is the equilibrium price and quantity for wheat?
b. Suppose the government wants to maximize the sales revenue for wheat farmers by setting a quota (a maximum physical amount of wheat that is allowed to be sold in the overall market). What quota would the government set?
c. Compared with a free market, how much does this quota policy cost society?

8. The demand curve for video tapes is given by Q = 10 - P, where Q stands for quantity in millions and P for price in dollars. Video tapes are produced in a competitive industry with constant costs, and the price is $4 each. When an excise tax of $2 per unit is levied on the sale of video tapes, it both raises revenue and imposes a cost on society. What is the ratio of the cost to society to the amount of taxes paid?

Chapter 4

9. Consider a firm whose short-run production function is given as follows:

Workers Hired	Total Output
0	0
1	20
2	35
3	45

The firm's product sells at a fixed price of $10. The firm has no fixed costs and must pay wages at the rate of $120 per worker each period. Use this data to determine the optimal quantity of labour to hire (relying on the marginal product (in dollars) equals wage rule), and to determine the optimal quantity of output to produce (relying on the marginal cost equals price rule). Since the firm only has one variable factor in the short run (labour), you must check that your answers are internally consistent (that is, once a certain quantity of labour is hired, the production function dictates what output is produced).

10. A firm can always increase its output by one unit at a marginal cost of $20. Its fixed cost is $200. The firm's average cost curve
a. crosses its marginal cost curve at the lowest point on the marginal costs curve.
b. crosses its marginal cost curve at the lowest point on the average cost curve.
c. never crosses its marginal cost curve.
d. is a straight line with a positive slope.

11. An airline is considering adding an extra flight from Toronto to Ottawa. The total cost of the flight including overhead is $5500. The variable cost of the flight is $2000. The revenue from the flight is expected to be $3000. Should the flight be added? Why?
a. No; the revenue ($3000) is below the cost ($5500).
b. No; the addition to profit is very small and not worth the effort.
c. Yes; profit is increased by ($3000-$2000).
d. Yes; profit is increased by $3000.

Chapter 5

12. Under perfect competition, price will equal minimum average cost
a. in the short run.
b. in the long run.
c. always.
d. never.

13. Consider a competitive industry that initially contains 100 identical firms. The short-run costs of each firm are:

Output	Total Cost
0	$30
1	120
2	150
3	200
4	270
5	360

and the industry demand function is $Q = 820 - 6P$, where Q and P stand for industry output and price in dollars.
a. What is the short-run equilibrium price? How much does each firm produce? How much profit does each firm make?
b. Assume that this industry has constant returns to scale - that is, if new firms enter, they will have the same cost function as existing firms. When this industry reaches long-run equilibrium, what will industry output be, and how many firms will comprise the industry? (To answer these questions, assume that firms cannot produce a fraction of a unit. With this restriction, full equilibrium will not occur exactly at the minimum point of the average

cost curve, but there will still be zero economic profit in the long run.)

14. Suppose good Y can be produced at a constant marginal cost of $4 per unit. Assume the demand function for Y is $Q = 100 - 5P$. Suppose the government takes over the production of good Y, and makes it available free to all users. Compared to the competitive market outcome,
a. there is a net gain to society of $40.
b. there is a net loss to society of $40.
c. there is a net gain to society of $20.
d. there is a net loss to society of $20.
e. non of the above statements are true.

Chapter 6

15. Suppose that a profit-maximizing monopolist facing a downward sloping demand curve and constant marginal cost suddenly becomes subject to an excise tax of $T per unit of output. In reacting to the tax, the monopolist will
a. not change her price per unit.
b. raise her price per unit by less than $T.
c. raise her price per unit by exactly $T.
d. raise her price per unit by more than $T.

16. Consider a natural monopolist with the following total cost and demand functions:
total cost $= 8 + 2Q$,
$Q = 6 - (1/2)P$,
where Q and P stand for quantity and price. If the monopolist chooses the largest output that is consistent with profit maximization, which output level is chosen? What is the maximum value of a license fee that the government can levy on this firm without causing it to shut down?

17. This question is designed to show the effect of a maximum price law that is imposed in a monopoly setting. Suppose that the monopolist's demand schedule and total cost function are those given here:

Quantity	Price	Total Cost
0	$18	$10
1	16	13
2	14	15
3	12	18
4	10	22
5	8	27
6	6	33

a. If the monopolist is an unregulated profit-maximizer, at what level does she set her price and output? How much profit does she earn?

b. Suppose a law is passed making the maximum price for this good $6. What output level will the firm choose? What will be its level of profits?

c. Compare what you have learned from this question with what you learned about maximum price laws in chapter 2.

Chapter 7

18. Detrimental externalities imply all but which one of the following?

a. The marginal social cost of an increase in output exceeds the marginal private cost.

b. A misallocation of resources will result from the fact that the private market supplies less output than is socially desirable.

c. Private firms will concentrate on private costs, ignoring the cost burden they are imposing on others.

d. Taxes that impose additional private costs on those causing the externalities are, in principle, capable of correcting the misallocation.

19. Education, especially at the primary and high school levels, provides positive external benefits. People who are illiterate or poorly educated are more likely to become a public burden or a criminal, so all taxpayers benefit from education. Economists therefore believe that

a. the provision of education should be left to the free market without interference.

b. education should be subsidized with public funds.

c. education should be provided only by the private sector.

d. teachers' salaries should be raised.

20. Under an emissions-tax program, the government sets _____; under an emissions-permit program, the government sets _____.

a. the price of the right to pollute; the price of the right to pollute.

b. the price of the right to pollute; the permitted total amount of pollution.

c. the permitted total amount of pollution; the price of the right to pollute.

d. the permitted total amount of pollution; the permitted total amount of pollution.

Chapter 8

21. Consider an economy with just two factors of production: labour and capital, which are both fully employed. Suppose that the supply of labour is 10 units, and that the marginal product of labour is given by:

$$\text{marginal product} = 16 - 0.8L,$$

where L is the quantity of labour employed. What is labour's share of national income in this economy?

22. Assume the following demand and supply functions for a commodity:
      demand: Q = 21 - 2P
      supply: Q = P.
Assume an excise tax of 3 per unit is imposed on the sellers of this commodity.
a. What percentage of the tax collected is paid by the buyers?
b. What is the ratio of the net cost to society of this tax to the magnitude of the tax collected?

23. Consider a negative income tax scheme with a guaranteed minimum income level of $6000 for a family of four and a tax rate of 50%. Which of the following statements is false?
a. The break even-level of income is $12,000.
b. Reducing the tax rate below 50% would increase work incentives and increase the break-even level of income.
c. Increasing the minimum guarantee without changing the tax rate will increase the break-even level of income.
d. If the Upton's earn $4000 in wages, their total income (earnings plus negative-tax receipts) will be $10,000.

Chapter 9

24. If the benefits of dropping a country's tariffs have been estimated to equal 3% of that country's overall output (its GDP), if the annual growth in that country's GDP is 3%, and if its interest rate is 7%, what is the present value of the move to free trade?

25. The domestic demand and supply functions for good X are:
      quantity demanded = 10 - P, and
      quantity supplied = P,
where P is the price of X in dollars. The world price of X is fixed at $6. If free trade is allowed, this small country
a. will import one unit of X.
b. will export one unit of X.
c. will import two units of X.
d. will export two units of X.
e. none of the above is true.

26. The domestic demand and supply functions for good Y are:
      quantity demanded = 20 - 2P, and
      quantity supplied = 2P,
where P is the price of Y in dollars. Y is available from the rest of the world at a fixed price of $3, if this country imposes no tariff. Compared to free trade, what is the net loss to society when a tariff of $2 per unit is imposed?

Chapter 10

27. In 1981, nominal GDP was $356 billion. In 1982 nominal GDP increased to $375 billion. On the basis of just this information, which of the following statements is true?
a. The total real output of the economy was greater in 1982 than in 1981.
b. The whole increase in nominal GDP was the result of inflation.
c. Real GDP increased from $356 billion to $375 billion.
d. It is impossible to determine what happened to prices and real output from the data on nominal GDP alone.

28. Consider a country that taxes interest earnings at a rate of 33.3%. Suppose the nominal interest rate in this country is 6% when there is no inflation. If inflation rises to 6% and remains there indefinitely, what increase in the nominal rate of interest is required to keep the after-tax real rate of return unchanged? What does this example illustrate about the costs of inflation?

29. True or false: "A period of excessive aggregate demand is likely to be followed by a period of stagflation (falling output combined with rising prices) as the inflationary gap self destructs."

Chapter 11

30. Assume that consumption and investment expenditures are determined by the following decision rules:
$$C = 100 + 0.7Y$$
$$I = 200 + 0.1Y$$
where Y stands for real GDP. What is the equilibrium value of GDP?

31. The self-correction process for a recessionary gap includes (I) a downward shift in the short-run aggregate supply curve; (II) an upward shift in the total expenditure line.
a. I and II.
b. I, but not II.
c. II, but not I.
d. Neither I nor II.

32. If the horizontal shift in the aggregate demand curve is $10 billion and the multiplier is 4, then what must have been the vertical shift in the total expenditure line?

Chapter 12

33. An increase in income tax rates will lead to all but which one of the

following?
a. a decrease in the size of the government spending multiplier on GDP.
b. a movement along the aggregate demand curve to a lower price level.
c. a reduction in the level of GDP.
d. a shift of the total expenditure line.

34. If all of every dollar of increased income goes to either savings, taxes or imports, the government expenditure multiplier on GDP is
a. zero.
b. one.
c. infinity.
d. 1/(1-MPC).
e. none of the above.

35. True or false: "Government deficits may impose a burden on future generations if, as a result of crowding out, there is less private investment and a smaller capital stock in the future."

Chapter 13

36. If banks hold currency as reserves in an amount equal to 30% of their deposit obligations, if households and firms hold $1 of currency for every $10 of deposits they have, and if there is $1000 of currency in existence, what are the total amounts of bank deposits and loans?

37. True or false: "A large switch in government deposits from the Bank of Montreal to the Bank of Canada will cause an increase in the Bank rate."

38. Deposit insurance
a. reduces the likelihood of a run on a bank.
b. protects the shareholders of a bank from losses.
c. Both (a) and (b) are true.
d. Neither (a) nor (b) is true.

Chapter 14

39. After reviewing the day's activity in the government bond market, analysts attributed the rise in bond prices to the activity of the central bank. This means that the central bank was probably (I) trying to lower interest rates (II) by purchasing government bonds.
a. I and II.
b. I, but not II.
c. II, but not I.
d. Neither I nor II.

40. Which of the following statements is not true, if Mexico and Canada have a flexible exchange rate, and a Mexican peso that used to cost 2 cents now costs 1 cent.
a. The Canadian dollar has depreciated relative to the peso.
b. Mexico's aggregate demand curve has shifted to the right.
c. Canada's aggregate demand curve has shifted to the left.
d. Mexico has a balance of payments deficit equal to zero.

41. Consider a country that is attempting to peg its currency at an unrealistically high value. Which of the following is not true.
a. Inflation will not be a serious worry for this country.
b. The country will have a balance of payments deficit.
c. The country will have a balance of payments surplus.
d. The country will be forced to use foreign exchange reserves - gold and holdings of other currencies - in order to buy its own currency.

Chapter 15

42. Which of the following is not a valid reason to oppose activist stabilization policy?
a. Doubts about the accuracy of forecasting.
b. Uncertainties about the response of the private economy to any change in policy.
c. A concern that activist policy necessarily means a growing public sector.
d. A strong belief that the economy, if left alone, is apt to correct most problems by itself quickly.

43. In what ways do policy makers have to face a trade-off between inflation and unemployment?
a. The cost of reducing inflation via restrictive fiscal and monetary policies is a permanent rise in unemployment.
b. The cost of reducing inflation via restrictive fiscal and monetary policies is a temporary rise in unemployment.
c. The cost of reducing unemployment via expansionary fiscal and monetary policies is virtually nonexistent.
d. The inflationary cost of reducing unemployment via expansionary fiscal and monetary policies is higher in slack times than in boom times.

44. The economy's self-correction mechanism to eliminate a recessionary gap relies on
a. increasing prices, which shift the aggregate supply curve inward.
b. rising wage rates, which shift the aggregate supply curve inward.
c. falling interest rates, which shift the aggregate demand curve outward.
d. falling wage rates, which shift the aggregate supply curve outward.

Chapter 16

45. Following an increase in government spending in a small open economy with a flexible exchange rate, there will be
a. a lasting increase in the price level and a lasting depreciation of the domestic currency.
b. a lasting increase in the price level and a lasting appreciation of the domestic currency.
c. a lasting decrease in the price level and a lasting depreciation of the domestic currency.
d. a lasting decrease in the price level and a lasting appreciation of the domestic currency.

46. For a small open economy on a flexible exchange rate, a depreciation of the domestic currency can be caused by all but which one of the following events?
a. an increase in the money supply.
b. a switch in government deposits to the central bank.
c. an increase in income tax rates.
d. a decrease in exports.

47. If Canada has a fixed exchange rate, a lasting increase in real GDP can be caused by either
a. an increase in exports or a decrease in income tax rates.
b. an increase in the money supply or a decrease in exports.
c. a decrease in the money supply or an increase in income tax rates.
d. an increase in the money supply or an increase in income tax rates.
e. a decrease in the money supply or a decrease in income tax rates.

Chapter 17

48. Over the longer run, lagging productivity growth in a single country is likely to lead to
a. a large increase in that country's unemployment.
b. greater exports from that country.
c. lower exports from that country.
d. a lower standard of living relative to other countries.

49. True or false: "Deficit reduction (which is an increase in national saving) helps capitalists more than labourers in a small open economy."

50. One ounce of the exhaustible resource Zenon now sells fro $200 in a competitive market. If the interest rate is 10%, and if there are no changes in the Zenon market over the next two years, how much will one ounce sell for?

Answers

1. c

2. Before the minimum price law is enacted, P = 4 and quantity (Q) = 8, so total expenditure by households, PxQ, is 32. After the minimum price law is imposed, P = 6, quantity produced is 12, and the quantity sold (demanded) is 6. Thus, total household spending is 6x6 = 36.

3. b

4. a. P = 10, Q = 60

b. Before the government purchase plan, PxQ = 600. After, PxQ = 11x66 = 726, so the producers' sales revenue increases by 126.

c. (i) shortage = demand - supply = (100-4P) - 6P = 20, so P = 8.
(ii) surplus = supply - demand = 6P - (100-4P) = 50, so P = 15.

d. (i) At P = 6, demand = 76, domestic supply = 36, so 40 is imported.
(ii) At P = 12, supply = 72, demand = 52, so 20 is exported.

5. P = 200, Q = 100

a. P = 220. To produce 80, firms need a price of 160. Total willingness to pay for the quota rights is (220-160)x80 = $48 million.

b. 60 cents per bottle, $48 million.

c. Consumers of beer would be indifferent. The two policies differ only if the quota rights are given away, in which case the firms (not the government) get the extra revenue.

6. $80.

7. a. Substitute P = 5 into the demand equation: Q = 7.5.

b. To determine maximum sales revenue (the maximum value for PxQ) try substituting several values of P into the demand function. You will find that the combination P = 10 and Q = 5 is the one that yields the biggest value for PxQ (equal to 50). Thus the quota is that Q not exceed 5.

c. By cutting output from 7.5 to 5, some resources are saved. The value of these resources is 5 per unit, so the saving is 2.5x5 = 12.5. But when these 2.5 units of wheat are lost, there is a loss of satisfaction equal to the people's willingness to pay for these units. The area under the demand curve over the 5 to 7.5 quantity range is the amount of this willingness to pay. This area exceeds the value of resources saved by 6.25. Thus, the net loss to society of the quota is 6.25 each period.

8. The ratio is one quarter. The tax collected is $2 on each of 4 units ($8), while the burden to society is the excess of the area under the demand curve (in the Q = 4 to Q = 6 range) over the cost of those two lost units.

9. In dollar terms the marginal product schedule is $200, $150 and $100 for employment levels 1, 2 and 3. Since the price of each worker is $120, 2 workers should be hired. The marginal cost schedule is $6, $8 and $12 for output levels of 20, 35 and 45 units. Since the selling price is $10, it pays to expand to 35 units of output, but not to 45. Thus, only two workers should be hired.

10. c

11. c

12. b

13. a. P = $70 and industry output is 400. Each firm produces 4 and earns profits of (4x70) - 270 = $10.

b. The lowest point on the AC curve that can be reached is $66.67, which occurs at an output level of 3 for each firm. Full equilibrium exists when enough firms have entered the industry to make economic profit equal to zero at this level of output. From the industry demand function, P = $66.67 implies Q = 420. The number of firms is then 420/3 = 140.

14. b

15. b

16. Profits are highest (at 4) when Q=3. The maximum license fee is 4.

17. a. MR = MC at Q = 4. The firm charges P = $10 and profits are $18.

b. The maximum price law makes the average and marginal revenue lines coincide over the Q = 0 to Q = 6 output range. They become a horizontal line up to Q = 6. Beyond that level of output, consumers are unwilling to pay a price as high as $6, so the law has no effect there. With the law, MR = MC = $6 at Q = 6. Thus, the firm charges $6 for each of 6 units and receives a profit of $3.

c. With competition, a maximum price law must reduce the quantity available while pushing price down. With monopoly, a maximum price law can simultaneously push price down and increase the quantity avaiable.

18. b

19. b

20. b

21. 2/3

22. a. Supply equals demand implies P = 21 -2P, so P = Q = 7 before the tax is levied. If P denotes the price received by sellers, P+3 is the price paid by buyers. Thus, with the tax involved, supply equals demand implies P = 21 - 2(P+3), so P = Q = 5. The tax collected equals tax per unit times the Q, or 3x5 = 15. Since the producer price falls by 2, and the consumer price rises by only 1, one third of the tax burden is borne by consumers.

b. The payment of tax is not a net loss to society; it is simply a redistribution of funds. But there is a net loss to society involved with this tax, since there are 2 fewer units of the good being produced and enjoyed. The loss in satisfaction is the area under the demand curve in the Q = 5 to Q = 7 range, and the value of the resources freed up by this cut back is equal to the area under the supply curve over this same range of output. The net loss to society is the amount the former exceeds the latter, which is 3. Since the net loss is 3, and the tax collected is 15, the net loss is 20% of the taxes collected.

23. d

24. Let n and r stand for the economy's growth rate and the interest rate. The flow of benefits coming from free trade equal:

$$\text{(Initial GDP)}(.03)[1 + (1+n) + (1+n)^2 + ...].$$

But each one of the future benefits must be discounted back to the initial period to make them comparable, and to calculate the present value:

(Initial GDP)(.03)[1 + ((1+n)/(1+r)) + ((1+n)/(1+r))^2 + ...].

As explained on page 135, the term in square brackets is equal to one divided by one minus (1+n)/(1+r). This term simplifies to (1+r)/(r-n), which is often approximated by 1/(r-n) since both r and n are rather small fractions. In this example, with r = .07 and n = .03, the benefits of free trade equal .75 of an entire year's total output (if the approximation is made) and the benefits are estimated to be 0.80 of a year's output if the approximation is not made.

25. d

26. $8

27. d

28. The real after-tax yield with no inflation is 6(1-0.33) - 0 = 4. With 6% inflation, the nominal rate of interest would have to rise to the value given by i as determined in: i(1-0.33) - 6 = 4. That value of i is 15%. Since nominal interest rates only tend to rise about one-for-one with inflation, this example illustrates that the real after-tax return to saving is reduced significantly even by modest inflation. Lower saving means less investment in new capital. With less capital, workers are less productive and the standard of living is lower.

29. True

30. 1500

31. a

32. $2.5 billion

33. b

34. b

35. True

36. The total currency in existence must be held in either of two places - in bank vaults as reserves, or in public hands. Thus,

currency = reserves + currency in public hands.

We are given that reserves = .3(deposits); that currency in public hands = .1(deposits); and that currency = $1000. Thus,

$1000 = (0.3 + 0.1)deposits

so deposits = $2500. The banks' balance sheets stipulates that liabilities (deposits) must be matched by assets (reserves plus loans). Thus, loans equal deposits minus reserves = (1 - 0.3)x$2500 = $1750.

37. True	**38.** a
39. a	**40.** a
41. c	**42.** c
43. b	**44.** d
45. d	**46.** b
47. a	**48.** d
49. True	**50.** $242

Index

READER REPLY CARD

We are interested in your reaction to *Economics: The Essentials* by William M. Scarth. You can help us to improve this book in future editions by completing this questionnaire.

1. What was your reason for using this book?
☐ university course   ☐ continuing education course   ☐ personal interest
☐ college course   ☐ professional development   ☐ other _____

2. If you are a student, please identify your school and the course in which you used this book.

3. Which chapters or parts of this book did you use? Which did you omit?

4. What did you like best about this book? What did you like least?

5. Please identify any topics you think should be added to future editions.

6. Please add any comments or suggestions.

7. May we contact you for further information?

NAME:
_____

ADDRESS:
_____

_____

PHONE:
_____

(fold here and tape shut)

MAIL ➤ POSTE

Canada Post Corporation / Société canadienne des postes

Postage paid
If mailed in Canada

Port payé
si posté au Canada

**Business
Reply**

**Réponse
d'affaires**

0116870399   01

0116870399-M8Z4X6-BR01

Scott Duncan
Publisher, College Division
HARCOURT BRACE & COMPANY, CANADA
55 HORNER AVENUE
TORONTO, ONTARIO
M8Z 9Z9